A THEOLOGY for AGING

A THEOLOGY for AGING

WILLIAM L. HENDRICKS

BROADMAN PRESS
Nashville, Tennessee

4217-12
ISBN: 0-8054-1712-5

Dewey Decimal Classification: 230
Subject Heading (s): THEOLOGY // AGING
Library of Congress Catalog Card Number: 8614710
Printed in the United States of America

Library of Congress Cataloging-in-Publication Data

Hendricks, William L., 1929-
A theology for aging.

Bibliography: p.
Includes index.
1. Aging—Religious aspects—Christianity.
2. Aged—Religious life. I. Title.
BV4580.H34 1986 230'.0880565 86-14710
ISBN 0-8054-1712-5

To

Paul and Carrie Lindsey

who

gave us an example

and to

Reid and Patsy Hutchens

who

have made the aging

process easier

Preface

This book is a closing parenthesis. The opening parenthesis was *A Theology for Children.* Childhood and old age are the parentheses of the human condition. The first book was written for—on behalf of—children. It was assumed that the age group for whom the book was written could not read it for themselves. The opposite is the instance in this book. I am assuming senior adults not only can read this book, but many of you have "lived through it." By that I mean that I hope this work will provide for you an expression of "things most surely believed" in a way that can be readily understood.

I will use the first person often in dialogue with you, the reader. There is an empathy and an identity between us. For I have written the work "from practical experience," the experience of aging. It is not a bad process, this aging. It is better than its certain, eventual alternative.

Let me tell you what this book is not. (1) It is not a scholarly, formal, academic theology. Although if you look carefully at the footnotes, you will find suggestions there to challenge the "brightest and best." (2) It is not an analysis of the science of geriatrics. That speciality must be left with the technicians in various fields, medical, sociological, and psychological.[1] (3) This book is not a special theology for aging and aged persons which is different in substance from other Christian theologies. The substance of Christian theology is a single message for all persons and all times. The substance of any Christian theology is the fact and its implications "that God was in Christ reconciling the world to himself" (2 Cor. 5:19).

Let me tell you what the book is:

1. It is an elemental Christian theology from a conservative, Protestant, conversionist perspective. I trust the work will speak to all audiences, but it was written from a confessional viewpoint. There is within these pages a genial and fraternal attitude toward all who name the name of Christ. There is likewise an evangelistic fervor and a missionary concern. The book was written on a mission field during

a sabbatical leave. There is a "listening love" toward all world religions and the diffuse truths they embody. There is an attempt toward understanding the "secular mind" and an intention to portray it accurately and to speak to it compassionately.

2. This is a theology based on revelatory insights as filtered through the experiences of older Christians. The authority of God through Scripture has been assumed from the first page and explained in the last chapter. The experiences of normal, everyday life have been used as analogs to express the content of theology. I hope that these metaphors will be illuminating and not confusing. These analogs are: the singing of gospel songs (chapter 1) and hymns (chapter 8), the asking of questions (chapter 9), taking a journey (chapter 2), looking for identifying marks (chapter 3), looking in mirrors (chapter 4), looking into a kaleidoscope (chapter 5), enjoying children (chapter 6), and breathing (chapter 7). My growing interest in the arts is evident in many of the illustrations.

3. The book is a labor of love. It is a word of gratitude to those who have nurtured me and helped to sustain me through my nearly thirty years of teaching Christian theology to Baptist ministers. It has been my joy to serve on the faculty of three nurturing institutions: Southwestern Baptist Theological Seminary, Fort Worth, Texas; Golden Gate Baptist Theological Seminary, Mill Valley, California; and Southern Baptist Theological Seminary, Louisville, Kentucky. Generations of students have taught me theology by their perceptive questions and by their willingness to learn. They are my inheritance. There have been congregations which cared for my ministry and my person. Fortunate are those who can minister and be ministered to by the people of God.

No task is ever accomplished "single-handedly." My wife, Lois, has shared the journey. My son, John, has enriched it. Immediate and fervent thanks are due to Onida Norman who typed the very rough handwritten draft, to Charles Scalise who put the notes and references into coherent form, to Rejeana Cassady who did good and faithful work on this book as well as in the other tasks in a busy academic office. This book is dedicated to Paul and Carrie Lindsey of Dixon, Missouri, my parents-in-law, and to Reid and Patsy Hutchens of Tishomingo, Oklahoma, who have been friends of the years.

Their support in trying times has indeed made the process of aging easier, and I am happy to acknowledge my indebtedness to them.

The guiding love in this labor has been "the vision glorious" seen in the face of Jesus Christ, who is the focus of God and the hope of the world.

WILLIAM L. HENDRICKS

Taipei, Taiwan
Pentecost, 1985

Notes

1. See the brief, selected bibliography on aging at the conclusion of this book, p. 361.

Contents

1

Last Things First

We, the aging, have the best of both worlds. We have retrospect and hope. Most older people, contrary to popular opinion, do not live in the past. But they do remember it! Neither do we "hanker after heaven" although we anticipate it. Ours is a present-oriented life which can look comfortably in both directions if the circumstances of life are reasonably secure.

I want to do theology in reverse because older persons can perceive the beginning from the end. Furthermore, they can talk about the end and the beginning more realistically because their experience provides a basis for understanding Scripture and relating it to life. It is God, through His Word, who provides our authority and our surety in things religious. And it is our experience and application of biblical insights that makes religion real. This tried and tempered authority gives us many chances to interpret and comprehend what Scripture means and what life is about.

We can be somewhat bemused and tolerant because we know that what young and middle-aged success-oriented religious leaders often declare is not what is important for us or realistic to us. We have, to be sure, a stake in the future. But we reckon how quickly stakes of the tents of Zion can be pulled up as God, moving with us and beyond us, goes out ahead of us making all of life a more temporary dwelling than younger folk suppose. For example, it is precisely because we believe in God and leave the future to Him that we do not constantly have to be anxious about and dwelling on the last days (2 Tim. 1:12). These are already our last days, for we know that these days are all we have in which to serve Him. Rather than scanning future skies, we delight to see the dawning of each day and the surprises it can bring.

From this experienced and more relaxed stance, let's work back and ahead. It is wise to begin with the ahead part, for that is where God really and fully meets us with the meaning of our lives.[1] Theological ideas which surface when we think of the future include all of the traditional terms. What do we believe about: heaven, hell, death, resurrection, judgment, the ultimate coming of Christ, the millennium, and the kingdom of God? It is the tendency of immaturity to work out all of the details of all of these topics. It is the wisdom of faith to dwell on the essentials. I would like to use, largely, musical phrases as topics for the final things. Perhaps this is so because like music these are the things that make the heart rejoice.

Heaven's My Home, but I'm Not Homesick Yet

The story is timeless and faceless. It's like so many of our legends, attributed to everyone. An old woman was asked if she was looking forward to heaven. Her reply was: "Heaven's my home, but I'm not homesick yet." She was realistic and honest. *Heaven* is a word which gives content to the spiritual gift of hope. Jesus speaks of it as His Father's house (John 14:2); the Old Testament makes us aware that God dwells in the heaven of heavens (2 Chron. 2:6; 6:18; Ps. 68:33), that is, beyond our world, its limitations and its circumstances. The theological word which expresses that God is different from and removed from His creation is *transcendence.* Transcendence is God's otherness, His thereness. Heaven is "up" in Scripture. That spatial term conveys more than geography. It talks about the way God is God. As we shall see later, His difference from us and our world is one of the foundations of hope. For if He is different and other, then maybe, in His time, we and our world can be different also. God's time is called eternity. God's place is called heaven. Of course we know that God cannot fully and finally be described in terms of time and place. But we also know that *we* cannot think of real and important things without giving them time and space meanings.[2]

Since all we do know and relate to is in time and space, it is natural that the old woman's remark would express our dilemma. We anticipate heaven because it is for us the term that conveys hope and final security. Yet, on the other hand, we are somewhat anxious because to reach heaven we must leave this familiar time and space. We must miss the usual and those people and things that are loved. And, most difficult of all, we must undergo death. It was for good reason Paul called death the last enemy (1 Cor. 15:26).

Most persons, in reasonably good health and if given a choice, would not opt to go to heaven right now. This strange wanting to but not wanting to yet is not a lack of faith. It is an affirmation of life. It is an opting for the familiar and the God-given which we now have. Much study about heaven is purely academic. Such study is an intellectual curiosity. Every grandparent knows that every grandchild can ask questions about the particulars of heaven which even the wisest minister cannot answer. If one is a wise minister, one will not even try to answer.

The images Scripture provides for us about heaven can be reduced to essential expressions. God's tree of life in the garden (Rev. 22:2) speaks of His eternal provision for us. The walled city (21:11-27) indicates His protection to us. The tabernacle of God signifies His presence with us (21:3). What more do we need than His provision, His protection, and His presence?[3]

Furthermore, His presence with us is of an intimate, family sort. Jesus, the elder brother, speaks of the Father's house. Being with God finally is to be at home. All of these are warm and positive expressions. Home has had to become where the heart is, for we live in a mobile society. Being a senior citizen has not exempted us from frequent moves, willing or nonwilling. *Home* is a very warm word about heaven. The image of God's people as a pilgrim people was given in Israel's experience in the wilderness. The idea is extended in Jesus' ministry. Of Him it was said that He had no place to lay His head (Luke 9:58). Through countless moves, after several cities and beyond clinics, hospitals, and convalescent centers it is good to be able to think of a solid base called home. Heaven! We couldn't do without it even though we are not yet quite ready for it.

Another idea about heaven is its sense of completion. Unfinished tasks tear us up inside. To start but never to complete is to lack something. Psychologically, we can't continue with beginnings only. There have got to be some finishings. Heaven stands for "finishings." If life is to be really finished, it requires, for us, the people with whom we began it and with whom we have moved through it. "They" will be there as part of their finishing and ours. We are a part of all we have met, and they a part of us. The more intimate and longer the association, the more vital is the warp and woof of relationships. Heaven is a place of corporate society. The full body of Christ is necessary, and this full-body concept in Paul takes precedence over isolated individuals (Eph. 1:22-23; Col. 1:17-24).[4] Heaven is not just a relationship between God and the individual believer. It is the finished product of all our relationships. It includes our family and the family of God.

The reunion and the reuniting aspects of heaven are part of the promise. The biblical promise that God will make all things new is predicated upon the former things which are passed away. In their place is not the utterly new, for if this were the case we would not know Him, ourselves, or them. The making new is the renewing of the old and its radical reconditioning so as to permit us to live in God's time and place and under His conditions. If we have cooperated with the Father here and now in beginning our salvation, we will cooperate with Him in the completion of it. God's way with His creation has always been to lead it along by promise and fulfillment. Every fulfillment brings a further promise and an enlarged vision as well. It is on this basis that we speak of heaven as a place of growth. In biblical thought perfection is dynamic. It is being like God. In Greek pagan thought, perfection was a static state one received instantly. The bulk of biblical evidence and the confirmation of our experience teach us that we will grow by our relationships and their ongoing quality. There is every reason to believe that this is as true of heaven as it is of earth. Completion and consummation are continuous just as all of our life and experiences are continuous.

The practical implication of this for our present life seems apparent. Many Christians, attached too much to earth and its material benefits, will indeed require some weaning away from "earthly" things to grow in receptivity to God's kind of life. One preacher put it in an unsophisticated but correct way when he said: "God will not fill us initially any more than the bucket we bring will carry." It makes sense to realize that both here and there we will enlarge "the bucket." Growing in grace is the pattern of our life, here and there. A mature Christian reflecting on this truth will realize that it makes sense, given the various stages of spirituality and dedication among Christians. There is, therefore, a deeper meaning to the old woman's saying "but I'm not homesick yet." There is the awareness of a need for further growth. Many of us know that we are not ready for heaven yet, in the sense of our being unwilling to be weaned away from the pull and the possession of earth.[5] It is a condition God will help us to outgrow.

These warm words of hope, the idea of family and home, the promise of finishing with the body of Christ what we have begun all provide enormous impetus for evangelism. Evangelism is telling the good news. Most older people share this good news in natural ways which respect the decisions of others. We are aware that getting heated up about heaven and arguing the point is a quick way to cool down the interest of those to whom we are trying to witness.

Heaven is the word of hope. We believe in the reality of it according to the promise of a trusted friend. The essentials about heaven are: a sure promise, a loving Father, an elder brother, a full body of Christ in which we fit, and a completion of what life is about. We can wait for the specifics beyond these things. And knowing these things, we can wait as those for whom heaven is the home for which we long, but for which we are not ready yet. We are not ready because of our imperfections. We are not ready because we are enjoying the previews of heaven in the life that is ours on earth, and this we were meant to do.

"Everybody Talkin' 'Bout Heaven Ain't Going There"

Two kinds of people would not enjoy heaven: (1) those who only talk about it but whose allegiance is not to the Lord of heaven; (2) those who refuse to talk about it and whose dedication is to the self only.

The black spirituals contain much good, elemental theology. They were born out of pain and deprivation. They look at life with a simple, biblical realism. One of these songs, "I've Gotta Shoes," has a very perceptive statement. "Everybody talkin' 'bout heaven ain't going there." This is a perceptive commentary on the religious society of our day. The Bible is keenly aware that there is good religion and bad religion. Good religion brings unity, peace, wholeness, healing and life. Bad religion brings divisions, war, fragmentation, dis-ease, decay, and death. (See Gal. 5:16-26 and Jas. 1:17 to 2:20.) It is not easy or instantly possible to discern good from bad in religion. This is so because the evil one appears most deceptively as an angel of light (2 Cor. 11:14). Or as one elderly, astute observer said: "The devil goes to church."

The question must be asked: If everyone and not even religious-talking people aren't going to heaven, where are they going? There have been several answers to this question. All of them have sought biblical support. The first answer grows out of the realism of the Old Testament. The Old Testament experience lay on the other side of Easter. There are, especially in the Wisdom literature, expressions about death being the end of man. Death does us in. One older gentleman said to me, while defending an extravagant life-style: "I'm enjoying it now. Because when you're dead, you're dead for such a long, long time." Job, in his despair, expressed that viewpoint (Job 14). People in the Old Testament dreaded death because it cut them off from the living, the familiar. They went down into the pit (*shachath,* Job 33:24,28; Ps. 30:9), the grave (*qeber,* 1 Kings 13:22; 14:13; Job 5:26). They went to *sheol,* the shadowy place where they could not be seen (Num. 16:30,33). Most important of all, they felt cut off after death from the worship and service of God.

This preresurrection realism is sometimes expressed by older folk today. They have seen loved ones and friends "going down the valley one by one," and they have never experienced one return. A theology based solely on experience might well conclude that the dead are dead, and that that is the end of the story. They would answer the question Where are the dead? with the blunt, final, and experienced observation: "They are nowhere. They are dead. They cease to exist." We all know people who believe this. A mature faith must acknowledge this expression of many of the aging. Often this view is born of depression, despair, long observation, or even an intense courage that dares to face nonbeing. Frequently this view is born of compassion because alternative views as to where the ones are who are not in heaven are too difficult to comprehend emotionally. Proof texts can be found in Scripture to bolster this opinion. This view of death as moving into nonexistence applies to all, the good and the bad together. This perspective would deny both heaven and hell. But this experiential realism is not the New Testament view.

A second answer to the question where are those dead who are not in heaven is a variation of the first. This answer says that the "wicked dead" are annihilated. They cease to exist. God does not call them into being beyond the grave. The theological name for this is conditional immortality. Conditional immortality believes in heaven as a reward for faithfulness. It believes in nonexistence, annihilation as the punishment for disbelief and refusal to believe. Those who take this view use two lines of argument. They argue theologically from a perspective of the justice and mercy of God which will not permit eternal punishment.[6] They argue biblically from the Greek word for destroy (*apollumi*) which they believe means to annihilate. The annihilationist view is compassionate and favoritist. This view permits one to have one's cake and eat it too. Mature belief often looks sympathetically toward this view, but two problems arise. Where then is there any final, corporate, and individual justice and judgment? The wicked often do prosper and hold on to their prosperity all through this life, and that at the expense of the poor through ill-gotten gain. Second, how does this view deal with the New Testament teachings about hell?

The third answer is the traditional one. People who are not in heaven are in hell. This answer, when it is not adequately explained, is emotionally devastating to the aging. Most older people have more friends and loved ones who have died than they have friends who are living. The last things are not always, in that situation, the best things or the most comforting things. The plain situation is that not all of our acquaintances and loved ones die in the Lord. When one combines this grim reality with the larger-than-life preaching of some who seem to be spiritual sadists in their descriptions of hell, the situation is emotionally and psychologically intolerable for the aging. As one elderly lady said about her pastor, "He preaches on hell and all of its particulars like he was born and raised there." To the extent that he was describing all of hell's particulars, he was getting his information somewhere else than from the Bible. A sober biblical analysis on hell reveals the following insights: hell is the absence of fellowship with God; hell is the consequence of our freedom to turn away from and resist the God who made us; hell is likened to the loneliness and separation of darkness; hell is analogous to the pain and unpleasantness of a smoldering dump.[7]

One often hears older persons who have been through or are in great trauma say: "Yes, there is a hell. I've been through it in this life." Just as blessing is a preview of heaven, so bane is a preview of hell. Just as one grows outward toward the body in heaven, so one grows inward toward the self in hell. Just as heaven is enlarging, hell is restricting and confining. The fellowship of heaven is counterpart to the centering on the self which is hell. Hell is not so much of God sending as it is of the self confining. This life is, indeed, the start of and a parable for the "world to come."[8]

Yet, we cannot gloss over nor hold back the pressing questions of justice, the "fate of the heathen," or the plight of those "who have never heard." The biblical examples of Jesus concerning Sodom and Gomorrah (Matt. 10:15; Mark 6:11) and the queen of the south (Matt. 12:42; Luke 11:31) give much help to these problems. These "gradation" examples give us every right to assert that there are degrees of rewards and punishment in God's time and space. The problem arises when we polarize heaven and hell into absolute, static states rather than dynamic states. The essential belief about heaven and hell is that God is in charge. It is He who is just and merciful. It is He who bids us to share. It is not we who will determine others, but God. It is we who are under command to share the good news of Jesus and who will be rewarded or punished for doing it or for not doing it. His justice and His mercy are His, and in the last analysis He may and will do what He desires. This essential fact about God is the determining fact about heaven and hell. Wherever what is "true, . . . honest, . . . just, . . . pure, . . . lovely, . . . and good" (Phil. 4:8, KJV) may be found, it is there because of Him. Wherever death, decay, disunity, disease, and destruction are found, it is because of our free choice to distort the good God has given. What I suggested for children is also good for second childhood. Hell is a great loss; it is a lacking of what might have been.[9]

Hell has lasting consequences. God with these dissidents feels the pain. Hell is the ulcer in God's "stomach." As long as a portion of His creation suffers, He will feel the pain. Hell is not just a categorical counterpart to heaven for purposes of discussion. It is a necessary context for confining evil, in all of its manifestations, to keep evil from utterly and finally destroying creation. Sober reflection among those who have lived long and suffered much will acknowledge there has got to be a place like that. Deep observation about the application of religion in life will lead us to know that "everybody talkin about heaven ain't goin there." Jesus said, "Why call ye me, Lord, Lord, and do not the things which I say?" "Lord, when saw we thee? (Luke 6:46; Matt. 25:44, KJV).

"You Must Walk This Lonesome Valley": Death

Folk sayings, Negro spirituals, and Appalachian songs provide some of the chapter divisions about the last things. This is appropriate, for the romance and poetic power of songs can help us to reflect on the reality of our deepest experiences. The final experience is death. A very brilliant philosopher made a profound, simple statement: "Life is unto death." That is obvious. It is true, and it is a good way to describe life. Life is bounded by our nonbeing before birth and our death at the end of life. The Bible states the situation even more succinctly and adds a second necessary situation. "It is appointed unto men once to die, but after this the judgment" (Heb. 9:27, KJV). There are two necessary things every living person must do: die and be judged. We have all heard the facetious saying that we must die and pay taxes. This is a way of stating civic and social responsibilities. If we are to maintain an adequate social relationship we must, indeed, pay taxes. But it is possible to escape our social obligations. It is not possible to escape death. Death is the one sure fact of life. It is also the certain termination of life.

The Bible looks at death in two directions. Most older people do also. Death is an enemy, a curse. Death is also a blessing, a release. From time to time and from circumstance to circumstance we can see first one view and then another. Death is a curse because of sin (Rom. 5:12-21). We are unwilling to say that everyone dies just because of Adam's sin. We know that we too have contributed to the stockpile of wrongdoings that bring about death, even our own death. In our advanced, technological world we are aware that we can and have discovered and invented things that kill us and God's world around us. The industrial pollution of the world around us poisons the air, and we breathe the air. When nuclear wastes are not properly cared for, the heat we created for energy becomes the fire of death. The preservation of food for long-term sales can mean, in extreme instances, short-term lives. The ingestion of addictive substances creates all sorts of havoc ranging from emphysema to overdosing. Our society is very skilled in violating creation, and that is sin; and we must pay the consequences of it. We do. Social sin is no less sin than individual sin; in fact, it is more. Social sin is more sin than individual sins because it unites more powerful possibilities and combines collective forces in a way that becomes more destructive than any one individual's sin.[10]

To be sure, individual sins also contribute to our own individual demise. Intemperate schedules, even if they are schedules for doing good things—even God's work—can and do kill us. Gluttony will take its toll. Failing to obey God's laws, which are commonsense injunctions for preserving the self, will kill us. The frequent complaint "I'm killing myself with all of these things" is more true than we realize.

There is a second sense in which death is a curse we bring upon ourselves. This second sense is related to the first, but it is deeper, more serious, and long lasting. This second sense in which death is a curse we call spiritual death. Spiritual death moves along with all of those physical ways in which we bring about the shortening of our lives. Spiritual death moves beyond these physical ways in the rejection of life, God's life offered to us. God's kind of life—eternal life—is His highest blessing. Physical life is His first gift to everyone, and everyone who has life is graced by God. Eternal life is God's highest gift, and everyone who "has the Son has life" (1 John 5:12, RSV). The opposite of this gift of eternal life is eternal death. In this sense to die is to refuse God's purpose for life and God's completion of life. The refusal of this life results in a "second death." Second death is a qualitative expression that means we die in this life by rejecting the life-giving purpose of God, and we die after this life because we are not redemptively related to God's kind of life.

Spiritual death, as we shall see in chapter 2, can be corrected and overcome in this life. In fact, it can only be corrected and overcome in this life. For spiritual death, according to Scripture, is sealed by physical death. All of this sounds paradoxical and terribly complicated. Simply stated, it means that we miss out on meaningful life here and hereafter if we reject God's gracious gift of life in Jesus, God's *logos.* Death is a curse. We contribute to it. Death is a curse because it removes us from the familiar. We lose sight of our loved ones. We do not complete life's goals. We don't finish what we've begun. We dread the pain which comes with sudden tragic death and even more with lingering illness leading to death. Most elderly people in good health are sympathetic to the poet's words, "Do not go gentle into that good night, . . ./Rage, rage against the dying of the light."[11]

Remember one reason we are not homesick yet is because we do not want to die.

Death is, nevertheless, also a blessing. A lovely interpretation of the "tree of life" in Genesis 3:22-23, Acts 5:30, 10:39, and Revelation 22:2 will help us to see this. By eating of the tree of the knowledge of good and evil, man became guilty. God drove man from the garden so that man would not eat of the tree of life. To eat of the tree of life in our stage of guilt and disobedience would mean that we would have to live forever in our fallen condition. We would have all of our weaknesses and afflictions, but we could not die. This was a gracious exclusion indeed. What hell on earth it would be to have to live forever in our finite and painful bodies! God closed off the tree of life. But He has granted it to us again in Jesus Christ, through the tree of the cross. And He will make its effects most completely known when in the garden of God we see the tree whose fruits shall sustain us and whose leaves shall heal us. This interpretation is more than a spiritualizing of the biblical accounts. It is seeing the deeper layer of meaning which is embodied in God's purpose.

Death can be a blessing because we have been blessed by the death of His Son. Death can also be a blessing because we are released from the sufferings of this life. Death, for Christians, is a blessing because it is the way home, to the Father's house. This is the double meaning of death in Scripture, curse and blessing. Those who are in frightful pain welcome the falling asleep that brings relief from that pain. We have all seen the blessing of death in the end of friends and loved ones. Some of us may come to know it for ourselves.

Modern medical technology has raised a serious question in our time. What is death? Earlier, less technological societies did not have to deal with this question in the same way as we do. I once heard a pioneer physician tell about elemental medical experiences in which the determination of who was dead was an easy thing. It was the frontier method of placing a mirror before the nostrils of a body to see, in cold climates, if there was a frosting of breath. The biblical materials speak of death as a losing of the spirit, the breath, the energizing force of life. In both elementary and advanced ways this is true. When breath is not present or possible, death occurs. We went full cycle from the nostrils to the pulse, to the heart beat, to brain death because of lack of oxygen. Therefore, not to have breath or to be able to breathe is death. That seems simple enough. The problem arises because we have invented machines which enable people to breathe indefinitely. This artificial breathing is helpful to those who do not have the heart or lung power to breathe on their own strength. In such cases, the machine may help temporarily or for an extended period. Breathing machines are a blessing to persons who are not in medically irreversible comas. They will survive and wake up. Beyond these points the issue becomes confused and not so clear. In medically irreversible comas, are breath inducing and sustaining devices helpful or harmful?

The arguments seem convincing on both sides. On the one hand, do we really know when a coma or unconscious condition is medically irreversible? On the other hand, when brain damage has been done, or when the possibility of active life is not present, and when one's limited financial resources are used up and loved ones may be obliged to pay exorbitant medical costs for an indefinite period, is it not better to permit death with dignity? My response is that each person should, before such conditions arise, determine that decision for the self. I have chosen the second alternative of not applying heroic measures in a medically nonhopeful case. I have registered that decision with my physician and my family. We have often accused the medical profession of playing "God." It is a role some of us have thrust upon them. It seems unfair to ask our immediate family to make decisions which may burden them with anxious guilt or incredible financial responsibility. These are serious words about death. Let me encourage you, the reader, to reflect and make some decisions of your own about these matters. In these extreme and final determinations we will find the encouragement of God and the courage to be responsible for the self.

There are three dimensions of our being. As best I understand Scripture, when any two of these dimensions cannot respond to God, the self, or others, some form of death is present. We have a biochemical dimension; this functions as our physical body. We have a psychosocial dimension; this functions as our "inner" self, and we have a spiritual or ultimate dimension; this functions as our deepest relationship to God, others, and the self. Perhaps the little scheme below will help in explaining these levels of death.

1. When we are able to respond to God, the self, and others at all

levels—biologically, psychosocially, and spiritually, *we are fully alive.*

2. When we are not able to respond to God biologically, psychosocially, or spiritually, *we are dead physically, psychosocially, and spiritually.*
3. When we are unable or unwilling to respond to God spiritually but respond to others and ourselves at the biological and spiritual stages, we are *spiritually dead.*
4. When we are unable or unwilling to respond to God, the self, or others psychologically or socially, we are *psychosocially dead,* as in persons who have withdrawn from reality.

What this means is that there are many types of death. Those people who have "cut out of reality" psychologically because they cannot cope with reality are also "dead." But they certainly should not be considered dead physically. People who are spiritually dead may be very vibrant physically and psychologically. What they need is spiritual life to be fully alive. These distinctions help us to understand the complexity of death and to realize that there is death and/or dying even in the midst of life. Furthermore, all of us, even the newborn, are in the process of dying. Dying is a process. Death is a condition. For those who are aware that they are actually dying biologically, Elisabeth Kubler-Ross has written a helpful book which describes the stages of the process.[12] For those who feel themselves threatened by or in the grip of the psychological death of depression, there is M. Scott Peck's *The Road Less Traveled.*[13]

For both of the above and for all who lack spiritual life, there are the Scriptures. The wealth of insights from Psalms to the Song of Solomon and from Job to John can give wise counsel and a way to salvation.

Seniors are often troubled by one aspect of death that is seldom, if ever, faced and discussed directly by our churches and their leaders. That problem is suicide. Suicide, self-induced death, is well known to all who have lived for a long time. Suicide used to be a smaller problem than it is today because there were fewer suicides. Moreover, there were only a small number of suicides among younger persons. Today suicide is the third highest cause of death among college students. And the alarming facts are that children in their teens and even younger are committing suicide in large numbers.[14]

There have been many attempts to gloss over instances of self-induced death. I feel we should discuss it plainly together. And I hope this brief discussion will help many seniors who have had to struggle alone with theological questions about suicide.[15] I want to make five suggestions that are implicit from the biblical materials.

1. Actively and violently taking human life is wrong. This includes traumatic suicide.
2. Gradually and knowingly contributing to those things which limit, shorten, and impede the full life are also wrong. This is gradual suicide, and most of us, in some way, fall in this category.
3. Suicide is not the unpardonable sin (Matt. 12:32; Mark 3:28; Luke 12:10). The reason that it was assumed by some to be so is because one who commits suicide is not able to ask God's forgiveness through the earthly church. We do not believe that forgiveness is contingent on the acquiescence of any earthly church.
4. Not all Christians have confessed all of their sins to the Father before they die. We have every reason to believe that when those who take their own lives are in God's presence with Jesus as Mediator, they can unburden their lives before Him, directly.
5. What is true of other sins we have not confessed on earth is also true of a final sin in taking one's own life. The important thing is to establish a relationship of forgiveness with the Father through Jesus Christ.

Suicide may be traumatic or gradual. It is not unforgivable.

"We Shall Rise, Hallelujah, We Shall Rise!"

The title of this section is from an old gospel song. The reality of which this section speaks is from the newest act since creation. In the creation, God gave all the possibilities of existence which we are still discovering. By the resurrection of Jesus Christ, God did a completely new thing.[16] The resurrection of Jesus is the basis and sole security for the resurrection of all persons.

There have been several ways that people have attempted to resolve the dilemma of death. One way is the way of reincarnation. It is one of the oldest attempts. It is characteristic of Asian religions.

Going around again and again could be more of a hell than a heaven. In Buddhism one resolves the problem of existence by eliminating all desire and eventually passing into nothingness.

A second way of resolving death is to affirm that we live on through the memory of our descendants who keep us alive by keeping us and our deeds in mind. This perspective is shared by such diverse groups as modern Judaism and traditional Chinese religion. Many ancient peoples felt that we could take it with us, hence the elaborate treasures and retinues of Egyptian pharaohs and Chinese emperors. But this journey to the other world was the prerogative of a royal few.

All of these attempts to resolve death are less than satisfactory. At best they illustrate our longing for life after death. In the resurrection of Jesus Christ, we have the only example of one who breaks the bonds of death and who is given a new kind of life by God, the Creator of life. Christ is the firstfruits of the resurrection (1 Cor. 15:20-23). Paul was at pains to point out in 1 Corinthians 15 that Christ's resurrection is the guarantee of ours. We do not have an automatic, innate immortality.[17] God graciously calls us into life after death. And this bringing of life out of death is the province of God alone, the Author of life and the Lord of death.

We all ask more questions about the resurrection life than the Bible gives plain answers. Several things are clear about our resurrection.

1. Our resurrection is based upon and made possible by the resurrection of Jesus Christ.
2. Jesus is the firstfruits of the resurrection and the only one who has been fully resurrected.
3. God will raise all persons at the last day to face judgment.
4. Resurrection life is analogous to but qualitatively different from earthly life. Paul says it is like the acorn to the oak (Compare 1 Cor. 15:35-49).

These simple affirmations leave scores of questions answered. Will we know one another? Apparently so since the apostles recognized the resurrected Jesus. Will we be sexual beings? Yes in the sense of being intrinsically male and female,[18] else how could we know one another? But no in the sense that we will not exercise physical sexuality, for we will not be physical in our present sense.

If Jesus is the only one truly resurrected, what of those who have died or will die before the last day? Three answers have been given by the Christian community to this basic question: (1) They are asleep. (2) They enter a different form of time, and they are resurrected immediately after death. (3) They go immediately into the presence of God in a formed, conscious intermediate state, and they are given their full resurrection bodies at the general resurrection on the last day. My interpretation of 2 Corinthians 5:1-5 leads me to prefer the third viewpoint. This is so because all of the biblical passages which deal with the dead speak of their being conscious. And the biblical, Hebraic way of looking at people, even the dead, assumes that they have some form or shape.

These secondary affirmations should not keep us from losing sight of the primary fact. Because He lives, we too shall live. Only God who brings us life can bring life out of death.

The old gospel song does well to rejoice: "On the resurrection morning when the dead in Christ shall rise, we shall rise, hallelujah, we shall rise." And this rising is not a mere resurrection of a corpse. It is a bringing of the total being into a new type of life. Resurrection is a new creation. This leads us to ask: Are our chemical components required to be kept intact in order for us to have resurrection? The answer is no. The mutilation, amputation, and disintegration of our human chemicals will in no way affect the resurrection of our selves. For He who holds us in life does not need these specific ashes and dust to reconstitute us anew for His time and space. This is encouraging to those who have lost loved ones in disastrous ways.

I am often asked: What is a Christian attitude toward cremation? My specific answer is that it does not in any way hinder resurrection. And ecologically and economically it may become the predominant form of burial.[19] Yet I do understand the reasoning of those who prefer traditional burial as a purely formal way of symbolizing their affirmation of the resurrection of the body. All of this discussion is to say something rather than nothing to the questions older people have asked and reflected on. Perhaps we have said too much and dwelt too much on the worldly, physicalist aspects about which many approaching death have asked so frequently. Resurrection, although it involves the total self, is a spiritual condition and a spiritual state. And it is into the hands of the Father of life that we, no less than Jesus the Son, must commend our spirits, our breath of life, in order that He may breathe life anew into us that we may know what it truly is to be children of life. We may know this because of Jesus who is the way, the truth, and the life (John 14:6).

Judgment

To judge means to make a decision, to discern, to decide. In this sense we all are judges, and we all are judged. But there is a final decision made about us by one whose discernment counts and whose decision is just. We speak of this absolute decision as the final judgment of God. This decision is inevitable (Heb. 9:27), involving all (Rom. 14:10; 2 Cor. 5:10), and right (Rev. 16:7).

Just as there are preliminary insights of heaven and hell in this life, so there are preliminary, significant judgments. We all tend to judge ourselves, and we vacillate between two decisions. Sometimes we are too hard on ourselves (1 John 3:20-21). More often we are too quick to justify ourselves; we are not then open to being justified by God. To justify means to render a favorable decision for someone or to declare that she is right. If you want to hear self-justification at its surface level, listen to motorists who have just had a "fender bender." Each seeks to justify himself. Self-justification and self-judgment will not do, for we are too prejudiced to render a fair judgment.

There is the other possibility that we are judged by our fellows, our family, or other people. This is inevitably true and necessary. One of the hardest tasks of being a parent is to learn to be nonjudgmental. One of the largest burdens some people bear through life is the judgment their parents make about them. Low self-esteem results when we have been judged unfairly and unrealistically by others. Jesus spoke truly and compassionately when He told us not to judge one another (Matt. 7:1).

The human community suffers when there are corrupt political judges. From the dawn of recorded civilization, people have found it necessary to have laws and to have judges to interpret and give judgments. Lack of good human justice is a major concern of the Old Testament. Lack of justice in matters of religion and society was a primary concern of Jesus in the New Testament.

Why judgment at all? If we cannot finally and realistically judge ourselves, and if we are not always justly judged by our fellow persons, maybe we should all be content to go our own way. Live and let live is a familiar slogan. In many matters most of us would accept that old adage. However, good and evil, right and wrong, and the vindication of these and the establishment of justice is what is at stake. It makes no sense to sew without a knot at the end of the thread. In a world like ours, there is no ultimate sense or meaning unless it is given by someone from beyond ourselves. This is as true of societies as it is of individuals. The whole thing is up for grabs if there is no judgment. It should be obvious by now that there must be judgment, and there must be, somewhere, a fair and correct Judge.

Few would deny the need for justice. The statement is often heard: "We are judged in this life." Most seniors have lived long enough to see the fallacy of that statement. The biblical Job and millions like him call into question that there is justice, in this life, for all persons.[20] Many of us have seen the wicked prosper and die peaceably in their beds while suffering saints have had a tough go of it even to the very end. Judgment and justice are necessary, and they are necessary in an ultimate sense.

One only is sufficient to establish justice and to render just judgments for people and for nations. That one is God. God only and finally will judge us, and that is both good news and bad. His just and final decision is, as always between Him and us, a cooperative decision. We do have to decide. And He confirms our decisions in a way that establishes justice. Our primary decision is in relation to Jesus Christ. The judgment of God's Spirit is on the basis of our decision for or against Jesus (John 16:7-11). The decision of Christ concerning us is along the lines of our decision for compassion and kindness toward the needy (Matt. 25:31-46). We are being judged in this life; God is confirming what we decide. When we break His laws in a physical realm, we suffer judgment. When we refuse the ethics of compassion, we are judged as nonloving, selfish people. When we reject Christ, we reject the Father who sent Him. When we acknowledge Christ but are not obedient, we are disobedient children who must be judged as such. God Himself in the threefold fullness as Father, Son, and Spirit is our Judge. Graciously, He has provided for us a favorable judgment in Jesus Christ.

There are those who would separate the various biblical statements about judgment and have several kinds and times of judgment in the world to come. It seems to me that all of the biblical statements regarding judgment can be fitted into the basic affirmation that at "the end" God will decide. Our decisions and those of others are important. But God's determination is final. Let's leave that final determination up to Him. The claim for ultimate arbitration and discrimination concerning ourselves and others belongs to God. I, for one, am willing to leave it with Him.

"When He Shall Come with Trumpet Sound"

Several gospel songs and special musical selections come to mind when considering the ultimate coming of Christ. I have used a phrase from "The Solid Rock." "Victory in Jesus" is another song about Jesus' coming that is widely sung and enjoyed. There is also the popular tune, often done by choirs with special accompaniment, "The King Is Coming." It is appropriate that we should think of music and joy in relation to Christ's final coming. This attitude of joy is a prelude to the music of heaven (see the various hymns in the Book of Revelation) which is celebrated in musical works such as Handel's *Messiah.*

Some theologians and scholars have taken away the music and joy of Christ's final coming by insisting on programs and charts. I will not permit that to happen. Systematic theology is a subject dear to my heart, and I have taught it for nearly thirty years. The first thing a theologian should know about God is that one cannot know all about God. God can and does do more and does it more mysteriously than we can capture or imagine. The first thing a theologian should know about the Bible is that it is the inspired Word of God. It has coherent insights about God. But Scripture is not a book of systematic theology. Scripture is most plain in its expressions about salvation. It is most unspecific about areas that lie beyond our history, that is at the beginning and at the end, when eternity turns into history and when history turns back into eternity. I have never envied those who "know all" about God's beginnings and endings. I am not interested in a theology which has no mystery and no dimensions of otherness about it. I am not interested because I am convinced that such a theology is not a biblical theology. Such a theology is a theology which has been put together to make things come out well. "Things" will come out well. The Bible is certain in its teachings about that. But Scripture does not, in my opinion, detail the *how* of that outworking. Scripture is more concerned with the *who* and the *purpose* than the *how* and *when.*

There is no mistaking the *who* of the final coming of Christ. It is Jesus, this *same* Jesus who comes again (Acts 1:11). It is important to stress this sameness of the one who comes for two reasons. On the one hand, there are religious groups today who are quick to nominate their leaders as contenders for the second coming of Christ. I had a spirited, public debate with the leader of one such group. Acts 1:11 was a primary passage in my arguments. Finally, my opponent asked what it would take to make me believe his candidate was the lord of the second advent. My reply was: "Call me when he comes out of the tomb." It is the earthly, resurrected, ascended Jesus Christ whom we are expecting and not anyone else.

The second reason we need to stress the sameness of the returning Christ is that some in the Christian community have portrayed the returning Christ as different in character from the earthly Jesus. This will not do! The popular joke is phrased in the good news/bad news format. According to this view the good news is that Jesus is coming again. The bad news is that He is as "mad" as He can be. Much preaching about the second coming has fortified this view. Granted, Jesus came in the framework of our human limitations the first time. Granted also, He is coming in power and glory with force to bind evil the second time. Nevertheless, it is the *same* Jesus who comes. His love for children, the dispossessed, His compassion for the helpless, His identification with sinners—these will be the same. His quickness to point out insincerity and hypocrisy, His eagerness to declare and defend the Father against all religious idolatrous claims—these too will be the same. The love that He bears to all will be perceived as wrath by those who reject it. The chains of love forged in the crucible of Calvary will bind the evil one absolutely (Rev. 20:1-10), even as they are able to do now proximately (1 John 4:4). The familiar hymn "What a Friend We Have in Jesus" would be a cruel joke indeed if the returning Friend were not also the Friend of children and the One who values the beauty of flowers. The triumphant Lamb of Revelation cannot be essentially different from the Lamb of God John the Baptist recognized (John 1:29).

It is *He* who comes in the name of the Lord. And His coming should have all of the winsomeness and anticipation of a friend eagerly awaited. The New Testament uses a variety of appealing terms to indicate the final coming of Christ. He will appear a second time "to bring salvation for those who are watching for him" (Heb. 9:28). He will come; He who is present will give us His full presence; He shall appear. These ideas are implicit in the basic New Testament terms presence (*parousia*) and appearing (*epiphaneia*).[21] His parables[22] about the Kingdom in the Gospels suggest several things about the final coming. It is sudden, unexpected (in the sense of the exact time), and an act of finality and judgment. The ancient religious word *glory* is connected with His coming. And closely associated with this is the brightness of celestial light. This consummation is God's third great cosmic event; the others were creation and crucifixion. His coming is universal in significance. It involves all (John 19:37).

It is appropriate to ask why Christ is coming again. One response often given is: "Because He said He would." Then, with the persistence of a questioning grandchild, we must ask: "Why did He promise He would come again?" The specific response to this is to receive His own (John 14:3), to bring salvation (in the full completed sense) (Heb. 5:9; 9:28), to judge (Matt. 25:14-46), to put away wickedness (Rev. 20:1-7; 11-15), to bring the millennium (Rev. 20:2-7), and to institute fully the kingdom of God (Mark 13). In other words, His coming is the last day. It is that time when time shall close, and history will be turned into eternity. As Peter put it in the earliest Christian proclamation, He comes to conclude the age (compare Acts 2:14-36).

It is part of the our legacy to hope. Hope is the gift of God's Spirit which enables us to live beyond the past and through the present. Hope holds out the possibility that things can be different. It is natural for us, as we grow older and we function at lower levels than we used to, to want a quick and easy way out. Older people and those in difficult circumstances understand one of the earliest urgent cries of the first Christians. *Maranatha!* Our Lord comes, or O, Lord, come quickly. Yet we also feel ambiguous about not being homesick yet. The parents of one of my church members illustrated this ready/yet-not-ready tension of healthy belief. The mother was painfully ill, and she asked the father to pray that God would take her in death. The obedient husband, faithful Christian, started to kneel by her bed to pray. The wife's response was: "Bert, maybe not yet!" That is how it really is with us about the second coming, and that is how it ought to be. For Jesus is the one "who is and who was and who is to come" (Rev. 1:4,8). We must not let the gift of hope become an all-consuming passion that robs the present of meaning or the past of significance. To anticipate Jesus' coming too avidly is to deny His presence with us through the Spirit. The *parousia* (coming) is not an escape clause. It is an honorable finish. And He will finish it. He will finish what He began in His own time and in His own way. Even so, Lord Jesus, come!

"O Land of Rest, for Thee I Sigh"

I mentioned that one of the purposes of Jesus' last coming is to bring the millennium. The very mention of the word brings apocalyptic shivers to some and shudders of confusion to others. The word itself is easy to define. The description of the content and meaning of the term has had a long and checkered history.

The English word *millennium* means a thousand years. The Greek term *chilias* also means thousand. A millenarian is one who believes in a millennial concept. Millennialism is to believe too much in the concept—at least that is what "ism" ordinarily means. *Chiliasm* usually refers to physicalist concepts of a utopian dream that has been set up somewhere as an attempt to bring in the peaceable kingdom. Sociologists have almost equated the idea of millennium with utopia. *Utopia* is a Greek word which means literally no place. The usual use of utopia is that it is a visionary place which is so good that there is actually "no place" which could live up to the dream. Knowing all of these words and their derivative meaning can help us define what we are talking about. But definition is only the first step. It is, however, an important step; and you would be well advised to ask people who are always talking about "the millennium" to define what they mean by that term.

Historically, there have been three insights concerning what those brief, illusive references in Revelation 20 mean: the institutional view, the physicalist view, and the symbolic view. Generally, these positions are given temporal or descriptive names. The institutional view is called postmillennial; the physicalist view is called premillennial, and the symbolic view is called amillennial.

The institutional, postmillennial view applies, as far as I am concerned, to all of those beliefs and practices which suppose that the church, some sect, some social experiment or some religious theocracy on earth is equivalent to the millennium. The excessive pride with which some earthly, religious, and secular institutions regard themselves is an implicit part of millennialism which is far from dead. This kind of religious kingdom building is prevalent even among formal pre- and amillenarians. Nationalism, particularism, and prideful triumphalism of all sorts are postmillenarian in their implication. Older, spiritual postmillenarians had a strong biblical point in their favor when they stressed that martyrs only participated in the millennium (Rev. 20:4-5). Their weakness was the assumption that evil had been confined.

Premillennialists affirm the literal, earthly 1,000-year reign of Jesus Christ. There are basically two views within premillennial circles. There are those who feel that Christians will suffer the final tribulation. There are those who feel Christians will be "raptured" before the final tribulation. The idea of "rapture" comes from the phrase "caught up" in 1 Thessalonians 4:17. If one looks at the broadest teachings and examples of Jesus in the New Testament and of Christians throughout the centuries, one is likely to realize that Jesus and His disciples are around when suffering happens.

The most difficult aspect of premillennialism for me is its physicalism. For some years I have taken tourists to the Middle East and especially to Jerusalem. These pilgrimage visits never fail to excite me and give me a renewed appreciation for Scripture. But I have watched some staunch and starched physicalists' convictions wilt with the high temperatures of Jerusalem in summer. After two weeks most Americans are ready to return to the comforts of home. A physicalist view of the millennium must speak to the implications of what literal, physicalism means. The response can be, of course, that God will provide ideal, nonthreatening conditions during the millennium. And the response to that would be that those conditions would not be like any literal, physical conditions we know.

The strong points of premillennialism are its insistence that evil intensifies as the full manifestation of God draws near and the understanding that Christ comes before the millennium, that is, at the time of the millennium. The weaknesses are its physicalism and the implications that God gives a second, almost irrefusable, chance to those who live at the end of time.

The third millennial view is the symbolic view or the amillennial view. This perspective holds that the millennium is a symbol which indicates a metaphorical time in which God rules and reigns. This is generally understood to be the perfect period of time between the first and the second coming of Christ. This view avoids the triumphalism of the institutional view and the physicalism of the physicalist view. But its weakness is that it does not, in some instances, adequately interpret the meaning of Revelation 20:1-7 in the sense that Christ comes prior to millennial expectation. The strengths of this view are that it avoids the weakness of the other views, and that it consistently takes the apocalyptic symbols of revelation symbolically. As you may have guessed, none of the views is completely satisfying. As you surely know, the arguments over all of these views have sometimes brought a spirit of dissension among Christians that would make us all believe that the devil is active indeed.

My personal perspective, which certainly does not answer all the problems either, combines elements from each of the above positions. Institutionalism is right in affirming the power and gifts given to the body of Christ by the Spirit. Any who await the millennium in a sense of powerlessness and despair and fail to do what we can do with the promises of Jesus and the power of the Spirit are missing the New Testament teaching about the church.

Jesus does bring the millennium with Him at His coming, and His coming will be, as it was the first time, in a period of deep difficulty and darkness. In this sense I am a premillennialist. But it is difficult for me to see the purpose of a physical millennium with favoritism toward those living in the last days.

Jesus brings the millennium, which is the gift of messianic peace, which is simultaneous with judgment, which is simultaneous with the bringing in of the Kingdom. In this sense I am a symbolist, but I am a symbolist who believes that symbols are as real and as important a way of expressing reality as any other way of expressing reality.[23] In this composite view there remains one clear and essential fact, that is, His kingdom will come on earth as it is in heaven. The kingdom of God, according to the teaching of Jesus, is the height and depth of what we ourselves and the realities beyond ourselves are all about. The millennium, whatever else it may be, is definitively an interlude on the way to the Kingdom.

"Thy Kingdom Come, Thy Will Be Done"

Malotte's version of the Lord's Prayer is familiar to most Western Christians. The petition "thy kingdom come, thy will be done" is a part of the regular litany at the beginning before the tune swells to its crescendo. It is good music. But it is bad timing, for the phrase about the Kingdom coming is regulative of all the other petitions. It should be the most memorable phrase and have the largest musical embellishments. Jesus' central message was about the kingdom of God and believers' duty of absolute obedience to the command of God to love.[24]

The biblical words for kingdom are simple. There is one term (with several variations) in the Old Testament and one term in the New. The words are simple. But the usages are complex.[25] Modern American seniors sometimes find it difficult to relate to ideas of sovereignty, kingship, and all of the royal trappings; although it has been observed that Americans who have never, since independence, had any royalty are terribly romantic about everyone else's royalty. The biblical notion of God's sovereignty and kingship is a unique concept and cannot really be compared to earthly royalty. God's sovereignty grows out of creation and redemption. As we shall see later, the power and authority of God are of a distinct kind which involves more than human kingship. Granted, we Americans may not "cotton up" much to royalty. Nevertheless, there is a final authority and power which resides in God which is not determined by "majority vote." The processes of the kingdom of God involve cooperation. But their ultimate decisions and boundaries are determined by God. The philosophies of absolute egalitarianism which rebel at any jurisdiction outside of humans or any authority larger than human will are not compatible or comfortable with notions of the kingdom of God. These views are as old as the first temptation to be as gods. And they are as full of pride as the first sin.

Whatever our politics or form of government, we cannot undo the biblical metaphor of kingship and kingdom. The idea of kingdom of God is open to a variety of interpretations. There is the view that the kingdom of God is coterminous with the physical kingdom of Israel, especially in its highest moment—the Davidic period. This physical view has merit in that the land of Israel was a promised inheritance from God. And it was from Israel, the nation, that God's redemptive history would be displayed, and God's fullest revelation, Jesus Christ, would come according to the flesh. Yet there is a problem in equating the kingdom of God and the land of Israel. This problem is the explicit statement of Jesus that His kingdom is not of this world (John 18:36). This physical Israel view also misunderstands the doctrine of election which means that the one stands for the many. The Elect One, Jesus Christ, died for all. The elect nation Israel was elect to bear witness to God's love for all the earth, not His exclusive concern for one portion of it. Whenever we equate the election of God with the chosen individual, we fail to see the representation and the responsibility of what it means to be chosen. Chosenness is about service and bearing witness more than it is about particularity and prerogatives. Israel, the land and the people, bears testimony to God and to His faithfulness. But physical Israel either in the Davidic period or in the present State of Israel is not the kingdom of God.

A second line of interpretation grows out of the first. This second view stresses that the church is spiritual Israel and is therefore the inheritor and manifestation of the kingdom of God. I shall have much to say later about both election and the church. The church, the body of Christ, is indeed the "elect lady" (2 John 1). There is a Pauline passage (Rom. 9—11) which can be construed to mean that the church is the New Israel, the spiritual Israel. But it is too easy to identify the body of Christ with some historical, particular institutional church and thereby make the kingdom of God a very small and restrictive place indeed. Israel, ancient Israel, the Israel of the Old Testament, must also be included in the Kingdom. And the rulership of God must extend to the entire cosmos. God is Lord to those who call on Him. He is King, and "his kingdom ruleth over all" (Ps. 103:19).

Twentieth-century discussions about the Kingdom have been obsessed with the temporal aspect of the Kingdom. One group of scholars affirmed that the Kingdom was already present and fully realized in Jesus.[26] This makes the Kingdom primarily past and present. Another group has insisted that the kingdom of God is totally future.[27] One has even suggested that Jesus taught that the Kingdom was totally future, but that He was mistaken.[28] There is a type of scholarship that reduces things too much to only one possibility. There are New Testament teachings of Jesus that indicate a relationship between the Old Testament kingdom of Israel and the work of Christ, that indicate a relationship between Jesus' historical ministry and the kingdom of God, that suggest that the Kingdom is both present and future. We do not have to settle for a reductionist view of the Kingdom.

The best way, it seems to me, to understand the kingdom of God is not in terms of time. The best understanding is in terms of *right.* The kingdom of God is God's right to rule over the creation He has made. In that sense, the kingdom of God is synonymous with and invested in the person of the King. The kingdom of God is the rule of God. And that is always in effect. It means different things to different persons, depending on their relation to the King. The Kingdom will be seen ultimately by all; and, if we only would acknowledge it, the Kingdom is already in effect because the King is effectual. The future, final manifestation of the kingdom of God waits upon Christ's termination of the age and judgment. The present, persistent implications of God's rulership may be seen, even in our fractured world, and be celebrated especially in the church. Certainly, His kingdom has not yet "come . . . . on earth as in heaven" (Matt. 6:10). But we who perceive what it is supposed to be like in heaven can and ought to be busier than we are about making earth a heavenly kind of place through our obedience to the King.

Benediction

We have come, at last, to the end of the last things. Through the idiom of music we have suggested the celebration and observations appropriate to the last and highest things. One persistent trait has come through: there is a relationship between the now and the then, the present and the future. Creation (the past) and consummation (the future) are tied together by the cross (the present). Lest you are confused by the fullness of the discussion, let me remind you of the essentials. Heaven is fellowship with God. Hell is rejection of God. Death is a curse and a blessing. Resurrection is God bringing His creation back to life through death. Judgment is God's final determination about His creation, and He alone is able to make that determination. Christ comes to turn time into eternity, to tie a necessary knot in the thread of all things. His coming brings peace and confines evil. Finally and finely, God's reign over His creation will be what it ought to be. Now that is something to think about, something to sing about, and something to live out of. Living out of ultimate affirmations is what the Christian life is all about. And the Christian life is what the next chapter will be about.

Notes

1. Compare Jurgen Moltmann, *Theology of Hope: On the Grounds and Implications of a Christian Eschatology* (New York: Harper and Row, 1967), especially pp. 15-36. Also see Moltmann's essay, "Introduction to the Theology of Hope," in Jurgen Moltmann, *The Experiment Hope,* ed. and trans. M. Douglas Meeks (Philadelphia: Fortress Press, 1975), pp. 44-59.

2. This dilemma was worked through in a technical, theological way sometime back in John A. T. Robinson's *Honest to God* (Philadelphia: Westminster Press, 1963), especially pp. 11-63.

3. See this symbolism expressed more fully in Ray Summers, *Worthy Is the Lamb* (Nashville: Broadman Press, 1951), pp. 211-215.

4. See J. A. T. Robinson, *The Body, a Study in Pauline Theology* (Chicago: H. Regnery Co., 1952), especially pp. 8-10.

5. See Richard Quebedeaux, *The Worldly Evangelicals* (San Francisco: Harper & Row, 1978), pp. 10-21.

6. For example, Le Roy Froom, *The Prophetic Faith of our Fathers, The Historical Development of Prophetic Interpretation,* 4 vols. (Washington, D.C.: Review & Herald, 1946, 1948, 1950, 1954), especially vol. 1, pp. 9-204.

7. Compare Jean-Jacques Von Allmen, *A Companion to the Study of the Bible,* trans. P. J. Allcock *et al.* (New York: Oxford University Press, 1958) pp. 79-83, 135-136, 468-469; Daniel P. Walker, *The Decline of Hell: Seventeenth Century Discussions of Eternal Torment* (Chicago: University of Chicago Press, 1964), especially pp. 3-70.

8. See C. S. Lewis, *The Great Divorce* (New York: The Macmillan Co., 1946).

9. See *A Theology for Children* (Nashville: Broadman Press, 1980), pp. 220-224.

10. See Reinhold Niebuhr, *Moral Man and Immoral Society* (New York: Charles Scribner's Sons, 1932), pp. xi-xxv, 1-22, 257-277.

11. Dylan Thomas, "Do Not Go Gentle into that Good Night (1952) in Dylan Thomas, *Collected Poems, 1934-52* (London: Dent, 1952), p. 116.

12. Elisabeth Kubler-Ross, *On Death and Dying* (New York: Macmillan, 1969).

13. (New York: Simon and Schuster, 1980).

14. Gabrielle A. Carlson reported: "Although the suicide rate in young people has fluctuated over time, . . . it has captured the attention of mental health professionals and the public in the last two decades because of its recent alarming increase. Accidents remain the leading cause of death in 15- to 24-year olds; however, death rates from malignant neoplasms [cancer] and cardiovascular renal diseases have been displaced in frequency by death from violent causes. In 1975, young people were killed in homocidal incidents at a rate of 13.7/100,000; suicide deaths were ranked at 12.2/

100,000. These two phenomena are now the second and third cause of death in the 15- to 24-year age group" (Gabrielle A. Carlson, "Depression and Suicidal Behavior in Children and Adolescents," in D. P. Cantwell and G. A. Carlson [eds.] *Affective Disorders on Childhood and Adolescence—An Update* [Jamaica, N.Y.: SP Medical and Scientific Books, 1983], pp. 335-352).

15. See Appendix A, "A Sermon on Suicide."

16. See my *Who Is Jesus Christ?* (Nashville: Broadman Press, 1985), chap. 5, pp. 69-85.

17. See Oscar Cullmann, *Immortality of the Soul or Resurrection of the Dead? The Witness of the New Testament* (New York: Macmillan, 1958).

18. Compare Karl Barth, *Church Dogmatics,* vol. 3, *The Doctrine of Creation,* Part One, eds. G. W. Bromiley and T. F. Torrance (Edinburgh: T. & T. Clark, 1958). See § 41 "Creation and Covenant," Section 2 "Creation as the External Basis of the Covenant," especially pp. 176-206. Barth declares, " 'He created them male and female.' This is the interpretation immediately given to the sentence 'God created man.' . . . Man can and will always be man before God and among his fellows only as he is man in relation to woman and woman in relationship to man" (ibid., pp. 184-186). For an analysis of Barth's interpretation from an evangelical perspective see Paul Jewett, *Man as Male and Female: A Study in Sexual Relationships from a Theological Point of View* (Grand Rapids: Eerdmans, 1975).

19. See Paul E. Irion, *Cremation* (Philadelphia: Fortress Press, 1968), especially pp. 51-72. A bibliography on the subject is contained on pp. 141-149. Also, see Jessica Mitford, *The American Way of Death* (New York: Simon and Schuster, (1963), chapter 2, pp. 161-172; and Leroy Bowman, *The American Funeral: A Study in Guilt, Extravagance and Sublimity* (Washington, D.C.: Public Affairs Press, 1959), pp. 118-119,116-168.

20. This is particularly true in Job's instance if we accept the decision of many scholars who suggest that both the prologue and the epilogue are inspired additions to the Book of Job.

21. For views about the second coming and word studies pertaining to it see: Ray Summers, *The Life Beyond* (Nashville: Broadman Press, 1959), especially pp. 95-146,209-216); G. E. Ladd, *The Blessed Hope* (Grand Rapids: Eerdmans, 1956), especially pp. 61-70. For a dispensational view see J. Dwight Pentecost's *Things to Come: A Study in Biblical Eschatology* (Findlay, Ohio: Dunham Publishing Co., 1958), especially pp. 370-426.

22. On the parables see Joachim Jeremias, *The Parables of Jesus,* trans. S. H. Hooke (London: SCM Press, 1954), especially pp. 120-157; Dan O. Via, Jr., *The Parables: Their Literary and Existential Dimension* (Philadelphia: Fortress Press, 1967); Madeleine L. Boucher, *The Parables* (Wilmington, Del.: Michael Glazier, 1981), especially pp. 63-86; C. H. Dodd, *The Parables of the Kingdom* (New York: Charles Scribner's Sons, 1936), especially pp. 34-110; Robert W. Funk, *Parables and Presence: Forms of the New Testament Tradition* (Philadelphia: Fortress Press, 1982), pp. 67-79; and Jan Lambrecht, *Once More Astonished: The Parables of Jesus* (New York: Crossroad, 1981), especially pp. 1-23,146-166. For bibliography in this area, see Warren S. Kissenger, *The Parables of Jesus: A History of Interpretation and Bibliography* (Metuchen, N.J.: Scarecrow Press [The American Theological Library Association], 1979).

23. See chapter nine and the discussion of language and its function, pp. 293-302.

24. See Norman Perrin, *The Kingdom of God in the Teaching of Jesus* (Philadelphia: Westminster Press, 1963), especially pp. 158-206 and Rudolf Bultmann, *Jesus and the Word,* trans. Louise Smith (New York: Charles Scribner's Sons, 1934), especially pp. 27-56, 120-132.

25. John Bright, *The Kingdom of God* (Nashville: Abingdon-Cokesbury Press, 1953), especially pp. 187-214.

26. Compare C. H. Dodd, *The Parables of the Kingdom* (New York: Charles Scribner's Sons, 1935); *The Apostolic Preaching and Its Developments* (London: Hodder and Stoughton, 1936); and *History and the Gospel* (London: Nisbet, 1938).

27. Compare J. Dwight Pentecost, *Things to Come: A Study in Biblical Eschatology* (Findlay, Ohio: Dunham Publishing Co., 1958), pp. 45-64, 129ff.

28. A. Schweitzer, *The Quest of the Historical Jesus: A Critical Study of Its Progress from Reimarus to Wrede,* trans. W. Montgomery (London: Adam and Charles Black, 1910), pp. 328-401; *The Mystery of the Kingdom of God: The Secret of Jesus' Messiahship and Passion,* trans. Walter Lowrie (New York: Shocken Books, 1964), especially pp. 84-93,106-126,253-273.

2

A Pilgrim's Progress: A Tourist's Manual of Important Questions

One of the interesting things older people get to do today is travel. There is more time. The cost of travel is lower. There are special tours designed especially for older people. Modern-day pilgrims are progressing through all parts of the world. As we travel, see different cultures, come face-to-face with other peoples and religions, we ask questions about who we are and about things we have always taken for granted. In this chapter I would like to give you a tour guide of important questions about the Christian life.

One of the best ways of gaining information is to ask questions. Having been a tour guide in various parts of the world, I like older people who ask questions. The questioning ones learn by observing and asking. Older people who question things are often younger than their years. There is curiosity and vitality in the question askers. Fortunately, most older people have lived long enough not be fooled by quick answers or to be squelched by those unwilling or unable to answer their questions. It is very depressing to be with persons of any age who do not take enough initiative and interest to ask questions about their surroundings, their beliefs, or their circumstances.

To ask questions is not to doubt, although questions may be born from doubting. Doubting is not a sin. The poet was right. There lives more faith in honest doubt, believe me, than in half the creeds. So come with me on a trip through what you thought was familiar terrain. Dare to ask your questions and to be open to mine, and you may be pleasantly surprised to see and understand things that have heretofore been taken for granted. The questions are simple. It's the simple questions and the little words which require the most explanation. I've picked a dozen questions you will want to ask on our journey: the pilgrim's progress through the Christian life.[1]

My questions are.

1. What is life?

2. What is the heart of the gospel?
3. How does one start the Christian life?
4. Am I OK?
5. Do I belong?
6. What's my part?
7. What is a "born-again" Christian?
8. Is it safe?
9. What does it mean to be ransomed?
10. What are the expenses?
11. Who is in charge?
12. What about other people?

What Is Life?

Some of us can remember when *Life* magazine was a weekly publication. Very few can remember when it cost only fifteen cents. There was a pointed joke in those days that went something like this: "That's tough!" "What's tough?" "Life's tough!" "What's life?" "It's a magazine." "How much does it cost?" "It costs fifteen cents." "I've only got a dime." "That's tough!" And it went on and on until one of the participants decided to stop going around and around. There is more than humor involved. The joke brings out the repetitiveness of our existence and something of our always falling short.

Life is like that. There are experiences we repeat: eating, sleeping, working, and so forth. Life does have its circularity. It also has some falling-short experiences. I once sat at dinner on a train with a man who looked very sad as we passed a certain piece of well-developed real estate. He remarked that his grandfather had sold many acres of that tract for a ridiculously low sum because he needed money. If he could just have held out! For many, life has had experiences where there was only a dime, and what was needed was fifteen cents. There are the experiences of falling short.

But there are the serendipities and the experiences of blessings too. We do eat and sleep to rise and eat and sleep again. But there are memorable meals, and there are times after intense pain when we have sleep "that knits up the raveled sleeve of care." Some of the best biblical expressions about the ongoing experiences of life, the good and bad together, are found in The Song of Solomon with its rejoicing in human love and Ecclesiastes with its true and humorous expression of what it is like to grow old (Eccl. 12). The Book of Proverbs also describes our life as human and how the young especially can get through it gracefully. Life is living, and the Wisdom literature of the Old Testament is wise indeed in describing it and in giving good advice about how to survive.

The creation account in Genesis also has some important things to say about life. According to Genesis, humankind is related to the earth, related to God, and related to others. Humans are distinguished from all other of God's creatures by the capacity for, intensity in, and quality of relationships. To be made in the image of God means to have the ability and the responsibility to relate to God, self, others, and the world around us. Life is living. But life is living because God, the source of life, has called us into being. The quality of life depends very much on how we relate to God, the self, others, and the world around us.

I will talk about relations with the self, others, and the world later. Just now I want to answer the question: What is life as it relates to God? Of course, this is regrettably an artificial division because our relationships with self, others, and our world enter into how we relate to God. And our relationship with God determines, to a large extent, how we relate to self, others, and the world around us. All of us are related to God because all life is the gift of God. Life is a biological organism undergoing experience. As biological organisms we are because God lets us be. The Christian faith starts its pilgrimage with the presupposition that God is He who creates, who lets be, who calls all things into being, enabling and sustaining them.

Our answers about the questions of life are two. Life is undergoing experiences. Life is the first gift of God.

The Greeks had a word for it. In fact, they usually had at least two words for everything. This is true of life. One Greek word for life is *bios* (we get our term *biology* from it). Literally, biology is the study of living things. The second Greek term for life is *zoe.* This term usually refers to meaningful life. For example, it is coupled with the adjective "eternal" in John's Gospel to speak of God's greatest and highest gift: eternal life. We sometimes make this kind of distinction in English. We use the words *existence* and *life.* The popular sayings bring out this distinction. We speak of someone eking out a miserable existence, and we speak of someone really living. We can answer the question about life for all people. They are undergoing experiences, and they are creatures of God. The question now occurs: Is there a more meaningful kind of life that can raise human existence to the level of really living? There is; we call this Christian life—eternal life. I want to spend the rest of this chapter talking about that kind of life.

What Is the Heart of the Matter?

Some guides I've had give too much information. If you ask about a plant, they describe all its parts, its horticultural habits, and its technical name. That all has a place but not in a quick tour of the terrain. This is not a technical, heavily documented theology. It is an overview, especially for the aging, put in the analogies of common experiences. Often the impatient and the appropriate question is: "What is the heart of the matter?"[2]

The heart of the matter is Jesus Christ and the basic message about Him. We have all heard many teachings and sermons on the Christian faith. Some theological discussions on matters of doctrine become terribly technical, and there are different interpretations in various denominations, and sometimes in the same one, about points of doctrine. I feel it would help most pilgrims if we simplified the essential points of belief in the Christian community. If quality life has to do with Jesus Christ and the message about Jesus Christ, what are the major points of that message? What is the heart of the matter?

The earliest churches knew the essential gospel. The sermons at Pentecost and during the time of the consolidation, empowering, and outgrowth of the churches contain that message. You dare not tell your pastor, but the longest of those sermons can be read or preached in less than five minutes. This early Christian message is found in Acts 2, 3, 4, 5, and 10 in the sermons of Peter. In Acts 7 and 8 Stephen gave a capsule summary of God's holy history and purpose. Paul in Acts 13 preached a summarizing sermon similar to that of Stephen. In these first words of proclamation, I believe we have the basic elements of what is the heart of the matter. These elements are the crux out of which the theology of the New Testament grows.[3] These proclamations (*kerygma*-preaching, what a herald proclaims) are simple and direct. Their salient message is this: Jesus came from God; He was crucified according to the plan of God; God raised Him from the dead; Jesus sends the Spirit; Christ concludes the age.

The mystique in all of this is God's love (John 3:16). The confession which grows from this is: Jesus is Lord. From first to last it is God's doing, and it is marvelous in our eyes. It is all there. There are three cosmic moments: creation, cross, and consummation. It is the Creator, God, the Maker of heaven and earth, the God of Abraham, Isaac, and Jacob, who sends His Son Jesus. There is the cross. It is wicked persons who caused Him to be killed. That includes all of us, for we all have contributed our part to making this the kind of world in which Jesus had to die. There is consummation. He comes to "judge the quick and the dead" (2 Tim. 4:1; Compare Acts 10:42 and 1 Pet. 4:5). There is the threefoldness of God. God the Father sends God, the Son, and the Son sends God, the Spirit. The trinitarian rhythm of revelation was an insight the earliest Christians understood and affirmed. What would later be called the mysteries of the faith, the incarnation of God's Son, and the threefold fullness of God, the Holy Trinity, is enshrined by implication from the first. Centuries of agonizing doctrinal disputes stated it more precisely. But the earliest Christians of the New Testament knew it more intimately and phrased it in terms of God's action rather than in philosophical discussions about God.

The earliest message was good news. It did not start by telling people how sinful they are. Most people know their problem. The basic Christian proclamation begins with a positive note. Jesus has come from God. Herein and in Him is love, God's own kind of love. Come to the feast. God unites Himself with us. Jesus came and called for all. He received them and us gladly. The unconditional love of God was proclaimed and embodied in Jesus, God's Christ. Accompanying this heart-of-the-matter message was a plea for repentance and a request to believe.

Repentance and belief are key words in our answer to the next question.

How Do I Start the Christian Life?

This chapter really is a tour, and so far we have begun where all people must start. We have stopped to reflect about life and what life is. Life is experience. Life is the gift of God. The next stop was a necessary one to start a Christian pilgrim's tour. It was hearing the essential message of God, as lived out by Jesus, and as proclaimed by the early church in the power of the Spirit.[4]

Having reflected on life and having heard the Christian message, it is now our turn to act. In one sense acting toward God is easy because God's Spirit helps us in the act. We do not come to God unless His Spirit works with our spirit in making our move toward Him. This is the affirmation which is important to a conversionist theology. We are enabled by God's Spirit to respond to God's Word, Jesus, as we hear the words of Scripture. And when this response-able moment comes, we are responsible to repent and to believe.

Repent is an interesting word. In the picturesque language of the Old Testament it means to turn around. The metaphor is an apt expression. We are going in one way, and then we turn to go in another. Conversion in adulthood is a more intensive experience than conversion in childhood. This is so because we have more experiences, more awareness, and more settled paths from which to turn.

We must not, however, leave the unrealistic impression that this turning makes us a totally different person. We still have the same conditioned responses, and we still deviate from the path; but we are now turned in a different direction. Repentance is being sorry for what we have done that was wrong, that was selfish, that was less than best. Feeling sorry is the psychological aspect of the theological experience of repentance. We will discuss the nature of sin later, but I want to be sure at this point that we see one thing clearly. Our feelings of guilt and sorrow can be misdirected. We can feel sorry because we got caught. We can feel sorry about things other people have told us we should feel sorry about. Sometimes we confess too much and too quickly. That is, we are quick to say we are sorry without doing any reformation of the things that are wrong. We also are so conditioned by what others tell us is sinful that we are confessing things that may not really be the deeper problems and dilemmas of our lives. Confessing some personal indiscretion such as gluttony may make us feel better, but that confession will not substitute for failing to confess our unethical business practices that may affect numerous people and structures in our society. Both types of confession, the too glib which does not reform and the too superficial which does not uncover the real problems, are less than adequate repentance.

Most older adults have been longtime people watchers. You have seen both kinds of repentance. There are the frequent repeaters who confess long and loud and often but do not seem to make any changes in their actions. And there are those who confess what it is convenient to confess but miss the really important things. It is easy to see these missteps in repentance in others. We also need to be honest enough to look just as closely at ourselves. I recall the indignant woman who was outraged at how dingy her neighbor's clothes looked on the line. When she went out to make some cutting remarks, she discovered that it was not her neighbor's clothes that were dingy. It was her own windows. There's a good lesson for all of us in that humorous incident.

As we grow older, repentance becomes a harder labor for most of us because we do understand it better. Repentance is one of the hinges on the wicket gate toward God. It is a swinging gate which we must use often and with much self-reflection. Repentance is a first step toward God. It is not a once in a lifetime thing. It is part of a daily process. It becomes harder to do with integrity, if we realize we are not going to do something about the wrongdoings we are confessing. Repentance indeed becomes "godly sorrow for sins" as we grieve over having to confess so often the same sins. There must be a first confession and a first moment when we consciously ask God for forgiveness. There should not be a last time we ask. Christian life has a beginning just as our physical life does, and just as physical life involves a process, so also spiritual life is process. There is the happy day on which a child is physically birthed. In a conversionist theology our spiritual birthday begins when we begin to repent. It is understood, unless it is a spiritual stillbirth, that there will be nurture and growth. One hinge on the gate to God is repentance.

The other hinge on the gate to God is faith. Just as God's Spirit enables us to repent, so also the Spirit enables us to believe. Faith is indeed the gift of God (Eph. 2:8-9). But, like all the gifts of God, it is to be used and exercised by us. It is appropriate to start where the Old Testament does with the faithfulness of God. Seniors who have seen so many things change so rapidly have a right to wonder if anything is secure and unchanging. Most of us have met enough people in life who did not keep their promises that we are, in our worst moments, highly skeptical. Our question is: Is there anyone who can keep a promise? Disillusionment and old age sometimes produce people who are suspicious of everyone and everything. If the mistake of childhood is to trust everyone, the bane of old age is to trust no one. There should be enough godly people who can be trusted to convince people that trust is a human possibility. There must be a central affirmation that God is trustworthy. In Scripture God is the God who keeps His promises. People who claim to be God's people should be trustworthy enough to give evidence that God can be trusted. It is difficult for disillusioned people, who are disillusioned by people, to be trusting. We must proclaim what Scripture says. God is trustworthy! We need also to try and embody what Scripture says. The people of God should be like God (Matt. 5:48). The foreground to faith is a firm grasp on the faithfulness of God.

In the New Testament the term for faith embodies at least three ideas. Faith includes knowing something to believe in. It includes trust and commitment. And it includes acting out of that trust and commitment. The Gospels and the Book of Acts are full of things most surely believed. The Book of Hebrews is an impassioned apologetic about the necessity and the blessings of belief. James is eloquent about how the person of faith is supposed to act. Faith is a total act. It involves the head (knowing the essential facts), the heart (making a decisive commitment), and the hands (doing something to demonstrate faith). It is a mistake to separate these dimensions of faith. Faith that is only knowledge is rational creedalism. Faith that is only commitment is emotional indulgence. Faith that is only good works is activist legalism. Faith is God's gift. Faith is also our act. It is a total act which involves the head, the heart, and the hands. Faith is the second hinge on the door that leads to God. We need always to repent. And we need to keep on believing. Repentance and faith are the beginning of the way to God. They are also the continuing path to the Father.

Am I OK?

As we continue to tour the pilgrimage of the Christian life, there are a variety of places we could stop and questions we could ask. These questions will concern the description of the Christian life. We will talk about what terms and insights are helpful in understanding what it means to continue the Christian pilgrimage, to be involved with the Christian way. How do the holy words and religious terms we use in church apply to the actual meaning of our life's experiences? Are we just talking, or are we talking about and living out of things that matter? Some few years back, churches were accused of answering questions no one was asking. That is a terrible indictment. The actual journey of life is too important to be cluttered with irrelevant questions and answers. I trust that you will see the application of the questions in this chapter to the reality of life.

A great deal has been written about self-esteem. Self-esteem is an important concept for older adults, and it is important that those who take care of those who cannot care for themselves recognize this necessity of self-esteem. In many geriatric centers, beauty-shop day is the most anticipated day on the schedule. All of us, from cradle to grave, want acceptance. We want to look OK and feel OK about ourselves. One of my most persistent concerns about major surgery was when I could get up and shave and shampoo my hair. Looking OK is one way of feeling accepted. Acting OK is another way. It doesn't take the residents of a convalescent center or nursing home long to fit into the routine and to do the expected thing. We do want to be accepted, all of us. One delightful part about many older folks is their tolerance for and acceptance of other people and perspectives. Many older people accept others, different from themselves, because they too know what it is to want to receive acceptance. The best-seller book on psychological acceptance *I'm OK, You're OK*[5] has increased our sensitivity toward affirming rather than criticizing others.

The most important affirmation of all is to be accepted by God, the source of our being. In Bible terms we call this being justified or justification. Paul especially had a pilgrimage toward acceptance. When he was Saul of Tarsus, he sought acceptance by keeping the law. Many religious people have the same pilgrimage. They work hard to please God. That pilgrimage is an all-consuming one. It is also a very frustrating one. We can never keep all of the rules. The problems that arise when we try to earn God's acceptance are: (1) pride in our accomplishments or (2) guilt because we can never do enough. Neither unjustified pride nor unnecessary guilt is a good basis for relating to the Father. In Jesus Christ, God accepts us as we are that He might help us to become what we ought to be. It is wonderful to be accepted by God. It is a necessary awareness for being a Christian.

God's justification is a forensic act. That is, He declares us to be right or what we ought to be because He sees us in Jesus Christ, who alone was what He and we ought to be. This idea of substitution and legal declaration has disturbed some people. They want to pay their own way and earn their own keep. This is the human cry for independence. But what God requires is perfection (Matt. 5:48), and none of us can attain it. Jesus is a substitute and a representative for us. He has done something for us we cannot do for ourselves. People who cannot acknowledge this are not ready for God. Jesus phrased it this way: "They that are whole have no need of the physician" (Mark 2:17, KJV; compare Matt. 9:12; Luke 5:31). There are certain conditions of the human community which make us all unwell. Those conditions are: (1) sinfulness, (2) the need for ultimate acceptance, and (3) the inevitability of death. In these matters we all need help. As we shall see in chapter 7, this is exactly what God has done for us in Christ. At this point I am primarily concerned to point out that God accepts us unconditionally in Jesus Christ.

Some of you started in business with a small stake that someone gave or lent to you. Your effort built your business and made it successful. But that initial investment of trust made all the difference. You came to believe in yourself because someone else believed in you. That is a good illustration of God's acceptance. Through the life and death of Jesus Christ, God tells us that we are important. He suffers on our behalf. He declares us to be right. He accepts us, and we can live out of that acceptance and learn to accept ourselves. The God who made us and knows us believes in us and accepts us. That is good news indeed. Christians on their pilgrimage must return to this place often—this place of the awareness of acceptance. We have some occasion to ask daily, "Am I OK?" The answer is always reassuring. Yes, through Jesus Christ you are OK. In Jesus Christ, God accepts you. We must return often to the place of acceptance, but we must also always go on from that place to responsibility. The next stop on our journey and the next question to be asked is: What's my part? If we stay only at the place of acceptance, we become satisfied. We become spiritually flabby and refuse to move on toward the next step of the Christian life which is striving.

But before I talk about striving, I want to ask you travelers a provocative question. If God has freely accepted us, should we not learn to accept ourselves and to accept others more completely? Some people are always "putting themselves down." Do not do that. If God who made you and knows you accepts you, why can't you accept yourself? Sometimes our difficulties in self-acceptance go back to our childhood when our parents may have given the impression that we could never please them. Learn to forgive your parents for being too demanding. Forgive them in the name of God who filled His own demands for us Himself. Then learn to live the accepted life.

Often we older people find it difficult to accept others, especially younger people. Why should we be so unrelenting and hard on them since God has been so accepting and gracious to us? Must not every generation be given the dubious privilege of making its own mistakes? Remember the parable of Jesus about the man who had been given much but would not forgive his small creditor even a little? (Matt. 18:23-35). We are outraged by this inequity. We ought to be a little more outraged by our own inequities in failing to accept others. With this basis of God's acceptance, we find the courage and the strength to move on to other places on the journey and to ask other questions along the road. It is now time to ask: What's my part?

What's My Part?

You cannot earn God's acceptance. He grants it to us freely in Jesus Christ. That is the doctrine of justification. It is the first stop on the Christian pilgrim's progress. And we must come back to visit there again and again. But there is a second necessary place we must visit. This is the place of striving. *Striving* is a good term to describe the doctrine of sanctification. We must do an alternate journey back and forth between acceptance, the passive receiving, and striving, the active participating places of the Christian life. Justification is God declaring us right through Jesus Christ. Sanctification is our striving with God's help to be what we ought to be.

Sanctification is being set aside to God and gradually becoming like the God to whom one is set apart. The biblical word for sanctification is related to the terms for *saint, sanctify* and *holy.* Our holiness is not exclusively of our own doing. God helps us. It is in His strength and our struggle that we become like Him. "Ye shall therefore be holy, for I am holy" (Lev. 11:45, KJV).

There are at least two misunderstandings about sanctification. One misunderstanding is the God-does-it-all view. The other misunderstanding is the God-does-it-instantly view. There are some who insist that sanctification is all God's work. Their mottoes are: "I just let the Lord do it"; "I have turned it all over to Him." Most persons who have lived a long while remember the anecdote about the preacher and the farmer. A farmer had bought a very run-down farm and with great effort had worked it into a productive, flourishing place. The preacher came by and remarked, "My, how God has prospered this place." The farmer replied, "Well, you should have seen what it was like when He had it by Himself." The point was not to deny the blessings of God; it was to emphasize the fact that God wants us to work with Him.

Working with God is important not only in the care of the earth but also in our own spiritual development. Those who turn it all over to God and claim they have no part in their spiritual development commit the mistake of spiritual pride. One would be spiritually perfect if God were doing it. This would mean sinless perfection. We are not and will not be perfect in this life, and there is no scriptural validation for claiming such perfection. Or if one did not claim to be perfect, yet claimed God was doing it all, he would be open to the question as to why God was not doing better than most Christians seem to be doing. The problem of letting God do it all is that God wants us to work with Him in being what we ought to be. This is not a self-improvement campaign. But it is, with God's help, a living out of the practical implications of James. Even Paul, in one of his last letters, was still fighting the fight, keeping the faith, and striving to finish the course (2 Tim. 4:7).

The second misunderstanding about sanctification is the God-does-it-instantly approach. Life is a total and progressive experience. The problem with those who want instant perfection or all sanctification at once is that there is nothing left to attain. If you "get all of God" at one time, what will you do for an encore? A man who was expecting instant perfection prayed, "Fill me, Lord." His wife, who had lived through several previous fillings, was heard to say: "Don't do it, Lord; he leaks." Generally, it is God's way with His creation to let life develop. The best testimony about Christian sanctification or striving was given by a senior adult who confessed humbly, "I'm sorry before God that I'm not yet what I ought to be, but I'm grateful to God that I'm not what I used to be."

It is necessary that we commute back and forth between justification and sanctification on our Christian journey. If we bask only in His acceptance, we become flabby because we do not exercise the gifts of the Spirit. If we strive always without relaxing into the grace of acceptance, we become brittle and break. Nor are we to suppose that we are saved by grace and then transferred to a basis of works. It is a daily commute. God is with us on the journey. When we are accepted, we can do all things through Christ who strengthens us (see Phil. 4:13). When we have done our best and are discouraged with the results, we can "Commit [our] way unto the Lord; trust also in him; and he shall bring it to pass" (Ps. 37:5).

What Is a Born-Again Christian?

After beginning our journey and learning to commute between acceptance (justification) and striving (sanctification), there are other stops on the road. I will name three of these "stops" because one hears them called out so often and wonders what they are like. The first is "born again." This is an expression used by Jesus in John 3:3. It is a vivid metaphor which likens the Christian life to a new birth. The symbolism is carried through in the act of baptism which is likened to a death, burial, and resurrection. The idea is extended by Paul's expression: If any man be in Christ, he is a new creature" (2 Cor. 5:17 KJV).

The term *born again* speaks about conversion. It is a term that stresses how we got to be Christian. Most everyone understands that Jesus' expression "born again" means to believe on Him, means to start a new life. The question is asked: How are you born again? Two classical answers have been given. One is a sacramental answer. The other is a conversionist answer. The sacramental answer suggests that one is born again primarily by the Christian rites of baptism and the Lord's Supper. The other suggests that one is born again by making an intentional and conscious acceptance of the Christian message leading to a conversion experience. All of these could fit together, but it is an important distinction as to which comes first. Born-again

Christians are those who insist on the priority of a conscious and intentional decision for Christ preceding the ordinances.

The term *born again* came into popular, public expression in the late seventies in America. Sometimes it is used to describe a Christian life-style and/or politics. Technically and biblically, the boundaries of the born-again city are confined to the meaning of how one enters the Christian life. The born-againess stresses a disjunction or a difference of a Christian life from a non-Christian life. The term implies a time of conversion. For some, this time becomes the all-consuming idea. This placing of great importance on an exact moment of conversion can be very upsetting to the elderly. And it is easy to understand why they would be upset. On the one hand, this "conversion-moment" stress depends more on an adult experience or one in which one has known great sin before coming to a turnaround. And on the other hand, this conversion-moment stress tends to play down the process toward conversion which many children have who are reared in a Christian home or who came to Christ at a fairly young age.[6]

Another factor that enters into the discomfort of some elderly people is a weakening of memory and a loss of details. We may all be grateful to God that our salvation does not depend on our memory or on our having a thunderbolt experience. Our being born again depends on God bringing us to faith, our exercising our faith, and God and ourselves continuing the journey together. Any number of ordinary Christians have been very confused because they didn't have a Damascus Road experience. Neither did Peter. Many do not live an immoral life leading to a crisis experience; neither did Paul. We know we are born again as much by our continuing experience with God as we do by the beginning of the process. In fact, if a dramatic and overwhelming experience does not continue into a living relationship with God, there is much reason to question if it is a genuine born-again experience. Born again speaks of renewal, or new resources, of starting over. We all need that. And there was a first occasion. It brought us into a different relationship and gave us options we had not previously had. The answer to what is a born-again Christian should be given from the Bible. A born-again person is one whom God has renewed and who has accepted that renewal. Many Christians want to get off at this stop of the journey and rejoice again in their born-againness. This is appropriate. But you cannot stay there. The bus is leaving. Life is an ongoing process. So is the Christian life.

Is It Safe?

There is one word that appeals to all senior adults—safe. *Safe* and *safety* are important and much-used words. We all would like to take a pilgrimage to "safe" city. People whose strength is not what it was are, and ought to be, concerned about broken bones, tumbles down the stairs, and the violence of society. Crimes against the aged are on the rapid rise. White-collar crimes in financial institutions call for the question: Are our savings safe? If we are going to live longer, and the statistics say we can, we want a safe life. And that is not too much to ask. There are some helps such as special protected places for seniors. Safety seat belts are more used among the elderly than among other folk. The "Gray Panthers" are on the prowl mobilizing the combined resources of the older generation.

All of this is to the good. But how does this fit into a theological discussion? Very naturally. We seldom connect the everyday adjective *safe* with the theological code word *saved.* But we should. To be saved means to be in a wide, spacious place, to have room to breathe. *Salvation,* the religious term, applies to all of life. The final and ultimate dimension of salvation is spiritual. But the proximate and immediate implications of salvation apply to physical and psychical well-being. A church that is interested in the salvation of senior adults will care if they are fed and will do something about their loneliness.

Young pastors, who have no experiential awareness about physical limitations, will often use their friendship to encourage seniors to "come out" at night. I want to appeal to young ministers to keep the safety factor in mind. I still bear the marks of ancient anxiety when I think of an elderly woman who was badly injured, so badly that walking would never again be a painless thing. I had urged everyone to come out for a special Wednesday night meeting that was not worth losing one's health for. This woman was badly injured in an automobile wreck. Most seniors love the fellowship of the church and will come as much as they are able. A wise spiritual leader will let the aging be the judge of when they are able. If all of this sounds strange in a theological discussion, that is only because we have overspiritualized the biblical meaning of salvation. Biblical soul-winners are those who will be concerned about the total person.

God alone will ultimately save us. We are more aware than we would admit that there are no "safe" cities. Our salvation and our safety lies with God. In the meanwhile, all the things we can do for the comfort and peace of mind of the aging are "salvific" acts indeed. The most important thing we can do for the aging is to bear faithful witness to God in Christ, who is "the Shepherd and Guardian" of our souls (1 Pet. 2:25). Less important, but still extremely helpful, are the things we can do to make the world of the aging a safer world. Everybody wants to be safe. Nobody is absolutely safe in a world like this. All of us can be saved, finally, from a world like this. Most of us could be safer in this life, our only historical life. We owe it to one another to work for a safer world here and now; especially is this true for those who know the promise of ultimate safety. Just as we have a prelude of heaven in the joy of Christian living, so also we should have a preview of the safe city of God in a salvation which begins on earth and comes at last to the haven of rest.

What Is It Like to Be Ransomed?

This question has taken on new meaning since America was held hostage in the Iranian crisis. Before that crisis, redemption was something the thrifty housewife did with trading stamps. The trauma of the hostage crisis was real, and the act of redemption and repatriation kept us all glued to our television sets. In that crisis there were people, our people, illegally seized and imprisoned. The anguish of helplessness and the rage of inability to remedy the situation consumed much of our national energies.

The ancient world understood hostages and redemption very well. Hostage taking and ransom demands were a way of doing politics. Even royal princes were sent to Rome for education *and* to keep their fathers in line. But most hostages were not royal, and they were not given royal treatment. Caravans were held hostage until the owners of merchandise paid up. Women who fell into disrepute could be brought so low as to be sold on the slaver's block. Their only hope was to find a good man who would pay a price for them and treat them kindly (Hosea and Gomer). Widows had little hope unless a kinsman redeemer guaranteed their safety and security (Boaz and

Ruth). It is not a pleasant stop on the pilgrimage, this city of bondage. Yet it is one the entire human community passes through. It is more realistic than fatalistic to say that all persons have some choice in the kind of bondage they endure. Paul, the slave of Jesus Christ, rejoiced in the only kind of bondage which liberates. Jesus, the ransom for many (Mark 10:45), by His death gives evidence of the bondage all have in sin (Rom. 3:23).

All hostages have one question in common: "Does anyone care enough to do something about my plight?" This is a question many older people ask. The aging are often in bondage to pain, to insecurity, to those who care for them. Whatever Jesus' cryptic message to Peter may have meant for him historically, the prophetic words are literally true for thousands of aging persons in our world today. "Further, I [Jesus] tell you [Peter] this in very truth: when you were young you fastened your belt about you and walked where you chose; but when you are old you will stretch out your arms, and a stranger will bind you fast, and carry you where you have no wish to go" (John 21:18). The bondage of physical infirmity and helplessness in old age is a haunting specter to everyone who has attended services at a nursing home.

What do we as God's people say to the older, helpless people of God? We should say two things: (1) We should say that God in Jesus Christ loves you enough, finally, to deliver you from this bondage, and (2) we should say that we love you enough to do all we can to help carry your burdens and make your bondage as bearable as possible. There are many levels of meaning to the old gospel song: "Redeemed, how I love to proclaim it!" We all have a turn at living in the city of bondage. Spiritually, we have been released from it. For many, places of physical and psychological bondage may be a grim reality. Gerontologists tell us that living in a care facility is probable for many of us. All stops on the pilgrimage of the Christian life are not necessarily pleasant. The place called bondage, whatever its dimensions, calls forth from us the question: Does anyone care enough to do something about my plight? The cross of Jesus Christ is God's stark, final answer to that question. And the care and concern of the church should give all the realistic, practical affirmation to that question that we can. What is it like to be ransomed? It is like having someone care. It is like being set free. It is like coming home. It is like heaven!

What Are the Expenses?

The first question travelers ask is how much does it cost? That is an important question. Read the fine print before you sign on. Are there hidden costs beyond the basic tour price? Good travel agents and tour companies will put it all up front. As one who has traveled much, I always want to be sure my tour groups know the whole and total cost. Cheap marketing tricks have stranded hapless travelers around the world.

There are those selling the Christian pilgrimage at the front end with the astonishing claim: "It costs nothing." Some proclaiming this really put the bite on later. For a free trip they come back with some fairly heavy costs, financial, physical, and in high-priced loyalty. Older people are usually leary of this kind of sales pitch. They know that somewhere down the line the expenses will have to be paid.

Honesty at the front end is by far the best policy. If you become a Christian, it will cost you your life. Jesus repeatedly told His disciples to take up their cross, to expect to sacrifice, and not to look back. "In the world you will have trouble." There is a paradox on the Christian pilgrimage. It is contained in the titles of two gospel songs: "Jesus Paid It All" and "I Surrender All." A paradox is a seeming, logical inconsistency. It does not conform to straight-line thinking. Both parts of a paradox are true, and each part must be explained separately. We will talk about "Jesus Paid It All" in chapter 7. At this point it is appropriate to discuss the "I Surrender All" truth of discipleship.

The requirements of God are all-consuming. But they are all-consuming in such a way as to reconstitute, renew, and recreate the one who obeys. Obeying the first commandment of God will save us. The first commandment of God is to love Him with all our heart, mind, and soul (Ex. 20:1-3; Deut. 6:3-9). When we love Him supremely through Jesus Christ ("This is my Son, My beloved; listen to him," Mark 9:7), we permit Him to save us because we cannot save ourselves. God desires that we love Him for our sake, not for His. It is in losing ourselves that we find ourselves. It is in giving that we receive. An old and familiar prayer expresses this paradox very well.

Lord, make me an instrument of Thy peace;
Where there is hatred, let me put love;
Where there is anger, let me put forgiveness,
Where there is discord, let me put unity,
Where there is doubt, let me put faith,
Where there is error, let me put truth,
Where there is despair, let me bring happiness,
Where there is sadness, let me bring joy,
Where there is darkness, let me bring light.

O Divine Master, grant that I may desire:
To console rather than to be consoled,
To understand rather than to be understood,
To love rather than to be loved.

Because it is in giving that we receive;
In forgiving that we obtain forgiveness;
In dying that we rise to eternal life.[7]

This commitment sounds like a daring venture. One philosopher called it a leap of faith. Peter called it leaving all to follow Jesus (compare Matt. 19:27; Luke 18:28). Dietrich Bonhoeffer called it "costly grace."[8]

There is an element of risk in Christian commitment. This paradox of Jesus paying all and our surrendering all is illustrated for me by a journey I have taken several times. The journey is to Laity Lodge near Leakey, Texas. There is a river on the campsite. The lodges and retreat center with all of their comforts, delightful food, and inspirational possibilities are located on a bluff overlooking the river. In order to reach the lodge one has to take a shallow road through the river bed. First comers usually stop their cars and look dismayed. There is a sign at that point which says: "Yes, you do have to drive through the river." There should be a sign at the juncture of every conversion which bears that message. Commitment costs, and prospective Christians should be told about it.

The wonderful part about paying these expenses is that they are recoverable. They are recoverable both en route and at the end of the journey. Let me try to explain that point. Christians are, or ought to be, pleased with their pilgrim way. For example, obedience to parents and application of their wisdom can certainly lead to a longer life than the excesses of the prodigal son. Awareness of acceptance and assurance of forgiveness gives not only the power of positive thinking but also, and even more, a firm basis for facing life with its triumphs and tragedies. Obeying a basic Christian code should lead to a healthier life-style. Of course, if the mode becomes a restrictive legalism without grace or humor, it can lead to a less healthy life.[9] But the truth of obedience and its rewards are not to be judged by its misunderstanding and its misapplications. The first part of the first commandment is to love God.

There is a second part of the commandment, and that is to love one's neighbor as oneself. It is obvious that this part of the commandment has two parts, and they are inevitably interwoven. Next to our love for God is the cost of loving others as ourselves. That means we must love others, and that means we must love ourselves. It is only recently we have become aware of the necessity of self-esteem, if we are to esteem others. Love for self is generally supposed to be selfishness. An interesting battle has been waged within all of us at this point. We are aware that Scripture says we should esteem others better than ourselves. We have been taught to be self-effacing. Yet within ourselves, we could not help but feel kindly disposed to ourselves, even while we were practicing humility. Later I will describe how self-love can become obsessive and destructive. I would like to point out here that good self-esteem and a proper care and concern for the self (that is, the total being, physical, psychical, spiritual) is necessary to health. Such self-esteem is necessary to the kind of health that can healthily love others. If we love others instead of ourselves, they can become our idols. If we love self without loving others, we become our own idol.

But by loving God supremely and emulating His love as evidenced in Jesus, we can balance our affections and relationships. His self-giving love is related to the seriousness with which He is God for us. Our love to self and one another should grow from an honest and realistic appraisal of who we are. We must not let the transgressions, misunderstandings, and misapplications of the commandment do away with its truth. There are those who despise themselves. They have no integrity of love to offer others. There are those who adulate themselves. They have no love left over with which to love others. There are those who are so self-effacing that the love they offer others is too anemic to be helpful. The Master has said to love God supremely and to love our neighbor as ourselves (compare Matt.

22:37-40). This is the sum of the matter. And on this hangs the teachings of the law and the prophets (compare v. 40). It is also on this basis that Jesus fulfilled the law and the prophets and gave himself a "worthy sacrifice" for the sins of humankind.

This cost of loving self and others also brings its own rewards in the form of satisfying relationships. But it is a difficult task because there are so many deceptive and devious ways we love ourselves and others. What is needed is constant examination of our motives and God, the self, and others. That is a painful process. For these motives are always mixed. Sometimes our motives are based on fear, desire for gain, or desire to control. The attempt at manipulation of God and others is not always missing from self-effacing people. The Christian life will cost us a daily process of sorting things out and trying to be honest and fair with God, others, and the self.

The specifics of how this is worked out is Christian ethics. Ethics is, or ought to be, an integral part of theology. But it would require a separate book to enumerate and clarify the issues. Let me say here that the cost of full Christian discipleship will include: matters of *substance* (ecological concerns, income, outgo, sharing with others, determining an appropriate individual life-style, influencing social policies bearing on need and life-style), matters of *time* (personal schedules, social expenditures, including the amount of time that should be spent by working people in pursuit of the necessities of life, how best to assist youth in the expenditure of time, how best to help the aging make satisfying and useful the time left to them after their formal careers), and matters of *energy* (the wise use of natural and technologically produced energy, the demands and amounts of energy that society and individuals spend in protecting/preserving/destroying the race, the energy individuals expend on life-styles, and the relative benefit or harm of this to humanity). You may well remark that this impressive list will involve you all of your life. That is what it means to be a Christian, to be involved with God, the self, and others all of one's life in all of the relationships of life.[10]

I hope this frank discussion of price will not deter any honest seekers from the journey. I also hope this candid discussion of costs will be a point of clarification for those who have been on the journey for some time. But there is a consideration for the Christian pilgrimage which is more important than the cost. Who is the tour leader? Who is in charge?

Who Is in Charge?

One summer I was leading a tour through a beautiful country. A few people on the tour took exception to the way I was conducting the tour. I can understand that. They really wanted out. They wanted to do what they wanted to do, but we were in a foreign culture, and we were obliged to be together, for we had to move and relate as a group. It was difficult. I am certain that it must have been very hard for them.[11] Before you sign on for the Christian pilgrimage, it is important to ask: "Who is in charge?" The answer is simple: God is in charge. I am sure you're enormously relieved to hear that. It is good news. For He, like no one else, would like for you to enjoy the journey. And He will do everything within reason to make life pleasant. But God will not be untrue to Himself. He will not change the itinerary. He will not rearrange the bounds that are set to our existence.

We all live within constraints. We all come somewhat "determined" as to what kind of bodies we have, our physical makeup. No one would deny this kind of determination. Older people call it "the way life is." We often hear someone say: "She was just born that way!" In addition to these biological boundaries, there are social boundaries. We are as we are partly because we are born in a certain place with a given culture and at a particular time in history. We all are people of time and place. We call this social determination. It is also true that we reflect, even in old age and especially in old age, the circumstances in which we grew up. Our parents, or those who acted as parents for us, do tend to shape and color our lives. This is psychological determinism. It is often said: "He has his father's temper." That is not really true, for his father probably still has his own temper, and the son developed his temper using the father's model. Then may it not also be said that in and through and beyond these circumstances we are likewise "determined" by God. This is one side of the story; and it is true. God is in charge. We are determined. But if we stop here we have only part of the story.[12]

My dilemma with all of these is that they are one-sided. They do not adequately take into account the aspect of human freedom which

God has willed His creatures should have. It is a mistake also to take any one of these factors in isolation. God's determination of us does not come apart from the biological, social, and psychological aspects of our life. When the theological doctrine of predestination is applied only to individuals in matters of salvation of the soul, it becomes an unrealistic and nonbiblical insight. The guidance of God shapes not only individual destinies but also the courses of nations and the outcome of world history.

The truth of the freedom of people is expressed by an old theological saying, "It was the will of God that mankind should have a will." The will of nations can affect the outcome of world history. The strong or weak wills of kings and rulers have affected the way society went. The health of a people, physical, social, psychological, and spiritual helps to shape their destiny. The individual decisions of a person can and do help determine her way of life and her theological destiny. It is not easy to fit together the balance and interplay between what is determined and what is free. In ancient times Augustine took the determined side, and his opponent Pelagius took the freedom side. At the time of the Reformation, Calvin opted for determination and Arminius for freedom. The vast majority of the Christian community has realized that there is the necessity of both.

Scriptures have been found to support both views. The determinists quote the Old Testament (for example, Jer. 1:5), Jesus (John 15:16; 17:5-21), and Paul (Rom. 9—11). The freewill advocates do the same. "Choose you this day whom ye will serve" (Josh. 24:15, KJV). "If any man will come after me, let him deny himself, and take up his cross, and follow me" (Matt. 16:24, KJV). "That if thou shalt confess with thy mouth the Lord Jesus, and shalt believe in thine heart that God hath raised him from the dead, thou shalt be saved" (Rom. 10:9, KJV). Every attempt to make God the sole determiner of our destiny comes to serious problems with matters of injustice, suffering, and evil. Every attempt to hold humanity solely responsible for all that happens has no answer for providential patterns in history, and it ends up too prideful of the human condition. Even if we cannot make a clear-cut description in every case, we must affirm that God has set the boundaries and that within those boundaries both societies and individuals make meaningful decisions.

In trying to solve this dilemma of who is in charge, two circles have been drawn. One represents the will of God and the other the will of man. Extremists on the theological determinism side have drawn the circles like this:

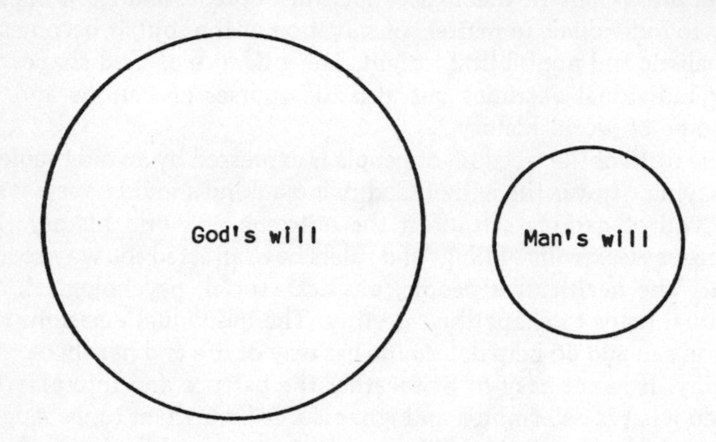

Obviously, in this kind of picture, the large will of God will overwhelm the small will of man. Extremists on the freedom side have drawn the circles like this:

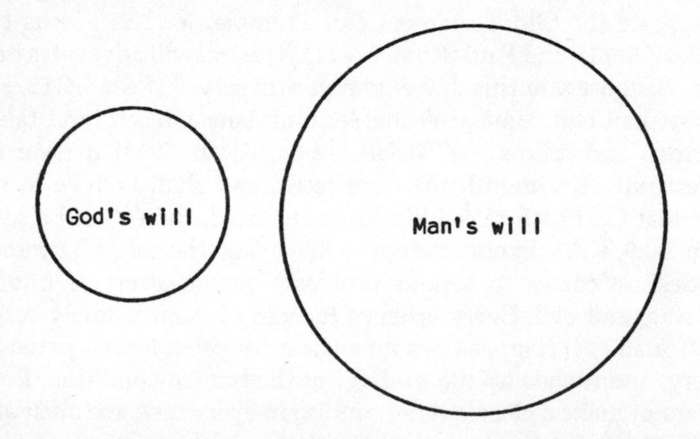

This reverses the position and is not very realistic about God. If the will of humanity is larger than God, then there is no point in having a "God" except to use the idea of "God" as a means of justifying one's own decisions and having one's own way.

I would like to suggest a third way in which the circles may be drawn. This third way requires three circles, not two:

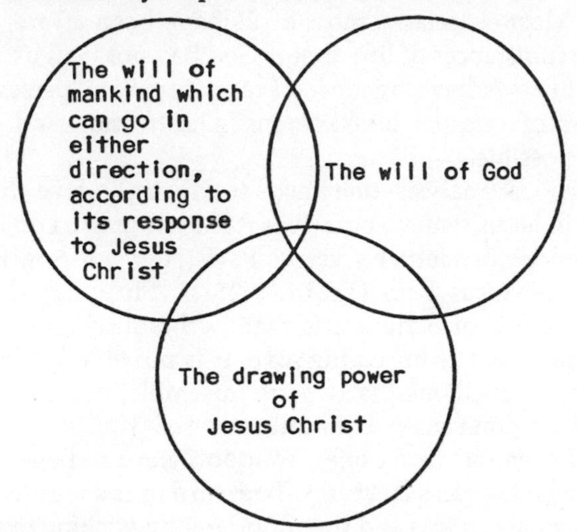

It seems to me a more biblical perspective to say that we are able to exercise freedom within our theological determination in relation to the drawing power of Jesus Christ. "And I, if I be lifted up from the earth, will draw all men unto me" (John 12:32, KJV). Nations and individuals are theologically bound and determined by decisions for and against Christ. This view, to be sure, raises an enormous theological question. But what of individuals and whole nations who have never heard of Christ? That is our final question on the Christian pilgrimage.

But before we answer it, we need to ask a secondary question. What about people on the tour, can they opt out? This too has been a great argument. Theologians speak of it as perseverance of the saints *versus* apostasy. Most ordinary church people would recognize the terms *once saved, always saved* versus *falling from grace.*

Once more, the long journey senior adults have made helps us to see Scripture in the light of life and vice versa. Most of us realize that it is relationship and not status which counts. Most of us have walked in such rocky terrain that we know the Christian life is sometimes up and sometimes down. All of us have lived long enough to see some who very early made professions of faith as children and then observed those children become consenting adults who have knowingly and intentionally denounced the way of Jesus in word and deed. Most especially, most of us have been aware, in the despairing circumstances of life, that if God had not held us and helped us we would never have "made it." Preservation and perseverance are not matters of celestial bookkeeping. Disaffection and wandering astray are possible.

But in the last analysis, one needs to ask if the love that will not let us go will let us remove ourselves from His grasp. I do not believe so. One can debate Hebrews versus Paul (Heb. 6:4-6 *vs.* Rom. 8:35-39) and Paul versus Paul (1 Cor. 9:27 *vs.* Phil. 1:6) all day. The prevalent opinion of Scripture is that God is in charge. Part of His being in charge is His unceasing love. It is possible while being His child to be so rebellious that we are miserable, and sometimes one wonders if we don't make Him unhappy too. But in our better moments, and even our worst ones, we don't want to be let go. We do not want to be hopeless creatures. To return to the tour leader analogy, we can spoil our trip and that of others by wishing ourselves out of the circumstances. In the last analogy, however, we are there, and He is there to see that we get home.

How does one explain those "spiritual stillbirths" that seemed to start but did not continue? There are two old expressions that may help. "Where there is life there is hope," or "God's not finished with me yet." A third expression can be added. "The faith that fizzles before the finish was faulty from the first." What we are talking about is not church membership or living by someone's culturally conditioned code. What we are talking about is the future of the world and our eternal destiny. Scripture is unambiguous about that (Ps. 8; John 17). These ultimate matters lie in the hands of God. And I, for one, am happy to let them reside there. For the God in whose hands the world lies is the kind of God who conquers through love and whose way is best for His world. He's in charge. God lets us, within the given parameters, decide on matters pertaining to ourselves and affecting our circumstances. So far as we can determine, death is the boundary of our individual freedom, and the end of the age is the limit of civilization's historical possibilities. The Spanish farewell *vaya con Dios* (go with God), the French *adieu* (to God) and even the English *good-bye* (God be wi ye) say something about our journey. But what of others and their journey?

What About Others?

Travel broadens our horizons. In our cosmopolitan, interdependent, satellite, jet-age world, we have become aware of others. It is easy to confine Buddhists to a realm outside God's love if one has never met a Buddhist. But when the Vietnamese family comes to us as a church project, and we see those adorable black-eyed children and realize they represent millions like them, then we begin to ask in earnest: "What about others?" Before some people travel outside their culture, they assume everyone is like them: "our kind of folks" is the expression. But if we travel very far and observe very well, we will know this is not the case. What about others? Does not Christianity feel that Christ is the answer? "For there is no other name under heaven granted to men, by which we may receive salvation" (Acts 4:12). The answer is yes. Within this yes there have been three viewpoints. One of them is distinctly and implicitly biblical.

One view about others is that they are in God, and with God; they are saved because the revelation which is given in Jesus of Nazareth is also given in and through other founders of religion and other prophets of God. Given this view, Christian missions is composed of pointing out the comparable and compatible points between world religions.[13]

A second view about others is that they are saved through their own religion because of God's compassion. This salvation is Christian, says this view, because, whether or not other religions know or acknowledge it, the cosmic Christ has been active in giving enough insights through that religion that full salvation is possible. In this view, Christian missions is designed to point how and which doctrines are true because they are related to Christianity.[14]

The third view is that for full salvation, everyone needs the message about Jesus who is God's Christ. Full and complete salvation is found supremely in Him. In this view the purpose and performance of Christian missions is to tell all the world the story of Jesus Christ. This view is the traditional Christian perspective. It should be noticed that this view says Jesus is the fullest revelation of God, not necessarily the only revelation of God. For God is opaquely found in the world around us and in the law of conscience within us. Likewise, we must affirm that wherever goodness, wholeness, happiness, health, unity, and life are found, God is the author of them. This third view can acknowledge that there are degrees of reward and punishment[15] and that Christ is the focus of all of God's other diffuse revelations of Himself. Early Christians used the idea of Jesus as the *logos* of God. One implication of this idea is that He is the touchstone which brings to full meaning all of the rationality and purpose in the world, wherever it is found. Jesus is God's final and fullest revelation of God. Jesus is the clearest picture of God the world has ever seen. This is a faith presupposition of the Christian community. That we share Jesus with all is important. How we do it may be even more important. God is "not willing that any should perish" (2 Pet. 3:9, KJV). Jesus comes to draw all the world back to God (John 12:32). We are given an awesome mandate to share the gospel of Christ (Matt. 28:19-20).

In the final analysis, He who leads the tours of life's pilgrimage and has set the parameters of existence will make the final determination. How is it possible in history to identify His purpose and His ways? Ultimately through Scripture. But, proximately, there is a community of God's purpose whose distinguishing marks we may describe. This is the church. We will move to the description of the community of Jesus in the next chapter. The analogy of a journey, a tour, a pilgrimage has, I trust, served us well. We are not done with the trip. There are more stops on the Christian tour than one brief book can express. Good traveling!

Notes

1. Go back and reread John Bunyan's *Pilgrim's Progress.* Some few years back on the occasion of the 300th celebration of its writing, I read it for the first time in thirty years. Bunyan's work, coupled with the poignant story of his hard life, has a remarkable meaning for those of us who grow weary, are tempted to give up, have flirted with Vanity Fair, and have dreaded the lions that we do not realize are chained. We understand better than we used to that the Celestial City is a goal not easily kept in mind and not readily attained. Besides, it is fun to match some of Bunyan's characters with some of our friends. If we look close enough into Bunyan's metaphorical mirror, we might even find something about ourselves.

2. For a theological work that combines technical scholarship and good factual material, see Hans Kung, *On Being a Christian,* trans. Edward Quinn (Garden City, N.Y.: Doubleday, 1976).

3. Compare C. H. Dodd, *The Apostolic Preaching and Its Developments* (London: Hodder and Stoughton, 1936).

4. See Juergen Moltmann's *The Church in the Power of the Spirit: A Contribution to Messianic Ecclesiology,* trans. Margaret Kohl (New York: Harper and Row, 1977). The strength of this title and this book is that Moltmann, a "theologian of hope," combines the doctrines of the church and the Holy Spirit.

5. Thomas A. Harris, *I'm OK, You're OK: A Practical Guide to Transactional Analysis* (New York: Harper and Row, 1969).

6. On children and conversion see *Children and Conversion,* ed. Clifford Ingle (Nashville: Broadman Press, 1970) and my *Theology for Children* (Nashville: Broadman Press, 1980), especially pp. 11-20,225-251.

7. Anonymous prayer attributed to Saint Francis of Assisi. Quoted from Frances R. Line and Helen E. Line, *Man with a Song: Some Major and Minor Notes in the Life of Francis of Assisi* (Garden City, N.Y.: Doubleday, 1982), p. 63. See also p. 67.

8. *The Cost of Discipleship,* trans. R. H. Fuller (New York: Macmillan, 1959), pp. 35-47.

9. On a positive and practical way of facing life with grace and humor, see the works of Grady Nutt: *Agaperos* (Nashville: Broadman Press, 1977); *Being Me* (Nashville: Broadman Press, 1971); *The Gospel According to Norton* (Nashville: Broadman Press, 1974); *So Good, So Far . . .* (Nashville: Impact Books, 1979).

10. For some good works in Christian ethics see: Henlee H. Barnette, *Introducing Christian Ethics* (Nashville: Broadman Press, 1961); Waldo Beach and H. Richard Niebuhr (eds.), *Christian Ethics: Sources of the Living Tradition,* 2nd ed. (New York: Ronald Press, 1973); Emil Brunner, *The Divine Imperative,* trans. Oliver Wyon (Philadelphia: Westminster Press, 1947); James M. Gustafson, *Christ and the Moral Life* (New York: Harper and Row, 1968); Stanley Hauerwas, *The Peaceable Kingdom: A Primer in Christian Ethics* (Notre Dame, Ind.: University of Notre Dame Press, 1983); Howard Kee, *Making Ethical Decisions* (Philadelphia: Westminster Press, 1957); T. B. Maston, *Biblical Ethics, A Survey* (Cleveland: World Publishing, 1967); Reinhold Niebuhr, *An Interpretation of Christian Ethics* (New York: Harper & Brothers, 1935); and Helmut Thielicke, *Theological Ethics* (Philadelphia: Fortress, 1964-69).

11. See the above discussion about hell and reflect on the play by J. P. Sartre: *No Exit.* (*No Exit and Three Other Plays.* [New York: Vintage Books, 1955]). The basic theme of Sartre's drama is that hell is other people whom we can't get away from, and we can't stand. Many of you will relate to this experience somewhere in life. Many have to work with people, live with people, and be around people that they don't like. You might want to reread the previous section with new appreciation for the difficulties involved in loving others as the self.

12. On genetic or biological determinism see Edward O. Wilson, *On Human Nature* (Cambridge: Harvard University Press, 1978) and *Sociobiology: The New Synthesis* (Cambridge: Belknap Press of Harvard University, 1975) and J. G. Murphy, *Revelation, Morality, and the Meaning of Life* (Totowa, N.J.: Rowman and Littlefield, 1982). On social determinism see B. F. Skinner, *Walden Two* (New York: Macmillan, 1948) and *Beyond Freedom and Dignity* (New York: Knopf, 1971). On psychological determinism see Sigmund-Freud, *Beyond the Pleasure Principle,* trans. James Strachey (New York: Liveright, 1950); *Civilization and Its Discontents,* trans. Joan Riviere (London: L. and Virginia Woolf at the Hogarth Press, 1930); *The Future of an Illusion,* trans. W. D. Robson-Scott (London: L. and Virginia Woolf at the Hogarth Press, 1928); *A General Introduction to Psychoanalysis,*

trans. Joan Riviere (Garden City, N.Y.: Garden City Publishing Co., 1938); *New Introductory Lectures on Psychoanalysis,* trans. W. J. H. Sprott (London: Hogarth Press, 1933); *An Outline of Psychoanalysis,* trans. James Strachey (New York: W. W. Norton, 1963); *Psychoanalysis and Faith: The Letters of Sigmund Freud and Oskar Pfluter,* ed. Heinrich Meng and Ernst L. Freud, trans. Eric Mosbacher (New York: Basic Books, 1964). For other writings by Freud, see James Strachey (ed.), *The Standard Edition of the Complete Psychological Works of Sigmund Freud,* 24 vols. (London: Hogarth Press, 1953-74). On theological determinism see John Calvin, *Institutes of the Christian Religion,* 2 vols. ed. John T. McNeill, trans. Ford Lewis Battles (London: SCM Press, 1960) especially book 3, chs. xxi-xxv, vol. 2, pp. 920-1008, and Henry Buis, *The Doctrine of Eternal Punishment* (Grand Rapids, Mich.: Baker, 1957), pp. 73-136.

13. Wilfred Cantwell Smith, *Meaning and the End of Religion: A New Approach to the Religious Traditions of Mankind* (New York: The New American Library, 1963); *The Faith of Other Men* (New York: The New American Library, 1963); *Questions of Religious Truth* (London: Victor Gollancz, 1967); *Towards a World Theology: Faith and the Comparative History of Religion* (Philadelphia: Westminster Press, 1981).

14. See K. Rahner and his intriguing but nonspecific ideas of the anonymous Christian: *The Christian of the Future,* trans. W. J. O'Hara (New York: Herder and Herder, 1967), especially pp. 85-88; *Grace in Freedom,* trans. Hilda Graef (New York: Herder and Herder, 1969), pp. 81-86; and also *Foundations of the Christian Faith: An Introduction to the Idea of Christianity,* trans. William V. Dyck (New York: Seabury Press, 1978), especially pp. 311-321.

15. See above, pp. 10-12.

3

Identifying Marks—The Church(es)

I have admired those people who can see a car and tell you its name, the year it was made, and evaluate its performance. Some men and boys can recite sports statistics by the hour. Women who sew a great deal can recognize a type of cloth at the drop of a stitch. Experts in plants amaze me at the way they recognize and call off the names of dozens of varieties of wild flowers. Many a farm woman can recognize the hillside plants to such a degree as to be the envy of a trained botanist. Most of us participate in the world of cars, sports, and plants without being able to recognize the identifying marks. It is that way for many of us about "church." For the majority of people, church is a place they go to worship. Specific buildings and familiar groups of people make up "church" for most of us. But there is a need to recognize and appreciate some more specific identifying marks. What is a church theologically? By function, church may be a place and a given group of people with its worship customs, but by definition and by essence we need to be more specific.

In the early history of the Christian community four identifying marks of "church" were suggested. These marks were: universality, oneness, holiness, and apostolicity. These marks continue to be important; unfortunately, they are more ideals than realities. The church ought to be one. Jesus prayed that it would be one (John 17:11). And in heaven the church will be one (compare Rev. 21:1-5). Nevertheless, on earth "the church" is so many different groups that it requires a large encyclopedia to list and describe, even briefly, its varieties in America.[1] "The church" ought to be everywhere. But it is not. I recently saw a map of an Asian island on which county after county was listed without any church of any kind. There are very few churches in Islamic countries; for Islam, where it is predominate, does not permit proselytizing or evangelization.

Holiness sometimes has a bad record even among conservative

Christian people.[2] All churches claim to be based on the doctrine of the apostles, but there is a great deal of doctrine and practice in all churches that goes beyond what the apostles clearly taught. For example, contemporary arguments about ordination are based more on tradition and practice than on the very sparse apostolic teaching and performance of ordination.

I very much applaud these classic four marks of the church. And it is important to uphold the ideal. While affirming these classic marks, I would like to suggest four others as the distinguishing marks of the essence of the church. These marks are: chosenness, corporateness, celebrativeness, and caringness. In and through these terms I would like to express our experience of "churchness" and raise questions we have had about the life and experiences of others within the many groups called churches. How do we identify a church? It sounds like an easy question. The answers are fairly involved.

Chosenness

One of the primary ways you can tell a church is by the sign. I don't mean the name sign with the particular name of an individual church; although that kind of sign helps, if you're looking for the place where a given congregation meets. The universally recognized sign of the Christian community is a cross. The cross is the Christian sign because it refers particularly to the way in which Jesus Christ died. The symbol, a sign with deeper and more involved meaning than appears on the surface, of the cross embraces all that Jesus was and did.[3] Paul's many references to the cross make this clear. In fact it was Paul, the first Christian theologian, who gave the sign "cross" its deeper, symbolic meaning. The cross is a good and obvious choice to represent Christianity.

The further question is how was Jesus Christ chosen? Paul expresses that also in a beautiful and wonderful way.

> Blessed be the God and Father of our Lord Jesus Christ, who hath blessed us with all spiritual blessings in heavenly places in Christ:
>
> According as he hath chosen us in him before the foundation of the world, that we should be holy and without blame before him in love:
>
> Having predestinated us unto the adoption of children by Jesus Christ to himself, according to the good pleasure of his will,

To the praise of the glory of his grace, wherein he hath made us accepted in the beloved.

In whom we have redemption through his blood, the forgiveness of sins, according to the riches of his grace;

Wherein he hath abounded toward us in all wisdom and prudence;

Having made known unto us the mystery of his will, according to his good pleasure which he hath purposed in himself:

That in the dispensation of the fulness of times he might gather together in one all things in Christ, both which are in heaven, and which are on earth; even in him: (Eph. 1:3-10, KJV).

John puts it more simply: "In the beginning was the Word, and the Word was with God, and the Word was God" (John 1:1, KJV). "So the Word became flesh" (v. 14). Jesus Christ, as God's manifestation, is God's chosen way of choosing us. If we want to know what it means to be chosen, we will have to look at the Christ event. There is an eternal dimension to Christ's chosenness. There is also an historical dimension to His chosenness, with all of the suffering that brought. And it was the climax of that suffering, the cross, that gives us the central symbol of Christ's chosenness.

But before I talk about the fact of Christ's chosenness and our relation to His chosenness, let me explain briefly what chosenness is all about. It often rankels us a little when someone is singled out for a special honor. There seems to be an exclusiveness about the idea of chosenness that goes against the democratic grain. Christians often associate chosenness with the Pharisaism of the New Testament. The term smacks of uppityness, privilege, and favoritism. That is because some chosen people, including Christians, have considered chosenness only from the point of privilege. When Christians talk about being the elect of God, and that is what the Bible word for chosenness means, they often stress salvation. Election, predestination, and all of those words we alluded to in the last chapter, from the viewpoint of the Christian life, are many times viewed from the side of privilege and favor. This is a mistake. In Scripture, to be the elect of God means not only to be cared for by God, it also—and especially—means service to God. And it preeminently means suffering for and with God. Christians can never hope to explain the biblical idea of chosenness to others as long as they stress the privilege and shun the suffering and service.

To be even more clear about chosenness, we need to reflect on the fact of choosing. To make a choice is to select or use one thing and not another. Choosing is the way things get done in our world. And choosing involves particularity. Nothing is done in general. Everything is done in particular. All farm chores are done one at a time using special, appropriate tools and instruments. All factory work involves special, particular, individual instruments. Everything we do, we do in particular. And every particular thing that is done begins with an act of choice. We may do what we do in a routine way because we are accustomed to it. But we do not do anything in general. Any-things are always some-things that are done by specific choice and action. God did not will to do things in general either. Creation is composed of several specific acts. So is redemption.

What makes chosenness seem so exclusive is that "the chosen" have interpreted their chosenness in terms of privilege. We have missed the truth of chosenness of God when we fail to see that He has always chosen for the sake of others and not for the sake of self. We sometimes make our choices based on what is best for others. God always does. Knowing this we can see and marvel that God chose Christ to accomplish what had to be done for giving eternal life. We marvel at this choice of Jesus Christ because God, who theoretically could have chosen a less painful and involved way of salvation, chose to involve Himself and to suffer in order to accomplish what had to be done. The why of the choice of Jesus is the nature of God's suffering love (John 3:16). It was a natural choice, this supernatural choice of Jesus, a choice which selfish human nature would not have taken. And Jesus chose the way of the cross (John 10:14-18). Therefore, the cross is a symbol of the church.

Let us carry the chosenness idea on to its logical conclusion and to its application to the church. Jesus chose disciples. He did not choose everyone in general. He chose certain persons in particular. It seems to me futile to ask why certain people were chosen to do certain tasks. In the instance of Jesus, it was because He was worthy and because He exclusively could do what had to be done. The humility of election and the exclusiveness of Jesus requires that we do not make the same claim fully for ourselves. We are not supremely worthy to be instruments of His choice, and we are not exclusively able to be involved in the task of redemption. In an absolute sense these things are true. But, in a qualified and in a different way, we can say that

God gives us a unique sense of worth and a distinctive sense of fitness in doing what we are asked, chosen, to do. There ought to be a genuine theological humility when we measure ourselves with the Master. There ought also to be a distinctive sense of worth in performing tasks and filling places in life which we, distinctively, can do. In this legitimate sense of worth and fulfillment of calling, we must look to Jesus to discern what our election is like.

The church, as the body of Christ, and we, as individuals in that body, participate in chosenness. We are chosen in Christ. We are chosen by Christ. We have, through Christ, chosen to participate in the chosenness of the church.[4] Our chosenness, like His, brings a sense of worth, of destiny, and of a distinctive task. Our chosenness, like His, also brings a sense of selflessness and service. Jesus did what He did for others. The church also must do what a church ought to do for others. The idea of the church as a gathering-in place for privileged persons to enjoy their status is a betrayal of the New Testament idea of the church. Our chosenness, like His, means service.

Service is a much overworked and ill-defined term. By service, I mean being on behalf of others. This kind of being is a very hard way of life to accomplish, for groups, as well as individuals, are selfish. Christian service involves using our substance to help others. Disaster relief is a significant dressing on the wounds of the world. But permanent solutions about how to help people help themselves and how to care for people who cannot care for themselves, wherever and whoever those people are, is a part of Christian service. Voting is a democratic privilege. Voting on behalf of others is a Christian use of that privilege.[5] Being on behalf of others is what a church should be. This kind of being does not sacrifice the self only. It also fulfills the self. This is characteristic of Jesus' chosenness. It should be characteristic of His chosen people. It is regrettable that both churches and individuals have not witnessed to their chosenness by this route of sacrificial (on behalf of others) type of service. Until we give recognition to this kind of chosenness, we do not understand what our chosenness is about. When we do practice the being-for-others responsibility of chosenness, others will begin to understand and appreciate what Christian chosenness is about.

There is that final aspect of chosenness which is to be dreaded but is to be undergone, as it too becomes necessary. There is the suffering dimension of chosenness. It is in this dimension that the symbol of the cross cuts deepest. When I speak of suffering as a distinctive part of the Christian mark of chosenness, I do not mean the suffering which we bring upon ourselves. I do not even mean the suffering which is brought about by others. And I do not mean the suffering of pain and problems which have no ostensible reason but which plague the entire human community. I will speak about those difficult aspects of our life later. Suffering as a mark of the church's chosenness is the suffering which we do willingly on behalf of others. This is the mark of chosenness which is most redemptive and Christlike. I do not know how to tell you how to "suffer" for others. To my dismay, I feel that I have done very little of this deepest mark of being chosen. The most profound aspect of suffering for others has, indeed, been done by Jesus on behalf of all of us. But I cannot agree that there is because of His suffering no need or occasion that we too may not be called on to suffer. He spoke often to His followers of taking up a cross and drinking a cup of suffering (for example, Matt. 16:24; 20:23).

In my opinion, there is no point where average American church life and average American Christians are so unlike "the true church" as at this point of suffering for others. This mark of chosenness is not to be self-imposed. Self-inflicted and self-imposed suffering gives rise to false martyr and messianic complexes. Even suffering occasioned by others may not be on behalf of others. Suffering imposed by others is more Christlike than self-caused suffering, but it is not necessarily a benefit to others. It was of benefit a generation ago when the stand of the confessing church of Germany and the heroic efforts of individuals to save Jews from destruction were widely known in some churches. The recent opening of the bamboo curtain in China has revealed stories of persecution and vicarious suffering throughout the last forty years. Isolated and tragic examples of suffering and martyrdom behind the iron curtain in Poland have won world admiration and possibly greater religious liberty for others. In America we have not often or deeply been in the circumstance of suffering, the deepest mark of Christian chosenness—suffering for others. We may well ponder if we are to avoid this mark entirely or permanently. We need to be faithful enough to Scripture to recognize that suffering is a mark of the chosenness of the church. Much of our easy triumphalism and rejoicing in our privilege is lopsided theology. It is also a poor witness to one of the biblical identification marks of the church of Jesus whose sign is a cross.

The chosenness of the church might be related to what Reformation Christians called the prophetic task of the church. This task was assigned parallel with the prophetic task of Christ's threefold office: prophet, priest, and king. The prophetic task of the church, like the task of biblical prophets, was to speak a word from God. And the well-known "prophet's reward" of service, suffering, and sent-by-Godness applies to both Christ and the church.

How do you relate to your own congregation at the point of the chosenness of God? There are moments when the track record of some Christians and some congregations is better than others. More specifically, how do you carry your chosenness? As a privilege to be enjoyed, a mark of divine favor to be exploited, a wonder to be amazed by, a gift to be shared, a service to be fulfilled, a possible cross to be carried when circumstances may make it necessary?

The question "What about others?" in the previous chapter leads to a discussion of how to look at world religions. The question raised about chosenness in this chapter is: What about the Jews? How does the chosenness of Christ and the chosenness of the church relate to the undeniable chosenness of the Jews according to Scripture? The story of the "church and the synagogue" has been a very troubled one. And the crux of that story lies in the understanding and meaning of chosenness.

There are no clear or totally satisfying answers to the relationship of Israel and the church. There can be no doubt that in the Old Testament Israel is seen as the chosen group designed to bless the nations. The original promise of God to Abraham (Gen. 12) is claimed by Jews, Christians, and Muslims alike. Each of these religions claims to be an inheritor of the promise: Jews through Isaac, Muslims through Ishmael, and Christians through Christ. Christians have sided with Jews in acknowledging that Isaac is the "true" heir. But they have disagreed with Jews that Isaac's descendants were faithful to the covenant. Some Christians feel that Israel's disobedience to the covenant and failure to recognize Christ have abrogated Israel's claim to be Abraham's true seed. In John, chapter 8, Jesus suggests that

Abraham's true seed are those who act in faith and who receive the Son. The lengthiest biblical discussion of the subject is in Romans 9—11.[6]

Various Christian interpreters have given four responses to these passages. One group speaks of two covenants—two ways of being saved: Israel through the law and Gentiles through Christ. The question I have with this position is: Why not then many ways to be saved? Buddhists through Buddha, and so forth. It seems to me that Scripture is clear in affirming that full salvation is through Christ alone. As I indicated above, there can be indirect and diffuse expressions about God in nature and other religions. But there must be one final focus through whom all meaning and full salvation is brought in perspective. This is Jesus Christ.

A second view is that of a twentieth-century theologian, Karl Barth. Barth believed that the synagogue was the necessary left hand of rejection to counterbalance the right hand of acceptance of Christ. This is a balanced "two-hands" view. This view is in contrast with the two-ways view in the preceding paragraph. Barth intimated that Jews will be saved because of their divinely appointed role of rejection, just as Christians are because of their divinely appointed role of acceptance. Romans 11:31[7] is his major text in this argument. In the last analysis, this two-hands view is a type of two-ways view. It also leaves unanswered the question of world religions and seems to place as much premium on rejection as on belief. This position would be hard to sustain in a general survey of biblical insights.

A third perspective is a merger view. This view indicates that the church took the place of Israel; and, as the new Israel, is the inheritor of God's covenant in both the New and Old Testaments. This perspective believes that Israel "according to the flesh" has abrogated God's covenant. Israel shall be saved like anyone else is saved, through Jesus, one at a time. The convincingness of this view depends on whether or not one believes that Israel, by a unilateral action, can do away with the covenant which God initiated.

The fourth view is called a final confirmation view. This perspective indicates that God is not yet done with Israel. The suggestion is that in some way—certainly Paul does not name it—God will confront Israel with Jesus as Messiah, and through this end of time belief (a confirmation of Israel's election), Israel will be saved by its belief in Christ. This perspective also faces the charge of favoritism. And in its defense, one can only say that this is a recompense for the special sufferings "Israel" has undergone in history.

Paul himself acknowledged the mystery in his benediction from Job, the Jew, and from the Stoics, the Gentiles.

> O the depth of the riches both of the wisdom and knowledge of God! how unsearchable are his judgments, and his ways past finding out!
> For who hath known the mind of the Lord? or who hath been his counsellor?
> Or who hath first given to him, and it shall be recompensed unto him again?
> For of him, and through him, and to him, are all things: to whom be glory for ever. Amen (Rom. 11:33-36, KJV).

This discussion seems a long way from arguments about which is the best church in town, the biggest church in town, or the most active church in town. This discussion seems a long way from the particulars of church membership, the assignment to a Sunday School class, or the choice of a Church Training seminar. This discussion *is* a long way from these considerations. This discussion of chosenness can involve those topics and help you make choices about your specific church life. But this discussion of chosenness, Christ's and ours, must precede and have precedence over these other decisions, if the church is to be the church. "From heav'n he came and [*chose*] her/To be his holy bride,/With his own blood he bought her,/And for her life he died."[8]

Corporateness

As we grow older we think more about our bodies. We have to because we can no longer take them for granted. We realize that our bodies are our way of being in the world. Furthermore, various parts of our bodies wear out. Some parts can be replaced, but usually at an awesome cost. We also begin to think more of other bodies. Some familiar forms are missing. Small bodies, our children, and even our children's children have grown larger, older, and often less familiar. Some of us grow more tolerant of the young because we see their lives paralleling our own half a century ago. Others of us grow less patient, because we envy them the basic things we no longer have: time, strength, energy. In our weaker moments we wish we could restore our bodies and live forever. In our better moments we are grateful we do not have to, in these conditions. One thing we long for above all. That is a sense of connectedness, of rootedness.

Corporateness is a second mark of the church. Whether we stress it or not, "church" is supposed to signify a group. Granted, groups are made up of individuals, but in Bible times individuals took second place to groups.[9] Much ink has been spilled over whether the age of corporateness or the age of individuality is better. The Bible makes room for both, but it puts a dominant stress on the corporate. The beginning of the race quickly speads out into nations. The sons of Jacob are the founders of tribes. The fate of nations often rests on individuals as evidenced by the "good and bad" kings of Israel and Judah. Hosea's individual story is important because it signifies a rebellious and sinful nation. In the New Testament Jesus' selection of twelve apostles is not mere chance. It is a recreation of a people of God. The apostles are distinctively individual. But they speak to and for the people of God. James advised church people how to act in such a way that economic distinctions don't carry over into worship (Jas. 2:1-9). Paul admonished whole congregations as part of the body of Christ (compare Ephesians 4:4,11-16) and called out the names of individuals who needed greeting and advice (for example, Rom. 16). John emphasized what the corporate witness of the apostles saw and experienced (1 John 1:1).

It is hard for us moderns not to think of church in terms of how many join, who belongs to which congregation, and which preacher is a better proclaimer or visitor. The New Testament metaphors for church favor the corporate idea of church. The church is the flock of God (John 10:1-18), a royal priesthood, a holy nation (1 Pet. 2:9), the extended family of Jesus (Mark 3:31-35; Matt. 12:46-50; Luke 8:19-21), the branches of a single vine (John 15:1-10). But most of all, the church is the body of Christ (Eph. 1:23; 2:16; 3:6; 4:12,16; 5:23,30).[10] These powerful biblical symbols for church invite us to think in terms of the well-being of the group before we think of the comfort and desires of our own individual wishes. The corporateness of the church involves: rootedness, representation, responsibility, and righteousness.

To be a part of the body of Christ means that we have "roots." Alex Haley's book by this title has struck a common nerve among all races. We all would like to know we belong and that we are a part of something more permanent and more lasting than our isolated selves. The genealogies in Genesis, Matthew, and Luke serve the purpose of showing how the people of earth are related to one another and how Jesus, the Messiah, is related to both Jews (Matthew) and Gentiles (Luke). Big families are not always happy, but they are seldom lonely. Being a part of the body of Christ is being some-*body*. It is being His body. We are rooted and grounded in Him through the faith of the apostles (Eph. 2:19-20; 3:14-19). The older and dearer terms *brother* and *sister* have deep theological significance. To be in Christ and in His church is not just "my God and I walk[ing] through the fields together."[11] Rather, it is more to be in the "company of the committed."[12] The strength of a plant is in its roots. The strength of a nation is in the solidarity and unity of its citizens. The strength of the body of Christ is in its rootedness in Him. But this belongingness is more than a good feeling. It is even more than the loss of loneliness.

The corporateness of the church speaks of representation. Representation is a vital and essential principle of biblical faith. Adam represents the race. So does Jesus. "As in Adam all die, even so in Christ shall all be made alive" (1 Cor. 15:22). Romans 5:1-12 and 1 Corinthians 15 are the primary biblical expressions of representation. One can and does stand for others. In the chapter on man we will refer to Adam as representative humanity. In the chapter on Christ we will speak of Christ as He who represents us before God. Here it is important to apply the biblical principle of representation to the church. As the body of Christ, the church is a visible manifestation of God in our world. The church does not extend Christ's presence, but it does represent Him in a tangible way in our world. He intended that it should do so. Matthew 16:16-19 gives sweeping powers of representation to Christ's believing community. "Binding and loosing" is not a papal or clergy privilege. It is a special obligation of the community of Christ. We said previously that God willed that we should have a will in our salvation. Christ has willed that we should have a part in extending the news of salvation. The church is Christ's representative. This does not mean that every congregation, or that all of them put together, knows perfectly the mind of Christ. But it does mean that we all share the commission of Christ (Matt. 28:9-20).

A popular poem by Annie Johnson Flint drives home this point. It may not be great literature; but it is good theology.

We are the only Bible
  The careless world will read;
We are the sinner's gospel,
  We are the scoffer's creed;
We are the Lord's last message
  Given in deed and word—
What if the line is crooked?
  What if the type is blurred?
What if our hands are busy
  With other work than His?
What if our feet are walking
  Where sin's allurement is?
What if our tongues are speaking
  Of things His lips would spurn?
How can we hope to help Him,
  Unless from Him we learn?[13]

Corporateness speaks of rootedness and representation. It also includes responsibility. It is hard today to find out who is responsible or to find anyone who will take responsibility. Not getting involved is the temper of the time. But disinterestedness and lack of involvement cannot be the position of the church. When this happens churches lose their witness and, in some measure, their right to be called Christ's church. This was exactly the situation of some of the churches of Asia Minor (Rev. 1—3). In such instances Jesus Himself threatened to remove the candle from the candlestick. Churches inevitably have sociological, cultural, and contextual dimensions. But to be a church, a called and chosen people of God—and that is what the New Testament term for church means—a church must be responsible.[14] This means that we are responsible before God on behalf of the world. This is the priestly function of the church. And it applies to all of the people of God, not just the ministry. We represent Him to them and them to Him (2 Cor. 5:14).

Such a task is not easy. It involves reflecting and representing the human community to God, through Christ. This representing involves praying for the world and sometimes paying for the world. The intercessory prayers of Abraham (Gen. 18:16-33), Moses (for example, Ex. 32:7-14), Paul (Rom. 9:1-5), and Jesus (John 17) embody this kind of responsibility. The self-sacrificial and unstinting devotion of their lives matched their prayers. It ought to be that way in His church. A famous Catholic order has as its motto *Orare et Laborare,* to work and to pray. Inherently, good praying leads to or involves diligently working. The theological term for the corporate responsibility of the church for the world is the priesthood of all believers. As we shall see later in the chapter, the priesthood of all believers means each person can come to God for himself or herself. The priesthood of all believers, likewise, means that each Christian is also responsible to God on behalf of others. The responsibility of corporateness means that we are responsible for those outside the church to assist them in all areas of their need. It also means we are to be responsible in the church to fulfill our functions within the body of Christ.

Our responsibilities in the church are as broad as the needs and the mission of the church. A primary responsibility in the church is worship. We are needed and necessary in the worship of the church. "Not forsaking the assemblying of ourselves together" (Heb. 10:25, KJV) is not the invention of a desperate pastor. It is the wisdom of an apostle of God who knew that the body could not exist without the visible and vital gathering of the members to exercise the body. All talk of worship in the woods, golfside meditation, and relaxing with the electronic church is spitting in the wind. A body has got to get its act together. And the body of Christ is no exception. Muscular dystrophy is a tragic disease in the human body and just as terrible in the church. Sharing talents and doing what has to be done are also ways of being responsible in the church. If fellow members of the body of Christ ask you to do what you can do, and if Christ requests your presence and participation to exercise your abilities, think hard before declining.

Sometimes the requests of our fellow Christians are not the same as the will of God for our lives. When that happens, decline with dignity for the sake of a larger good, which may well be the preservation of health and sanity. There is a feeling on the part of some of us that we have done our part. A wise pastor's wife once told me that she had learned that God's work doesn't come in parts. Sometimes some of the body of Christ wants to keep on presuming on and pressuring older parts of the body of Christ beyond reasonable measure. There is even the callous forgetting or growing disinterest in people when they can no longer attend church or sign their names to a check. It is the responsibility of us who are still somewhat able to see that our church is responsible to and for those who are no longer able to be responsible and to point out this responsibility.

The corporateness of the church also calls for righteousness in the church. This is not to be a smug self-righteousness. It is to be a rightness on the part of people who have been "right-wised" (a literal translation of the New Testament word for justification) by God alone, Who is right. The church must do what she discerns as right, always open to the fact that she can be wrong. If we are in Christ, then we will see through His eyes. We will be compassionate as He was compassionate. We will be indignant about things that deserve indignation.[15] This righteousness of the church extends beyond personal piety.[16] The righteousness of the church must apply to the corporate and social issues of society. Politics may be dirty business. But Christians in politics and involved in political issues should strive to clean things up. I am not talking about blue laws or imposing narrow mores on large elements of society. I am talking about matters of life and death, poverty and wealth, health and happiness, dignity and equity, war and peace.[17]

The second mark of the church, corporateness, involves our rootedness, representation, responsibility, and righteousness. Corporateness speaks of the priestly function of the church even as chosenness speaks of the church's prophetic function. Chosenness is comparable to the ancient mark of the church called oneness. Corporateness is analogous to the classic mark of universality. The corporateness of the church includes all Christians of all time, everywhere. The journey of the Christian life, in chapter 2, raised the question of other religions. The chosenness of the church in section one above raised the question of the Jews. The corporateness of the church raises the question of our relationship to fellow Christians.

Since we are speaking of the body of Christ, let me extend the family analogy to describe four ways in which Christians relate to one another. I am referring to inter- and intradenominational groups.

1. There is the view of spoiled exclusiveness. Not all only children are spoiled. But spoiled only children are usually pretty badly spoiled. The spoiled exclusiveness of some Christians says that our

group is the only one that is Christian. Agreement on all points is usually demanded. Diversity is not desirable or permitted. We all know people, churches, denominations, and theological perspectives like this. Their standards are built to order, their order. These have a copyright on God. There are usually rude awakenings for the spoiled exclusive child on that first day of school. It is possible that the first moments of God's eternal order will require some adjustments while the exclusivists are getting used to their neighbors. God has a sense of humor.

2. There is the sibling rivalry way of looking at other Christians. Sibling rivalry is, it seems, an inevitable stage of childhood development. It is especially acute among close siblings. Some items of theological debate and the acrimony with which they are carried on remind us of sibling rivalry. A timeworn joke illustrates it well. On a hot summer Sunday in a small town, before the days of airconditioning, the Presbyterians were heard to sing "Will there be any stars in my crown?" The Methodists intoned the gospel song: "No, not one!" To which the Baptists responded with gusto, "O that will be glory for me." Sibling rivalry can be made light of, so long as it is an elementary and temporary affair. But it is a sad and divisive trauma when families are separated, communities disjoined, and energies wasted on justifying oneself at the expense of others.

3. Occasionally, we hear a sad word among brothers and sisters. The saying is: "We are not close." This usually means that each has become so preoccupied with his or her own existence that the dimensions of the family have gone begging. This, it seems to me, is a pity. The mutual encouragement and the deepening of natural ties and shared experiences is missing. What could have been family has become isolated individuals preoccupied with their own concerns. This too will require some mending in heaven. There are churches who are not close to others in the family of God.

4. There is a happier, healthier way. It is embodied in the expression "We are family." That means we belong together. This does not mean that we are all alike or see all things eye to eye. It does mean that we confess a common elder brother and offer our gratitude to our Heavenly Father. We are related, and the fact of our relatedness is more important than the differences which pertain.

Conviction and correct belief are to be considered in determining who is family. I have already given you my understanding of what is minimal to basic Christian belief.[18] The acceptance of this shared good news and this common calling upon Jesus Christ as Lord speaks to me of family. Other Christians require more. Some require conformity on all points of an elaborate theological system. "One Lord, one faith, one baptism" (Eph. 4:5) speaks of a unity we need. What is meant is the fact of baptism. What is intended is "the faith which was once delivered unto the saints" (Jude 3, KJV) by the witness of the "apostles and prophets" (Eph. 2:19-20). And no Christian would have to be told to whom the one Lord refers. Jesus is our unifying center. He is the head; we are body (Eph. 5:23; Col. 1:18). This is Christological corporateness. It is an identifying mark of the church.

Celebrativeness

Celebration used to be a secular word in some religious circles. I hope it is not for you. I am glad that contemporary Christians are discovering this term of joy as one of the primary marks of identifying the church. The church was born in joy (Acts 2). The birth of Jesus, her Lord, was announced in joy (Luke 2). The Fourth Gospel and all the Epistles are full of the joy of Jesus. The missionary apostle Paul highlighted joy in his first correspondence (1 Thess.) and made it the keynote of a letter from prison (Phil.). The church is the body of Christ. He is the head. We are the members. The Spirit is the energizing breath. And one of the primary gifts whereby the Spirit energizes the church is joy (Gal. 5:22). A contemporary musical *Celebrate Life*[19] speaks in a lively way of Christian joy. A classic hymn called "Joyful, Joyful, We Adore Thee"[20] is becoming popular in many worship services. The psalmist used six different words for *joy.* Joy is a major mood of the Christian faith.

It is appropriate and natural that we associate music with joy.[21] Job suggests that creation is a hymn of joy. To celebrate creation the "morning stars sang together" (Job 38:7). The harmony of music and the harmony of God's creation fit. American pioneers treasured two books: the Bible and a hymnal. Music is a distinctively theological art. Christians usually do not remember much about the sermons they hear, a sad acknowledgment from a preacher. But tunes and texts are retained and sung by most Christians. The fact of Christian joy is deeply ingrained in Scripture and worship through music.

The primary acts which celebrate Christian joy are the distinctive acts of the Christian community, namely, baptism and the Lord's Supper. The reality for which these symbols stand express better than any other Christian act the source and significance of our joy. Unfortunately, it is exactly these acts which have also divided the Christian community most deeply. Let me try to express first why each of these acts is an intrinsic symbol of joy. Then I will point out the different ways in which these symbols have been understood in the Christian community.

Baptism is a joyful occasion. It celebrates the death, burial, and resurrection of Jesus (Rom. 6:1-4). The fact of Jesus' death seemed, at first, an unspeakable tragedy. The reality of resurrection turned it into triumphant joy. The historic fact behind baptism is Jesus' "crossing a line" to stand with sinful humanity.[22] The theological significance of baptism is the believer accepting the identifying sign of Jesus as the signification of his or her life.[23] The joyful singing of hymns and gospel songs at the time of baptism is a Prostestant custom which reinforces the time of baptism as a time of celebration.

The Lord's Supper also is an expression of joy. Like baptism, the history which gave rise to the Supper had the makings of a tragedy. The young man Jesus, who had not only a "reverence for life" but also a great joy in living, spoke of the New Covenant (Matt. 26:26-30. Compare Ex. 19 [esp. vv. 5-6] and Jer. 31:31-34). This bond between God and humanity was sealed at the price of Jesus' broken body and shed blood. Where then is the joy? In the promise of a continued presence and in the foreshadowing of a new and final meal in the kingdom of God (1 Cor. 11:23-34; compare Matt. 26:26-30). For a long time Catholics have spoken of celebrating the Eucharist (a term which means a thanksgiving taken from Jesus' prayer of thanks offered before the bread and wine). The verb *celebrate* is an appropriate one for this meal in which Jesus gave thanks for the cup and the bread and in which Christians give thanks for what they mean.

These acts, baptism and the Supper, are the cause and way of celebrating our Christian confession. The meaning and form of these joyful acts differ widely in the Christian community.

The use of water in religious ceremonies is universal. The general understanding of the use of water is as a cleansing agent. It is thought that Naaman's dipping of himself seven times in the Jordan (2 Kings

5:1-19) was a type of Jewish proselyte baptism. The cataclysmic and redemptive experiences of the Old Testament in which the race (in Noah's case) and Israel (at the Red Sea) were saved from the peril of water are considered, in the New Testament, to be a prototype of baptism which symbolizes our salvation (see 1 Pet. 3:19-22 in the case of Noah and 1 Cor. 10:1-5 in the case of Israel). The Essenes of New Testament times around the Dead Sea practiced immersion as a cleansing act of the community. Some scholars feel that John the Baptist may have been related to this community.[24] John was the first in biblical record to practice baptism on others. The baptism of John was preparatory to full Christian baptism and its meaning (Rom. 6:1-4).

The most literal belief about the meaning of baptism is that it is the actual washing away of original and all actual sins. Obviously, those who hold this view would also logically feel that a child at any stage of human development ought to be baptized. There is a less literal view which does not suggest the actual washing away of sin. This less literal view of baptism nevertheless feels that an infant should be set aside to God and have this Christian seal placed upon him/her in order to mark that child as a Christian child. Both of these views would argue that a vicarious form of faith is present through the belief of parents or godparents. (Originally godparents were those who pledged to rear the child in the Christian faith if the parents should die or be unable to do so. In many instances today it is a more social, relational status which binds friends or family to the infant.) One staunch adherent of this view, who strongly proposes salvation by faith alone, suggested that infants might have faith and declared that it could not be proved that they did not.

In all instances where infants are baptized, either as a means of salvation or a mark of salvation, religious education of the child is required. This training is designed to teach a child about Christian doctrine and practice. It includes the elements of the earliest Christian kerygma. It is ordinarily done by a series of questions and answers which the child is expected to learn, to understand, and to affirm for the self. The process is called catechesis. The teaching that is given is called a catechism, and the one who is learning is called a catechumen. The baptism of an infant is seen as a time of joy and gratitude for the families, and there is a celebrative occasion which rejoices in the birth of the child and the child's being commended to God.

The other way of looking at baptism in the Christian community is the practice of beliver's baptism. In this view baptism is seen as the testimony of the one baptized. This means that the person being baptized has consciously and intentionally, by the guidance of the Holy Spirit, understood the meaning of the gospel and accepted Christian salvation and the experience of forgiveness. In believer's baptism, the one baptized consciously reenacts the death, burial, and resurrection of Jesus as a way of giving up the old self and identifying with Christ. This baptism is often prepared for by individual or group instruction. And those churches which practice believer's baptism also conduct classes, sessions, and one-on-one instruction for the newly baptized. The meaning of baptism in believer's baptism is that it is a symbol of salvation. The mood of such baptismal services is also one of joy. Usually, joyful music is sung in such services. Greetings from the congregation are given to the newly baptized.

Obviously, I have placed these two primary understandings of the meaning of baptism, agent or mark of salvation and symbol of salvation to the believer, in their most favorable light as to their meaning and ideal practice. My tradition and my own understanding of Scripture lead me to affirm and practice believer's baptism with the meaning of a symbolic act illustrating a vital, individual, and conscious response to God's good news.

Baptism is always an act upon an individual. But the meaning and practice is always, and ought to be, a corporate act. This corporate act is important at two levels. Any incorporation into the body of Christ is an act that involves the whole body of Christ and should be an occasion of great joy and celebration (Luke 15, especially v. 32). The performance and practice of baptism is, and ought to be, by a portion of Christ's church out of its own understanding and interpretation. Baptism is not an isolated, individual act done by one person on another. Baptism is an act of the body of Christ. It is for this reason that baptism is considered as the door of the church, the incorporating act of the body of Christ. Discussions of church membership and individual privileges and practices of diverse church groups are all post-New Testament concepts of the form and organization of practical church life.

There is one additional meaning of baptism. Baptism, in the New Testament, was one's identification with Christ and was usually also a public profession of faith.[25] Often accompanying the act of baptism was a verbal confession of Christ (Rom. 10:9-10; compare Acts 8:36-38). There were the early Christian confessions, *Kurios Christos,* Christ is Lord, and *Maranatha,* the Lord is coming, or O, Lord, come. First Peter is considered by some to be a baptismal sermon which was, in part, intended to be read to believers at the time of their baptism.[26] Words and symbolic acts are a very biblical way of celebrating important moments of faith. It seems to me particularly appropriate that the person being baptized should repeat one of the New Testament confessions of Christ or give a personal word of confession upon which he/she is then baptized as a "confessing" Christian. In the traditions of infant baptism, this is done by others. In the tradition of believer's baptism, this needs to be done by the believer.

The form of baptism has been an occasion for various perspectives in the Christian community. All scholars agree that the Greek term means to dip, plunge, or immerse. Some traditions feel that the symbol of baptism is best preserved by immersion which physically is analogous to a scene of death, burial, and resurrection. I agree with them. Other traditions sprinkle water instead of pouring. Baptismal fonts are not always separated between the cause/mark of salvation and the believer's/confession view. In some traditions, both pouring and immersion are used on different persons and on different occasions. One tradition practices the immersion of infants. It seems that the body of Christ will have to live on earth with a variety of forms of baptism. What is essential is that baptism and faith go together. It seems to me that the biblical materials are clear in affirming that faith precedes baptism. It is to be hoped that when this is not the custom, faith will be expressed individually after baptism. In either event, baptism is merely a ritual unless it is vitally related to faith. Joy and celebration are appropriate attitudes about baptism. This distinctive symbolic mark of the Christian community, which speaks of the beginning of the Christian life, is an occasion of celebration.

The second symbolic act of the Christian community, the Lord's Supper, speaks of the continuing and the consummating of the Christian life. This act too is the occasion of great celebration. In early times feasts were important as occasions of celebrating both sacred and secular occasions, although those kinds of distinctions were not made in Bible times, and I am not sure they should be today. All creation and all life was special and came from God. We would do well to remind ourselves of this. It would keep us from thinking the sacred is what we do on Sunday while the secular is the rest of the week. Nevertheless, there were special meals that were celebrated because of some particular thing God had done for His people. The Passover meal was such an occasion. The anticipation of a messianic banquet when the Messiah came was another. Both the Passover meal and the anticipated messianic banquet figure in an understanding of the Last Supper. Passover (Ex. 12:3-28) was associated with God's deliverance of His people from Egypt. The Passover and the Exodus from Egypt were preliminary to the covenant of God with Israel (Ex. 19, especially vv. 5-6). Jesus and the early church connected these events with His death (Mark 14:12-16; Matt. 26:17-19; Luke 22:7-18; compare John 13:1-5) as a means of deliverance of all of God's creation and the formation of God's New Covenant. The first written account of the Supper by Paul (1 Cor. 11), as well as the Gospels, stresses the future meaning of the Supper. The Supper symbolizes the Lord's death till He comes (v. 26). It anticipates a time when Jesus' followers shall drink and eat in His Father's kingdom (Matt. 26:29). The original occasion of the Supper was sad because of Christ's impending death. All subsequent occasions of the Supper are times of joy because of the deliverance His death effects and the promise His coming brings.

The meaning and purpose of the Lord's Supper, and even its terminology, have been even more diverse than views on baptism. All views agree that the Supper is a celebration of Jesus' death and an anticipation of His coming. Some call the Supper "Eucharist" (after the word Jesus used in giving thanks). Some call it Communion because of the interaction Christians have with Christ and one another on that occasion. The Lord's Supper is an apt and unambiguous term. This meal can be confused with none other. It speaks of the meal on the night on which He was betrayed (1 Cor. 11:23). There are four basic views as to the meaning of the Supper:

1. Some suggest the Lord's Supper is essential to our continuity with Christ. Therefore, they argue, it is to be taken daily. Related to this is the theory that the Supper is a sacrament (a vehicle of saving

grace). In earlier times it was believed that the bread and the wine, in their spiritual (substance) properties, were transformed into the body and blood of Christ. Extreme statements of this literalist position said that the very taking of the Supper by itself (*ex opere operato*) continued salvation. Other proponents of this view indicate that the faith of the individual must work with (*ex opere operantis*) the individual to continue salvation. When the Supper and faith are not combined, even as faith and baptism must be combined, we have mere ritual. It is difficult to prove from Scripture that the Supper itself is a means of staying in God's grace or continuing in salvation.

2. A second view as to the meaning of the Supper might be called the quasi-literal view. This perspective denies the substance of the bread and wine are changed. But it affirms that Christ is really present in, under, and around the elements in a mysterious way. It is hard to find nontechnical names for these views.

3. I would like to call the third view a semiliteral view. This view of the meaning of the Supper is that Jesus is spiritually present at the meal in a sense in which He is not at any other occasion. It seems to me that Christ, through His Spirit, is fully and equally present as the head of His body, the church. The difference in the presence of Christ is not from His side. It is from ours. It is problematic, for me, to talk about Christ Himself being more present with believers at some time than at others. I freely grant that we, participating in certain acts and refreshing certain memories, can be and are more aware of His presence in certain acts than in others. The Lord's Supper is one of those acts and one of those memories. This interpretation is related to the view of the fourth meaning of the Supper.

4. The fourth way of looking at the Lord's Supper is called symbolic or memorial. At times, my tradition has resisted the interpretation of other traditions to the extent that we seem to speak of a mere memorial. That is a mistake. The Lord's Supper is a meaningful memorial. The Supper does not, in this memorial view, act as a sacrament to keep us in grace. But the Supper alone is the distinctive act in the church by which we celebrate Christ's Passover and continue by symbolic action to remember what it means that we are sustained by Him and will be received and renewed by Him. The Supper is a fuller experience of grace because it is words plus act. It is a time of special memory and of joyful anticipation. Preaching about

Christ's death gives us verbal pictures of His sacrifice. Participation in the Supper gives us verbal and visual moments of memory and anticipation.

Like baptism, the Supper must be related to faith to be meaningful. Like baptism, the Supper is a corporate concern. Usually, the interpretation of the Christian community offering the Supper is the normative interpretation for those observing the Supper. One possible exception is the obvious and acknowledged presence of different views in the receiving congregation. In these circumstances Christians especially bring their heritage and interpretation with them. All Christians as they receive the Supper should do so in a context of joy and celebration.

I want to talk with you earnestly about a circumstance in connection with the Supper which is arising because of aging, infirmity, and the presence of large numbers of Christians in convalescent centers. When possible, the elderly should go to church. Most of them want to. Unfortunately, many of them cannot. Some of these have loved the Supper and been faithful in the observance of the Supper. In my opinion, the churches have some obligation to provide the Supper for them. This should be done upon request. It can be done where several persons of the same interpretation are in the same center, or even for one person. A representative group of persons from the church can, upon church agreement, perform the service. The memorial view is as appropriate as interpretation for this practice as the sacramental view. In the sacramental view this must be done to be consistent with that theology. In the memorial view the extension of the Supper is nonsacramental, nor does it require a special minister or priest to perform it (the memorial view is usually held by those who affirm the priesthood of all believers and embrace a form of congregational government). What is needed is the request of the elderly or infirm person receiving it and the authorization of the congregation extending it. This special ministry is extended not to continue one's salvation. It is done to affirm and comfort those parts of Christ's body who desire it but can no longer continue this special celebration of joy because of their disabilities.[27]

Just as there have been many interpretations about the meaning of the Lord's Supper, so there have been many interpretations about the form and practice of the Lord's Supper. The form or practice of the

Supper usually follows the meaning held by the group offering the Supper. The practices differ widely. There are basically four views: The literal view which requires a special person (priest) to perform the Eucharist. This view is held in common with an episcopal (bishop-led) form of church structure. Sometimes, out of reverence for the "changed" bread and wine, the priest took the wine and the people took the bread. This is called communion in one kind, and it is accompanied by the belief that each element contains both the body and the blood of Christ. This practice is diminishing today. In most sacramental observances of the Supper a piece of bread or wafer is given to each participant, and a common cup is shared by all, being wiped after each use. In both the quasi- and semiliteral views of the Supper, a properly ordained minister (clergy—from a special kind of cloth that ministers used to wear) is required.

There is an interesting way of observing the Supper that I will mention at this point. It has been used by many different Christian communities at various times. It is called "intinction," and its particularity is to dip the bread, wafer, or cracker in the wine or juice. Each communicant then consumes a piece of the bread which has absorbed the wine.

The memorial view usually uses individual cups and a small piece of bread for each person. The congregation may appoint someone to preside at the Supper. Usually an ordained minister or deacon presides, but this does not have to be the case since the Supper is not a sacrament and does not require a special kind of person (ordained, apostolic, clergy) to preside.

There is an irony in all of this discussion of the rituals of celebration in the Christian community. What should be an occasion of joy and celebration has often become a cause of divisiveness and argument in the body of Christ. This is a fragmented witness to the non-Christian. The diversity can be accepted. The divisiveness and bitterness has turned many away from the Christian community and been a cause of misunderstanding to those within the body. Many aging people have grown more tolerant of the diversity, since they have seen committed Christians from all of the different views. Some people, as they grow older, become more persistent and defensive about the particulars of their faith. Wise ministers will seek to care for both groups. Caring is what ministry is about. And caringness is the fourth mark of the church.

Before going further, let me review the three marks we have discussed, their relation to the classic marks of the church and their analogy to the ministry of Christ. The chosenness of the church is comparable to the classical view of the oneness of the church. Chosenness is akin to Christ's prophetic ministry. The corporateness of the church is like the universal mark of classical Christianity. Corporateness speaks of Christ's priestly function. I wanted to keep together the notion of our common cause and our vicarious (on behalf of others) responsibility and representation of others. Celebrativeness has to do with the classical mark of holiness in that those who are set aside are those who celebrate the deepest meaning of life and the deepest kind (eternal) of life. Celebrativeness speaks to me of the kingship of Jesus Christ. It is appropriate that the community of faith celebrate the past, present, and future history of Him who is the royal Son in the kingdom of God. Chosenness raised the question of the relations of Christians and Jews. Corporateness raised the question of interrelationships among Christian groups. Celebrativeness raised the question of diverse meanings and forms in which the Christian community has participated in the distinctive Christian acts of celebration.

Caringness

The fourth and final mark of the church is caringness. Caringness relates to the classical mark of apostolicity. Caringness requires a discussion about the purpose, mission, and ministry of the church. Caringness raises the question of the Christian Community in its relation to the world.

God's Caring, the Model. Jesus was a walking parable of caring. The Bible nowhere gives a physical description of Jesus. But Scripture does characterize Him as a "man approved of God among you by miracles and wonders and signs" (Acts 2:22, KJV). The caring posture of Jesus is an extension of the loving concern of the Father (John 3:16). This caring and compassion was passed on in the commission of Jesus to His disciples (Matt. 28:18-20). Caring initiates with God, is carried out by Jesus, and is commissioned to the church.

The Old Testament contains many expressions of this continuous caring of God. He makes covenants and promises keeps them. He persists in His care of a rebellious people (Hosea, Jeremiah). God pities His people like a Father (Ps. 103:13). Perhaps the most vital caring image of God in the Old Testament is the root metaphor of God as Shepherd (Ps. 23). This idea is carried over in the New Testament with the idea of God as anxious householder, waiting Father, and seeking Shepherd (Luke 15). It is no accident that the deepest theological interpretations of Jesus' ministry in the New Testament is that of Shepherd (John 10:1-18). The head of the church—Jesus—cares. So should the body.

The Purpose of the Church. One aspect of the caringness of the church is seen in the primary purpose of the church. You who have lived a long time have learned to ask some of the right questions. One question it is always important and appropriate to ask is: "What is the purpose of a thing?" We call purposeless gifts "white elephants." We call purposeless people drifters. We might want to call purposeless organizations "superfluous." The church is not superfluous. It is necessary. Necessary for what? Necessary for proclaiming, embodying, and imaging the message of God.

Historical answers as to the purpose of the church are legion. Some say the church is to convey salvation. I would prefer to say the church is to announce salvation. Some argue as to whether the primary purpose of the church is evangelism or ethics. That is like asking if a body should breathe in or out. Another suggestion for the church's purpose is worship. Worship certainly is necessary to the inner life of the church, but so is education. It has been suggested that the church is to extend the incarnation. Technically, incarnation is a unique task embodied in Jesus only. The church can embody Christlikeness and even godliness, but it does not incorporate Godness. This is true because the church is made up of people who are both saved and sinful (*simul justus et peccator*). And the church is always given the task of reforming the world in which she lives and being reformed by her faithfulness to the head of the church, Jesus Christ (*semper reformata et reformandum*).

I believe the primary purpose of the church is to "bear witness" to Jesus Christ. In Scripture, witness bearing is not just a verbal testimony. The Greek word for "witness" (*martus*) is the same as that for martyr. Even as the chosenness of the church requires suffering, so the caring of the church requires service. Bearing witness to the Word—Jesus—is an extension of His bearing witness to the Father. Bearing witness to God in Christ involves worship, evangelism, education, ethics—and if need be, martyrdom. Every thing should have its purpose. The church, as the special thing which is the creation of God in Christ, has the distinctive and particular purpose to bear witness to God through the Holy Spirit. There is no other "thing" or group or arena of action in which this is the primary purpose. Literature and the arts can express both the greatness of God and the intensity of evil. Therefore, they should be appreciated, appropriated, and learned from by the church. But it is not the specific and particular purpose of the arts per se to be intentionally and exclusively a religious witness. Parachurch Christian groups share the purpose of the church with the church. But, in my opinion, they do so only fragmentarily if they do not spell out consciously and intentionally how they relate to and interface with the church. Church is God's people with a purpose. Purpose and mission are two sides of the same coin.

Mission, a word which comes from the Latin term *send* (*missio* from *mitto*) is the method by which the church carries out her purpose.[28] The discussion of mission method is much too involved to elaborate on in this book.[29] But some theological affirmations about mission, how the church carries out her purpose, can be stated. (1) The specific tasks of mission should be specifically related to the purpose of the church. (2) The Christian community is missionary by mandate, that is, it is the specific command and act of Jesus Christ to bear witness to God, and He commissions the church with this same task. (3) The message of the church in mission needs to be the central message of the New Testament witness and not the cultural context of the missioners. (4) The mission of the church is the responsibility of the whole body of Christ and is not entrusted exclusively to any one group within the body. (5) Christian mission is not verbal only. It is, as with Christ, a matter of words and deeds.

The Form of the Church. The form of the church is the way in which the church is structured for caring. Structure and form are not to be despised. Where they are overstressed, there is a loss of dynamic. Where they are understressed, there is a loss of effectiveness. Most discussions and designations about the form of the church have had to do with the type of ministry (in the sense of official personnel) a given church has. I, for one, feel that this is too narrow a focus for the form and ministry of the church. The caringness of the church and the way in which that is carried out in its entirety is a larger question than that of what type of clergy a given group has. I will discuss this larger dimension in the final question of the chapter, namely, what is the relation of the church to the world? But it seems expedient to lay out, at this point, the traditional discussion of ministry.

The Ministry of the Church. The New Testament notion of ministry is first and foremost a function and not an office. Ministry is about caring. The term for *minister* in the New Testament is the same word as *deacon.* A second New Testament word for minister is *pastor,* which is the Latin word for *shepherd,* the root metaphor for Jesus' caring. A third word which the New Testament uses to express ministry is the word for *priest,* and the function of a priest is to care for others before God and on behalf of God. A fourth New Testament word for the function of ministry is *overseer, bishop.* The primary meaning of overseer is spiritual concern, not structural hierarchy. The fifth and final New Testament word for ministry is *elder.* The basic insight in this word is the notion of wisdom through long experience. All of our current forms of ministry and organizational structures of the churches rest on historical, traditional understandings of these five words: *diakonos* (minister/deacon); *poime* (pastor/shepherd); *hieros* (priest/carer for "souls"); *episcopos* (overseer/bishop); and *presbuteros* (wise one/elder). Let me share with you how these have "factored out" in Christian history to form the varieties of ministry structures and types of churches in the Christian community today.

Episcopal. One form of church structure is the episcopal form. There are three or four types of episcopal church structures. The monarchical episcopacy has one primary bishop, the bishop of Rome. There are many other ranks and groups of clergy in this group, but the final authority is invested in one person. This is the governing form of the Roman Catholic Church. The clergy in the Roman Catholic Church claim apostolic succession. Ordination of the clergy can be done only by those who have been ordained by previous clergy who stand in a line of apostolic succession. Ordination conveys the right to perform the sacraments of the church. Cardinals, high-ranking clergy, are appointed by the bishop of Rome, popularly called Pope (derived from the Italian word for father). At the death of a bishop of Rome, the College of Cardinals elects a new bishop of Rome. Ordination is a sacrament known as Orders (not to be confused with various orders of congregations of religious groups of both men and women, such as the Franciscan Order). Only males may be ordained by the Sacrament of Orders. The ordained of the Roman Catholic Church have traditionally been celebate (nonmarried).

A second type of episcopal form of church structure is the patriarchal episcopacy. This is the structure of the Eastern Orthodox communities. A church, in the Orthodox sense, is all those gathered in a given territory or a certain group. Examples are Greek Orthodox, Russian Orthodox, Syrian Orthodox, and so forth. The ranking bishop of each group is called a patriarch. Theoretically, patriarchs are under the guidance of the patriarch of Constantinople (Istanbul). But practically each patriarch guides his own group. The Orthodox likewise claim apostolic succession. The clergy of the Orthodox are all male. There are two types of Orthodox clergy: the monks who must be celibate and the pastors who generally are married.

A third type of episcopacy is in the Anglican or Episcopal type of church government. Anglicanism has a state head of the church, the British sovereign, and a religious head of the church. The religious leadership of the Anglican church is theoretically divided among the bishops, who recognize the priority of the Archbishop of Canterbury and the Archbishop of York, with more actual authority invested in the former. American Episcopalians use a modified version of Anglican church government with the bishops electing one of their number as the presiding bishop for a stated term. Anglicans and Episcopalians have both male and female clergy.

A modification of the Anglican episcopacy is found in Lutheran churches and Methodist Episcopal churches. (M.E. is the abbreviation for Methodist Episcopal. Meth. is the abbreviation for Methodist.) Both men and women may be clergy in the Methodist churches.

Presbyterial. A second major type of church government is the presbyterial form. In this type of church structure, there is shared responsibility between the ordained and laypersons who form presbyteries in local congregations. These presbyteries, in turn, send representatives to a larger presbytery who decide matters of policy for all churches associated with it. The presbyterial ministry and its lay presbyters may be men or women.

Congregational. The third major structure of church government is the congregational type of church government. The theological premise behind this method of church government is the priesthood and equality of all believers. Authority in matters of faith and practice resides in local congregations which relate to larger cooperating groups called associations and conventions. Traditionally, the ordained ministry of this group has been male, although several bodies within the congregational form of government ordain women also. Ordination is at the discretion and policy of local congregations. In theory, there is no qualitative distinction between the ordination of a minister or of a lay leader (deacon) in congregational polity churches.

In recent years new forms, new customs, and structural changes have taken place in all of the traditional forms of church government. Roman Catholics are giving more attention to laypersons. Some congregational groups are moving toward presbyterial (binding associational) types of church government.

Ordination has become a major issue in most churches. The more power and privilege invested in ordination, the more important the discussion becomes. Varying forms of ministry, unknown until recently, have emerged. Questions are also posed by various relations between church and state that relate to ordination. The Bible says remarkably little about ordination. The specifics and qualifications of ministry discussed in the New Testament, if taken absolutely, are largely unattainable. These qualifications include: being blameless, being married (only once), being a parent of obedient children, one who always controls the temper, and so forth (Titus 1:6-9).

To me the larger point in all of the discussion is not the privileges of ordination but the caring on the part of the ministers of God. As one who holds to the congregational form of church government based on the priesthood of all believers, I do not feel that ordination conveys special privileges so much as it connotes particular responsibilities. The basic theological requirement for ordination, in my opinion, is a call from God corroborated by Christian commitment and caring. There are two practical commonsense requirements in addition. The first is a basic and acceptable awareness of Christian belief. The second is a specific situation in ministry. Ministry is not confined to the ordained. But all ordained ministers should be caring.

In a congregational form of church government, ordained ministry is difficult to regulate. The revocation of ordination should be possible and practiced in congregational-type church groups. A minister should be able to request suspension or revocation of ordination when that person leaves ministry for nonchurch-related work. A church should be able to request and insist on revocation of ordination in matters of recognized, blatant heresy or immorality. The church requesting revocation may be either the congregation which ordained the minister, the congregation being served by the minister, or the congregation of which the minister is a member. In every instance such drastic action should be accompanied by love and caring attitudes. I cannot stress too much that the caring mark of the church is more constitutive and important than the structure of the church. Caringness with its discussions of purpose, mission, and ministry relates to the classical mark of the apostolicity of the church.

Relatedness of the Church and the World. This discussion of the caringness mark of the church raises the final question of the relatedness of the church. What is the relatedness of the church to the world? You would expect the obvious answer. It should be a relationship of caring. But we need a more precise answer than that. To whom or what should the church be caring, and in what ways? The church could be caring of the entire cosmos in such a way that we relate to it in a conserving, constructive, and creative way. In this way we will give a faithful witness to God, the Creator of life. The church should relate to the entire human community, corporate and individual, in life-affirming ways so as to give a faithful witness to God, the Preserver of life. The church should relate to social and private problems in a way that will affirm the quality of life, thereby giving a faithful witness to God, the Redeemer of life. The church should relate in a caring way to all societies and persons who perceive themselves as uncared for or who demonstrate that they cannot care for themselves in such a way as to provide hope, and thereby give a faithful witness to God the Consummator of life.[30]

These are the marks of the church: chosenness, corporateness, celebrativeness, and caringness. Do you know any churches like this?

Some do better than others. Remember, God is not done with us yet. This has been a fairly involved discussion. Let me summarize it in outline. There are classical marks of the church, and there are classical offices of Christ's ministry. There are questions of relationship the church must respond to. My suggested marks of the church fit these classical expressions in the following way:

My Suggested Mark	The Classical Mark	The Offices of Christ	The Relational Question
Chosenness	Oneness	Prophetic	Christians and Jews
Corporateness	Universal	Priestly	Christians to fellow Christians
Celebrativeness	Holy	Kingly	Christians to our symbols of joy
Caringness	Apostolicity	Shepherd	Christians to the world

Thus far we have seen the last from the first, eschatology (the last things). We have asked questions about the pilgrimage of the Christian life, and we have learned to recognize the essential marks of the church. All of this could be somewhat detached, but I hope it is not for you. Now we must look in the mirror. And that is personal, intensely personal. Mirrors reflect who we are and what we look like. A look in the mirror will serve as the image for discovering ourselves and the doctrines of persons and sinfulness.

Notes

1. Compare John Gordon Melton, *The Encyclopedia of American Religions,* 2 vols. (Wilmington, N.C.: McGrath, 1978).

2. Compare Richard Quebedeaux, *The Worldly Evangelicals* (San Francisco: Harper & Row, 1978), especially pp. 15-17.

3. See below, Chapter 7, pp. 258-262.

4. See the discussion of the relation of divine sovereignty, the enabling power of Christ, and the participation of our wills in the discussion and diagrams of the last chapter (pp. 64-69).

5. See appendix B, "The Christian and the Ballot Box" from Christian Life Commission Seminar, Washington, D.C., 1984.

6. Compare Johannes Munck, *Christ and Israel: An Interpretation of Romans 9-11,* trans. Ingeburg Nixon (Philadelphia: Fortress Press, 1967).

7. K. Barth, *Church Dogmatics,* vol. 2, *The Doctrine of God,* Part 2, ed. G. W. Bromiley and T. F. Torrance (Edinburgh: T. & T. Clark, 1957), § 34 "The Election of the Community," especially pp. 301-305. Also *The Epistle to the Romans,* trans. Edwyn Hoskyns, 6th ed. (London: Oxford University Press, 1933), pp. 417-421.

8. Adapted from Samuel T. Stone, *The Church's One Foundation,* 1866, stanza 1, second half.

9. The shift toward extraordinary individuality arose in Western civilization in the eighteenth century in a movement called the Enlightenment. See John Herman Randall, *The Making of the Modern Mind: A Survey of the Intellectual Background of the Present Age* (Boston: Houghton Mifflin, 1926).

10. Compare Paul S. Minear, "Idea of Church" in George A. Buttrick (ed.), *The Interpreter's Dictionary of the Bible* (Nashville: Abingdon, 1962), vol. 1, pp. 607-617. Also, see Minear's *Images of the Church in the New Testament* (Philadelphia: The Westminster Press, 1960).

11. A phrase from a well-known religious song (Austria A. Wihtol [pseud. I. B. Serge], *My God and I,* c. 1935, 1963, Singspiration Inc.).

12. The title of a good and well-known book by Elton Trueblood (New York: Harper, 1961).

13. Annie Johnson Flint, "Christ—And We," Stanzas 2 and 3 in James D. Morrison, *Masterpieces of Religious Verse* (New York: Harper and Brothers, 1948. Published originally by Evangelical Publishers, n.d.), pp. 360-361.

14. See the work of Emil Brunner (*The Misunderstanding of the Church,* trans. Harold Knight [London: Lutterworth Press, 1952] and *The Christian Doctrine of the Church, Faith, and the Consummation: Dogmatics, vol. 3,* trans. David Cairns [Philadelphia: The Westminster Press, 1962], pp. 3-139.) in which he makes the distinction between church as a social, historical group and *ekklesia,* the Greek term for church, as the true people of God. See also this principle and its application in Jurgen Moltmann's *The Church in the Power of the Spirit: A Contribution to Messianic Eschatology,* trans. Margaret Kohl (London: SCM Press, 1977), especially pp. 1-65.

15. See James S. Stewart's *A Man in Christ, The Vital Elements of St. Paul's Religion* (London: Hodder and Stoughton, 1935), especially pp. 194-198.

16. *See* Carl F. H. Henry's *Christian Personal Ethics* (Grand Rapids: Eerdmans, 1957), especially pp. 201-208.

17. For a basic discussion of Christian social ethics see Paul Simmons's overview, "The Bible and Christian Ethics," in Paul D. Simmons (ed.), *Issues in Christian Ethics* (Nashville: Broadman Press, 1980), pp. 21-39, and the work of T. B. Maston, *Biblical Ethics: A Survey* (Cleveland: World Publishing, 1967).

18. See above, pp. 50-52.

19. Buryl Red and Reagan Courtney, *Celebrate Life* (Nashville: Broadman Press, 1972).

20. Henry Van Dyke, "Joyful, Joyful We Adore Thee," 1907. From *The Poems of Henry Van Dyke* (New York: Charles Scribner's Sons, 1911).

21. Compare S. Paul Schilling, *The Faith We Sing* (Philadelphia: Westminster Press, 1983) for a theological evaluation of Christian hymns and William J. Reynolds, *Companion to Baptist Hymnal* (Nashville: Broadman Press, 1976) for the stories behind hymn texts.

22. For a fuller explanation of this point see my *Who Is Jesus Christ?* (Nashville: Broadman Press, 1985), pp. 34-36.

23. See George Beasley-Murray, *Baptism in the New Testament* (Grand Rapids: Eerd-

mans, 1973), especially pp. 263-305, and Karl Barth, *Church Dogmatics,* ed. G. W. Bromiley and T. F. Torrance (Edinburgh: T. and T. Clark, 1969), 4, pt. 4 (fragment).

24. See W. H. Brownlee, "John the Baptist in the New Light of Ancient Scrolls," in K. Stendahl (ed.), *The Scrolls and the New Testament,* (New York: Harper, 1957), pp. 33-53. (Earlier published in *Interpretation,* 9 [1955], pp. 71-90.)

25. Compare Oscar Cullmann, *The Earliest Christian Confessions,* trans. J. K. S. Reid (London: Lutterworth Press, 1949), especially pp. 18-21, 35-47.

26. For a good brief summary of the liturgical hypotheses advanced concerning 1 Peter see J. N. D. Kelly, *The Epistles of Peter and Jude* (New York: Harper and Row, 1969), pp. 15-20. Richard Perdelwitz (*Die Mysterien religion und das Problem des I Petrusbrief* [Giessen: Topelmann, 1911]), Herbert Preisker (*Die katholischen Briefe* [Tubingen: Mohr, 1951]), and Frank L. Cross (*I Peter, A Paschal Liturgy* [London: A. R. Mowbray, 1954]) are important advocates of a liturgical view.

27. This custom should likewise pertain to the growing number of disabled younger people whom medical technology has saved from traumatic biological death but cannot restore to functioning life.

28. For a sustained and creative dialogue about the methodology of church mission see *Missiology, An International Review* (Scottdale, Pa.: American Society of Missiology, 1973-).

29. See Francis DuBose, *God Who Sends: A Fresh Quest for Biblical Mission* (Nashville: Broadman Press, 1983) and *Classics of Christian Missions* (Nashville: Broadman, 1979).

30. See my specific suggestions in some of these areas in the proceedings of the Christian Life Seminars: 1978 ("Lifestyle: A Theological Base," pp. 26-30); 1981 ("Power: The Subjunctive Possibilities," pp. 2-8); and 1984 ("Each Christian and a Vote," pp. 67-72) under the general topics of justice, power, and love. See Paul Tillich's *Love, Power and Justice: Ontological Analyses and Ethical Applications* (New York: Oxford University Press, 1954).

4

A Look in the Mirror

As far back as advanced civilizations go, we have found mirrors of one kind or another. We are fascinated from childhood with images and reflections of the self.[1] Mirrors are not just occasions for vanity, although they can be that. Mirrors are tricky things. They can be constructed so as to give distorted images. There are mirrors which give reflections on one side but permit those on the other side to have an undisturbed, in-depth view of what is going on. Three-way mirrors give us a full image of ourselves when we go to buy clothes. Cracked or unsilvered mirrors let us see very indistinctly. Imaginative stories for children, that are even better understood by adults, speak of stepping through a mirror into a deeper, more mysterious world. I would like to use all of these images and types of mirrors to express the theological doctrines of humanity.

Older people have not lost their fascination with the self. We have used mirrors longer. And we doubtless use them more critically. We may look to see if all the hairs of our head are grey, if we are properly shaved or "made up," if we are acceptable to be seen by others, and so forth. It is really disconcerting to gaze in a mirror, for we often find a "strange face" staring back. Sometimes we do not like what we have become. There are some who, from childhood, have not liked or felt comfortable with what they have seen in the mirror. There are even those very serious moments when we examine some part of us in a mirror to discover if there is some sinister, even fatal, growth that would herald the beginning of our end. This looking in the mirror is serious business. I am inviting you, through the metaphor of the mirror, to find out more about the human race and your place in it from a theological perspective.

"A Distant Mirror"

A Distant Mirror is the name of an important book written by Barbara Tuchman about fourteenth-century Europe.[2] Her point of view is that if we examine carefully that time we will find several analogies to our own time, and I think her argument is convincing.[3] There is a "distant mirror" for the human community. It is the figure of Adam. Adam was the first instance of what all of us have become. Adam stands as head of the human race and as an example of the human race. He is an individual and a corporate figure.[4] The rabbis indicated that Adam was composed of dust from the four corners of the earth. But Adam was not only "earthy." He was distinct from all other creatures in that God breathed into him the breath of life. There was an earthy and a heavenly dimension to Adam. There is with all of us as well. Adam represents a stage of the human race which we do not. That is the stage of innocence. Theoretically, it was possible for him not to sin. He was portrayed as having an absolutely free choice. Our lives are inclined in such a way that we inevitably turn out as those who disobey and transgress.

Most world religions and all Near Eastern religions have a notion of a remote ancestor, a representative of all of us.[5] The ancient world thought much more in terms of representative figures and corporate personality than the modern world does. Adam is the remote mirror who reflects the solidarity and the sinfulness of the human race. First figures are important paradigmatic figures. The mirror of Adam reflects our oneness with all humanity. It is important that Luke represents Christ as descended from Adam. Theologically, we all are. It is hard for older people with pride of place, race, tribe, clan, or family to acknowledge fully this deep and necessary theological truth. We have spent most of our lives cultivating, rejoicing in, and even defending our particularities. The Bible calls us to recognize our oneness with all humanity. In our deeper, better selves we recognize this oneness. Interestingly enough, the birth or plight of a child, any child, helps us to come to grips with our human condition.

The distant mirror shows us an Adam who is one, who was innocent, who made the wrong choices, who was punished, and who was loved of God (Gen. 1—3). So are we. Granted our innocence is not absolute, as in the case of Adam, nevertheless, there was a time for all of us when our choices were less conditioned in selfishness, self-deception, and self-justification than they are now. Perhaps I should add an explanation about Adam being loved of God that will refresh your mind about the discussion of death in chapter 1. Adam's punishment was exclusion from paradise. Ours too. We have only dreamed of it; we have never been there.[6] Adam was loved and protected by God lest he eat of the tree of life in his fallen state and have to live forever as a fallen, frail human, incapable of death and therefore not a candidate for resurrection. In this sense we are loved of God in that we too can die so that we can be raised in Christ.

Of course, all of this discussion of Adam is meaningful in Christian theology because of Paul's contrast of Adam with Christ. Paul's major references about Adam and Christ are Romans 5 and 1 Corinthians 15. Paul's references are individual and corporate. There is an exquisite parallel between the first of the old race and the first of the new race. The one represents sin, death, and disobedience; but Adam also represents a type of Christ who is to come. That is, Adam's corporateness relates to us all. So does Christ's. This point needs further discussion. A few of you may have seen in early American samplers the old motto: "In Adam's fall we sinned all." It is a paraphrase of Paul's famous paragraph.

> Therefore being justified by faith, we have peace with God through our Lord Jesus Christ:
> By whom also we have access by faith into this grace wherein we stand, and rejoice in hope of the glory of God.
> And not only so, but we glory in tribulations also: knowing that tribulation worketh patience;
> And patience, experience; and experience, hope:
> And hope maketh not ashamed; because the love of God is shed abroad in our hearts by the Holy Ghost which is given unto us.
> For when we were yet without strength, in due time Christ died for the ungodly.
> For scarcely for a righteous man will one die: yet peradventure for a good man some would even dare to die.
> But God commendeth his love toward us, in that, while we were yet sinners, Christ died for us.
> Much more then, being now justified by his blood, we shall be saved from wrath through him.
> For if, when we were enemies, we were reconciled to God by the death of his Son, much more, being reconciled, we shall be saved by his life.

And not only so, but we also joy in God through our Lord Jesus Christ, by whom we have now received the atonement.

Wherefore, as by one man sin entered into the world, and death by sin; and so death passed upon all men, for that all have sinned (Rom. 5:1–12, KJV).

No passage of Scripture has been more widely discussed and disputed than this one.[7] In the last analysis, it can mean two things if one applies the parallel consistently. It can mean that all persons are, in some unexplained way, automatically made sinners and die because of Adam's sin. Therefore, all persons are, automatically, made alive or redeemed because of Christ. This would mean universalism, that all of the race is saved. Universalism would mean that persons have no real or effective freedom of choice. The passage could also mean that all persons have a part in choosing to be sinful and that they also have a part in choosing to be saved. I definitely feel that the second meaning is more consonant with the bulk of biblical teaching and is more true to our experience. A third alternative is sometimes suggested. This alternative states that all the race is automatically condemned in Adam, but part of the race is either predetermined to be saved or must choose to be saved. I do not feel this interpretation is possible. It obviously does not fit the plain meaning of the passage.

Adam helps us. By looking into the mirror where he is reflected we see: (1) the theological unity and solidarity of the human race; (2) the reflection of a necessary stage of innocence that makes choice significant; (3) the reality and intensity of our decisions which lead to sin and bring estrangement from God; (4) the double composition and complexity of human existence—both earthly and heavenly; (5) the representative negative figure who is counterbalanced by God's second Adam, Jesus Christ. We could not do without Adam. Adam reminds us of us. He reminds us that we cannot come out well, so long as we have only Adam. The mirror of Adam has a certain convexity about it that makes the dim past close In Adam's distant mirror we seem very similar to humanity's dim past. And in the convexity of the distant mirror we see another mirror on the opposite wall. That is the true mirror of Jesus Christ, into which mirror we also will have to look if we are really going to know ourselves. Adam is in humanity's distant mirror. Adam might also be called the rearview mirror of humankind. Like the side mirrors on our cars, we need the mirror of Adam to see where we have been and to realize the threat of the "first Adam" which always is in danger of overtaking the human race.

A Cracked Mirror

Cracking a mirror is, according to an old superstition, supposed to bring seven years' bad luck. The cracked-mirror image I have in mind is worse than that. It brings us perennial bad luck. The "curse" never runs out. I want to use the symbol of a cracked or dimly silvered mirror to signify what happens to us because of sin. The theological ideas for this analogy of the cracked mirror are the image of God and what happens to it in "the fall." Now there are two terms which cry out for definition: *image of God* and the *fall.* Let me define these terms just after I have made clearer what I mean by "a cracked mirror." Glass mirrors are made with some kind of backing that will reflect an image. After a certain length of time this "silvered" back portion can disintegrate and begin to lose its capacity for sharp reflection. We can no longer use the mirror to reflect accurate pictures. They either have to be "resilvered" or discarded. A cracked mirror or a shattered mirror is even worse. One can still see in a cracked or shattered mirror, but the reflection is diffuse and broken up. It is hard to image wholeness in a cracked mirror. It seems to me that the unsilvered, shattered, cracked mirror analogy is an apt one for talking about the image of God in humanity after the fall.[8]

Now, let me have a go at defining what we mean when we speak theologically about "the fall" and the image of God (*imago Dei*) in humanity. You have heard the expression, this is a "fallen world." Obviously, that is a symbolic expression. To take it literally would mean that, at one point, our planet earth was physically higher in the atmosphere than it now is, and that, at some point, it dropped a physical distance lower. That is not what is meant by "the fall" in Christian theology. The fall is a metaphor which means that something is wrong with the world. It is not now the way it was supposed to be. In fact, the world is also not now what it is going to be in its redemption. It is a presupposition of the Christian faith that as the world is now, it is not as it was originally intended to be, nor is it as it is ultimately going to be.

Let me draw some lines that I hope will make this idea clearer.

the world as redeemed

the world as innocent

the world as fallen

Please notice that there are three levels. The world as God "originally" created it was good. Genesis 1—2 is unambiguous about that. This was the good creation of untried innocence. To put it another way, unfallen Adam was innocent. He was not perfect. Jesus, the second Adam, was perfect. Perfection implies testing, struggle, the exercise of the will, and successfully overcoming temptation. The world as redeemed will be "higher" (better) than original innocence or present fallenness. The world as it is now certainly is not what it was supposed to be. It is "less." It is something other than good. That is what fallenness means.

"The fall" is a way of saying that something is wrong with us and with the world in which we live. That something, as we will see in our next mirror, involves the very structure of our being. The physical, and the psychological, and the spiritual are all involved in "the fall." Even the world around us, which we often call "nature," is not what it ought to be. Mankind, as steward of creation, is responsible for these effects on nature. A phrase from the Christmas carol "Joy to the World" expresses it well. "No more let sins and sorrows grow,/Nor thorns infest the ground;/He comes to make his blessings flow/Far as the curse is found."[9] A fallen world does not so much refer to the biological structure of our world as it does to the ecological ruin which humanity is making of it.[10]

I want to add a further point here. Modern urban society (and that is becoming the predominant kind of society) knows very little of nature. Most people today dwell in a technological fabricated, or prefabricated, global village.[11] We seldom live in "nature" anymore. Ours is an industrial, product-oriented world. Even rural people participate in this kind of world *via* their machinery, television, transportation, and so forth. Given that we are a fabricated society, the point about the fall is even more appropriate. We have ruined God's original world. And we have ruined the fabricated world which we have produced. Neither of these worlds is satisfying or "good" in the biblical sense. Ours is a twice-fallen world. This is what it means to talk about "the fall."

The image of God likewise is not a thing. It is a concept which explains a relationship. There are really many words like that. It seems to me that all abstract words are concepts or terms to explain reality and relationships. Love is not a thing. It is a certain way of being, an intense kind of relationship. What you see in the unsilvered, shattered, cracked mirror is a broken image. There have been numerous suggestions about what the image or likeness of God in humanity is.[12] Many classical theologians said the image was our ability to think and to reason. The process of thinking and rational reflection is certainly one of the things that distinguishes people from animals, plants, and all the rest of God's creation. But I am a little wary of defining the image only as the ability to reason. I am wary because it puts too much emphasis on the processes of formal reasoning, certainly more than the Bible does. And the implication might be that people who reason best are most like God. That certainly is not true to experience. One is reminded of the sharp wit of G. K. Chesterton who quipped, "Education without Christ merely produces clever devils." One also remembers the popular piety of a whole host of saints who were better at being good than they were at being smart.

Some have made the suggestion that to be made in the image of God means that we literally look like God, or He looks like us physically. For God's own sake, I hope not. God became man. But He does not permanently reside in a physical body. And we who do have received the promise that we will be like Him and not vice versa. There has been the suggestion that the image of God is our ability to relate to others, especially the male and female relationship which speaks of community and intimate interpersonal relationships. This is, in my opinion, better than other definitions, but it is too closely bound with "sexuality" to be precisely appropriate to God. I would define the image of God as the ability and responsibility to respond to God, the self, and others.[13]

Christian theology, following Genesis 3, suggests that the image also was affected by the fall. This means that our relationships and our ability to relate are affected by our being out of step with God, ourselves, and others. There are three ideas as to how much and to what extent our being is affected by sin.

1. One view makes a distinction between the "image" and the "likeness" of Genesis 1:26. The assertion is that the likeness was affected by the fall but the image, our ability to reason, was and is basically unaffected by sin. This view would obviously have a strong view of the reasoning ability of mankind and would be optimistic about our ability to reason our way to God, at least up to a certain point. This is, in principle, the Roman Catholic view. This view is flattering. It is, in my opinion, too flattering. We can and do reason well about a lot of things. But how to find and understand God is not one of them. It is precisely in our quest for God that our "natural" reason is ineffective (Rom. 1:19–21).

2. A second idea about the image after the fall is that the image is totally obliterated. According to this view God has to recreate us from within before we desire or can respond to Him. Luther and Karl Barth held this view. It is difficult to affirm either from the Bible or experience that there is nothing in us which cries out for God.

3. The third idea is that a relic of the image is left "after the fall." Augustine and Calvin held this view. It is obvious from my metaphor of the cracked or shattered mirror that I agree with this perspective. There is an old saying of Augustine that is worth quoting on this point. "You have made us for yourself, and our heart is restless until it rests in you."[14] There is something about us that keeps looking in the shattered mirror. And there is something deep within us that recognizes, even beyond and behind the cracks of our own fragmented selves, that we are not what we seem. There is a longing for wholeness, a desire to set the reflection right. We see through a glass darkly. The glass is very dark, and it is marred. But we do see, and seeing, we long for a fresh vision and a whole picture. Unfortunately, the cracked mirror is not the worst one we have to look into. There is a deeper and more devious glass into which we must look before things are set right. That is the mirror of distortion.

The Mirror of Distortion

The mirror of distortion is an analogy to an old-fashioned fun house mirror. Such a mirror distorts the image of the viewer. Some make us look short and fat; others tall and skinny. The observers are always amused. But the analogy of the distorted mirror I am using is not funny at all. It is really a "trick" mirror in that when we look into it, we usually see what we want to see. We become accustomed to the image in this mirror, and we even come to believe that this image is what we are supposed to look like. To paraphrase a well-known song: We have grown accustomed to our faces. The theological term for the mirror of deception is sin. One of the characteristics of sin is to distort. Another of the characteristics of sin is the seductive way it has of making us think that its distortions are the way things are supposed to be. Alexander Pope expressed it well. "Vice is a monster of so frightful mien, /As to be hated needs but to be seen; /Yet seen too oft, familiar with her face, /We first endure, then pity, then embrace."[15] We are always embracing what we see in the mirror of distortion. The first seductive voice from the mirror was a distorted picture: "Of course you will not die" (Gen. 3:4). All of the sounds and sights from the mirror of distortion are what we want to hear and see. This is different from what we need to hear and see.

In exploring the picture we see in the mirror of distortion, we see that the image is wrong in all directions. It is wrong in all of the dimensions of each of us, and it is wrong in all of the particulars of the group image of all of us. Just as Adam reflects the corporate picture of all of us, so also the mirror of distortion is a crowded mirror. We all appear in it. The image is not a pretty family picture. We all are at our worst, and each of us comes off no better than the other. "For all have sinned, and come short of the glory of God" (Rom. 3:23). Group pictures are sometimes a delight. Go through some of your old class photos. Each individual looks first for himself. Unfortunately, one of the tricks of the mirror of deception is that each of us looks first to discover the distortions of the whole group or of individuals about us. It is part of the distortion of sin that we can find the distortion of sin so quickly in others and so slowly in ourselves.

One direction in which we are distorted is at the point of our height. We seem taller than we are. Babel (Gen. 11·1–9) is a collective account of our desire to reach the heavens. *Bab-el* means a gate to God. The distortion of sin leads to a heightened pride that presumes it can reach the heavens. This is as true of modern technological society and the pride of its achievements as it was of ancient Babel. And it is as true of each individual as it is of the collective society in which we live. "You will be like gods" (compare Gen. 3:5). There is another voice we need to hear. "God is in heaven, you are on earth" (Eccl. 5:2). The distortion of pride lifts us up to a very deceptive height.

Another direction in which the mirror of distortion deceives us is in the matter of breadth. We suppose ourselves very wide indeed. We want to incorporate it all. Like small children dressed in large clothes posturing before the mirror, we reach out to bring all things into the self. This is the sin of greed. One generation wants to use up all the natural energy for itself. Great world powers strive to control more territories and peoples. Individuals grasp for more than their share. Every one looks upon his image and proclaims it good and prosperous and feels as if the whole earth were a private possession. We need to hear another voice: "Whatsoever is under the whole heaven is mine" (Job 41:11). It is God who is speaking, and it is He alone who can make the claim. He can make this claim not merely because He created the world but because He is the only one who can handle "full property rights" without a sense of greed which calls for more. There are societies which consider fatness to be a desirable quality of prosperity and good favor. The mirror of distortion casts an image of obesity as handsome. The glut of greed, to which we all are prone even in spiritual things, is an "overweight" problem that will prove fatal if not corrected.

The third direction in which the mirror of distortion represents us is downward. The sin of a downward glance in the mirror is sloth. Sloth is a form of sin that makes us content with what we are. Sloth prevents us from seeing the whole picture, the true picture. Sloth only glances down to see if the underskirt is showing or if the shoes are polished. Sloth looks for the minimum and is satisfied with the self. Sloth comes to an uneasy truce with the level of our accomplishments. And that level is an abysmally low one in the light of our potential. The distortion of sloth disallows a standard that it should have owned. "Be ye therefore perfect, even as your Father which is in heaven is perfect" (Matt. 5:48, KJV). Sloth is the downward look in the mirror that is satisfied with the lowest level of achievement. Sloth has a soothing voice and a too-soon-satisfied standard.

The fourth direction in which the mirror of sin deceives us is in the dimension of the relations to others and to God. This is the sin of rebellion which holds others and even God out of the center of life. A medical analogy might be the tragic disorder anorexia nervosa. That strange disorder causes the victim to suppose that he/she is fat and needs no nourishment. It can be a terminal situation in which the sufferer starves to death. The sin of rebellion holds out others and especially God under the supposition of a sufficient self. The distorting sin of rebellion will not share the self with others. And the result is the isolation of loneliness and the arrogance of playing God. The distorted rebellious self needs to hear the Commandment, "Love the Lord your God," and "your neighbour as yourself."

Whichever way we look in the mirror of distortion, we are deceived. "If the eyes are bad, your whole body will be in darkness" (Matt. 6:23; compare Matt. 20:15; Luke 11:34). The fault is complete. It is both the mirror (the world around us) and the viewer (ourselves in trying to assess ourselves) who are faulty.

What is even more frustrating and deceptive is that the roots of sin *are* related to the image of what we ought to be. The elements of ourselves that are distorted are those that can give us worth and dignity. The roots of our sin are related to the roots of our sanctity. The wheat and tares have to grow together (compare Matt. 13:24–30) because if we uproot the one, we destroy the other. These statements seem confused and distorted. This unnerving paradox is a part of our problem. Both we and the mirror are faulty. Let me explain. Pride is a positive virtue that leads to a sense of self-worth and accomplishment. Without legitimate pride we could accomplish nothing. Bringing unto the self the things necessary for self-survival is the only way we will survive. Even looking down to slow down the wild expectations of life is necessary. Your own heart will teach you the necessary life affirming rhythm of contraction *and* relaxation. Without some restraint to the expectation of constant accomplishment, life would be intolerable and not worth the effort. There is even the necessity of retaining our own integrity with God and others. God has willed that we should hold ourselves as individuals before Him. He wants our free decision, not our automation. Others have a claim on us, but we can never be successful with others without first valuing and preserving the self.

So there you have it. The mirror does distort, but the reality it distorts is a legitimate reality. We cannot remove those elements which are exaggerated and distorted. We sometimes cannot even tell the point and degree of distortion. It is a very mixed up and ambiguous situation. The distorted mirror is the most difficult one of all. By looking only in it, we cannot be sure that what we see is or is not supposed to be what we see. We notice the distortions in others. Yet those same distortions are less apparent in the self. And, ambiguously, we are not sure what are distortions since all of the others have them too. Maybe we are automatically the way we are supposed to be. Maybe the image we have of ourselves is a true image. Maybe. But I do not think so. Nor did Paul think so. His most powerful expression of the divided and confused self who looks in the mirror of distortion is in Romans 7:15–24.

> For that which I do I allow not: for what I would, that do I not; but what I hate, that do I.
>
> If then I do that which I would not, I consent unto the law that it is good.
>
> Now then it is no more I that do it, but sin that dwelleth in me.
>
> For I know that in me (that is, in my flesh,) dwelleth no good thing: for to will is present with me; but how to perform that which is good I find not.
>
> For the good that I would I do not: but the evil which I would not, that I do.
>
> Now if I do that I would not, it is no more I that do it, but sin that dwelleth in me.
>
> I find then a law, that, when I would do good, evil is present with me.
>
> For I delight in the law of God after the inward man:
>
> But I see another law in my members, warring against the law of my mind, and bringing me into captivity to the law of sin which is in my members.
>
> O wretched man that I am! Who shall deliver me from the body of this death? (KJV)

Sin is more than sins. Sin is a distortion of the world around us and within us. This mirror is a true mirror because it shows us the way we are. It is a false mirror also because we have looked in it and lived with it so long that we suppose that the image we see in this mirror of distortion is also the way we are supposed to be. This is not the case.

I want to suggest to senior adults that we are particularly vulnerable when looking in this mirror. For we have gazed in it longer than others. We have become accustomed to our faces. If pressed, we would say that we like some of those habitual features which we have nourished so long. It may be harder for us, who have ingrained habits and familiar sights, to be convinced that the images of the self we have lived with so long are, in any sense, distorted. We may be more resentful than others about the charge of being sinful or other than we ought to be. Long experience of looking into a distorted mirror does not remove the distortion. It merely lets us become comfortable with the picture we see. What is required is a different mirror, a true mirror that reflects an image of how things are intended to be. It was necessary to look in the distant mirror; we had to glance into the cracked mirror and to keep looking in the mirror of distortion because these are mirror images of our lives. They are all pervasive in a world like ours. They are the tools of our seeing and the honest, if unwanted, reflections of who we are.[16] Attempts to avoid these mirrors are futile or self-deceptive. The answers to the dilemmas of the self—who we are, what we are like, how should we see ourselves—lie first in an honest use of these three mirrors. But the "real" picture lies in the fourth mirror, the mirror of truth.

The True Mirror

We would not know about the mistakes, the cracks, the distortions unless there was a true mirror. Christians affirm this true mirror is Jesus Christ. He is the image of God (Heb. 1:3) in a consistent and convincing way. But He is not only the image of God, He is also the image of what humanity is intended to be. Jesus brings us meaning by His life as well as by His death. I will discuss the doctrine of Christ in chapter 7. At this point I want to emphasize Jesus as God's truth. It is He who is the "true mirror." The reflection is right. It is right from the viewpoint of God and from the viewpoint of humanity.

The traditional doctrine we have used to discuss this point is called the sinlessness of Jesus. Arguments raged over whether Jesus was able to sin or not able to sin. Proponents of either side would argue from His divinity or His humanity. If He were divine, He could not sin. If He were human, He had to be able to sin. It seems to me this was starting from theory instead of reality. We know what Jesus was like from what Scripture says He was and did. We must not, as we shall see later, let His natures war among themselves. Jesus was a total, integrated person. We will have to assume, therefore, that if He was tempted, He could have yielded to temptation. We are told that He did not (Matt. 3:13–17; Heb. 4:15). What this means is that His reflection of God was authentic, and His reflection of humanity was not distorted. He faced a distorted mirror because of the kind of world in which He lived, but He provided an alternative which is a corrective to the distortion of sin in our own lives. The sinlessness of Jesus is not just a doctrine. It was a condition of His life. Sinlessness was not something "given" in His genes. It was something struggled for in His character. We are talking about a victorious experience, not a legal status.

Most Christians affirm His sinlessness on the biblical report of His experience. Some have suggested that if He really were human, He would have to have participated in sinfulness in order to be thoroughly human. This is a convincing argument if you are willing to define God's revelation by human experience. There is another way to put the problem. That is to say that Jesus is the only and authentic human. He is the model for humanity. He is what we are supposed to be. I prefer this view. This means that we are not confined to our distant, cracked, and distorted mirrors. There is another one, a true one, in which to see the measure and the model of ourselves.

There is another belief about Jesus, the man in God's true mirror, that enters into this discussion. That is the virgin birth, or more precisely, the virginal conception. The particulars of this doctrine will be treated below, but one function of the virginal conception should be mentioned here. Jesus' own struggle with sin and His triumph over it means that He does not have to reflect the distorted mirror of sin. His virginal conception is a way of saying He does not have to reflect the image of the shattered and cracked mirror. Virginal conception is a way of saying that God is starting a new line, a new creation (compare Paul, "if any man be in Christ, he is a new creature," 2 Cor. 5:17, KJV). The world around us contains us and confines us. We entered a fallen world, under fallen conditions. We must look through the mirrors of distortion and cracked images. Barth has rightly said that the miracle of Christmas is God coming to be with us in a new way, and the wonder of Christmas is the virgin birth.[17] The purpose of the virginal conception is to say that God has come to us in a new and different way, a way that will give the option of not having to look through our cracked mirror. Jesus entered a fallen world. But He was not a fallen person. Traditionally stated, this means that the image of God in Jesus was not a fallen image. He came intact from God to provide an option—a true mirror.

A third step is obvious and needs to be expressed. The preexistence of Jesus is a way of emphasizing His freedom from the "distant" mirror. All who come after Adam must bear the stamp of Adam, except the one Who came "after" Adam but was "before" Adam. "In the beginning was the Word, and the Word was with God" (John 1:1). In the incarnation, the Word of God was with us. And He is with us in such a way that He can provide an alternative. He is not bound by the "distant mirror" because He is from an even more distant time and place. Doctrine grows out of worship.[18] Both doctrine and worship are to be occasions of praise and reasons for giving thanks. The preexistence of Christ is not just a matter of the priority of time; it is a matter of the primacy and privilege God provided through Jesus Christ. There is an alternative. It is the true mirror. Now we must ask about the meaning of that often-used and seldom-defined word *truth*.

"What is truth?" asked Pilate. Truth is a five-letter word. Truth in lending and in advertising laws are passed by the government. *The* truth was an absolute abstraction sought by Greek philosophers. Truth is a mathematical equation to those to whom mathematical models appeal. Truth varies with the context according to the situationalist. Truth in politics is our preferred politics and its way of stating the case. Witnesses swear to tell the truth, the whole truth, and nothing but the truth. Only the "fool hath said in his heart" there is no truth, because there is no God (Pss. 14:1; 53:1). In an age of outrageous lying, official double talk, and double standards, we still must ask the truth question. And in a time of philosophical skepticism, religious pluralism, and competing ideologies, we must ask about the method of verification of truth claims.[19]

If there is a truth mirror, of what does it consist? Where is it to be found? In my opinion truth is grounded in and guaranteed by God. God is truth (compare 1 John 5:6). "Let God be true, but every man a liar" (Rom. 3:4, KJV) is the emotional cry of the apostle Paul. When I say truth is grounded in God, I mean that, in the last analysis, whatever is correct rather than incorrect, whatever is life inducing rather than life destructive, whatever promotes the unity, well-being, and integrity of the universe as a whole and the smallest particle of it in particular is related to the truth. Truth is not whatever is. Truth is the well-being of what is and the standard of what ought to be. Truth is related to goodness and to beauty. Goodness is not just what is nice. Beauty is not just what is pretty. I would want to affirm that truth is a realm of "oughtness," an ideal, an absolute.

All of this is high-sounding talk, but it is important talk. From these affirmations I would want to draw out several important points. (1) There are several kinds or fields of truth. There are mathematical kinds of truths. There are ethical kinds of truth. There are religious kinds of truth. For example, true love is different from true equations. (2) There is no one uniform way of unifying or proving all truth. You do mathematics and abstract logic one way. You prove character in another. And you prove God, if at all, in still another. (3) All truth is unified and grounded in God as source and guarantor of truth. But God as truth is a special kind of claim which cannot be proved outside of the realm of faith. The abstract noun *truth* is to be interpreted, in the arena of faith, by God and not by any other predetermined standards or presuppositions of what one supposes truth is.

In the light of all this heavy talk, one passage of Scripture comes to mind. It is Jesus' claim to be the way, the truth, the life (John 14:6). I take this to mean: (1) that the kind of truth which is important in talking about the Christian faith is a truth that is personal and relational. This does not mean that it cannot be expressed in accurate propositions, for it can. But it does mean that the truth of God *is* God as most clearly revealed in Jesus, the Son of God. That is where a Christian theologian would want to start all discussion about "truth"; (2) Jesus is God's truth at the point of being the way, a method for accomplishing God's purpose, and the life, interrelated experiences of positive, sustaining, and meaningful existence; and (3) Jesus as the truth has to do with God, His will, His way, and His purpose for the world and with humanity, its destiny, its meaning, and what it is intended to be.

We may now turn from the distant, the cracked mirrors, and distorted mirrors. We need to keep glancing at the true mirror, Christ. We also need to look away from the implications of Adam, original sinfulness. We need to look at Christ as the model image, the Truth. Holding all of these together we can the better look at who we are in all of our complexity. This requires a three-way mirror.

A Three-Way Mirror

How do you feel when you go to buy clothes? You try to feel your best because standing in front of a three-way mirror is very disconcerting. The experience of looking into a three-paneled mirror is, as Bobby Burns would say, "Seeing ourselves as others see us." When you are buying clothes, you need the full story. I want the image of the three-way or three-paneled mirror to stand for a holistic view of ourselves. We need the full picture because we are complete selves. We are body. We are soul. We are spirit. We become conscious of our stomachs when we are hungry. We pay attention to the body when it sends us pain signals. We think about how we think or do not think when we are asked to think. We finally recognize that we are in depression, unless we are having so severe a depression that we cannot recognize it. We are aware of our psyche when something psychical or psychological happens to us or goes on within us. We become concerned or convicted spiritually when we hear a good sermon, read Scripture, or go to church. We are aware of the spiritual dimension of life when someone or something calls us beyond the self. Most of the time we just are. We are bodies. We are conscious. We are spiritual.

Usually we do not reflect on these dimensions of our existence. Sometimes, when we do reflect on one dimension of our experience or another, we assume that we come in parts: a body, psyche, or a spirit. That view is too exaggerated or separated. What a three-way mirror shows us is that we are total beings who have various ways of relating. Good relationships involve all of each of us. We miss friends and loved ones when they are, to use a biblical phrase, absent in the body. True, we may remember them through our thought processes. But we could not even do this if we had not seen or known their bodies. Bodyness, embodiment, is a necessary item to our knowing and being. The working of the mind is necessary for all consciousness of the self. When the mind, or reflective abilities, are not functioning, we speak of the body being in a coma. When we are not sensitive to, enlivened by, and responding to God, the spiritual life, our push for self-transcendence, we speak of being spiritually dead. When we are conscious of our push for self-transcendence, the desire to go "beyond" the self, and when we exercise this part of us in unsatisfactory ways or direct the spiritual to something less than God, we speak of idolatry. The problem of idolatry is wasting our energies on the unfulfilling.

All our dimensions are not always harmoniously together. Much of the time we are just existing and not really living. Life, in the best sense, is all dimensions of the self being conscious and being integrated. That is the "whole look." The conscious integrated self is the way we ought to "look." We fit; the "clothes" look good when we have it all together and can see it all together.

There are theological words that describe all of these dimensions of us: body, self, soul, spirit. It will be helpful to see them all together in this three-way mirror, for that is how we are. Then we will need to take each dimension and let it be a kind of mirror we use to observe that dimension. But the whole comes before the parts. The whole is made up of the "parts." and, in this instance, the whole is greated than the sum of the parts. It is "greater" because it is a totally functioning self. None of the three dimensions is, strictly speaking, able to function alone, nor was it meant to.

The first word about who we are, according to the Scripture, is the obvious dimension of our existence. The term is *body.* The form or shape of a "thing" is the thing that lets you know anything is there. If you ask if John is in the garage, someone goes out, looks, returns, and says nobody is in the garage. You do not ask, "How do you know nobody is there?" The answer is obvious. Your friend would reply, "Nobody is there because I did not see anybody." We know that someone is born when there is a separation of that individual's body or form from the mother's form. We say one dies when his chemical form is no longer functioning.[20] In a special meaning, we speak of the corpse as "a body." If someone comes back and says to you "There is a 'body' in the garage," you are in trouble. The point is that body is the basic, constituent element in being.

There can be and are different kinds of bodies. There are different types of physical bodies: animal, vegetable, mineral, and human. There are also spiritual bodies (1 Cor. 15). But the preponderance of biblical insight suggests that nothing exists without a body. The Old Testament refers to God with bodily terms. "Behold, the Lord's hand is not shortened" (Isa. 59:1). This is a special use of the term *body:* we call it anthropomorphism, that is, God explained in human form. The

New Testament speaks of an embodiment of God in Jesus. "For in him dwelleth all the fulness of the Godhead bodily" (Col. 2:9, KJV). Body is the shape of whatever has actual being.[21] God "existed" before the incarnation, but we would not have known that unless He had used different "bodies" to express Himself. God used the bodies of the biblical writers to understand and express the realities of His message. Christianity is not a "spiritual" religion. That is, Christianity is a religion which is concerned about creation, about this world and its transformation, and about the redemption of the body. Body is the first thing we see in the mirror, literally and symbolically.

Self is the consciousness of the body. Self is the inner, reflective function of who you are. Self is conscious that you are you and not another. Self is apparently dependent upon the body. But it would be a mistake to say that the self of the individual is just a matter of chemical action and interaction. Self is thinking, realizing, reflecting, planning, making creative plans, or reading a book. All of these rational acts and all of our emotional acts also are the expression of the self. The "self" hurts even when the body does not. The self can be offended, satisfied, elated, or depressed. These things happen through the body, but they are not "just" bodily expressions. They are expressions of a self-consciousness. When we look in a three-way mirror, we are conscious of our bodies. We are also self-conscious in most instances, if we are really looking—looking not just at the body but also at the mysterious reflection of who we are, we, the "looking" persons.[22]

The third idea to express who we are is "spirit." I am going to use that term here to mean those aspirations, hopes, abilities, and desires that go "beyond" the self. This is what I mean by self-transcendence. Self-transcendence or spirit does not normally operate separate from and without regard for the body and the self. We are not confined to bodily chemical explanations. Spirit is that surplus of who we are that lets us relate to others. Spirit lets us relate to God. Spirit gives meaning, aspiration, and purpose to the self.

I trust that you are getting the picture of one complete person looking in a mirror and being conscious of different "layers" of what is seen. Superficial people see only the body. Too sensitive people see primarily the self. Overly spiritual people try to pretend that the body and the self are not there or do not count. There really are three dimensions of who we are. They are like concentric, interlocking circles. If you pry them apart, we are not the same. If you say they are one and not three, you are not looking closely enough. I have saved the biblical terms and discussion of these dimensions to use in the separate mirrors of each dimension. What I wanted you to see first is who we are altogether and who each of us is completely. Turn around a few times before a three-way mirror.

A Full-Length Mirror

Body Corporate and Individual. Let us start first with the central panel of the three-way mirror. This is the full-length mirror. I would like for the full-length mirror to represent the body, the most obvious part of us as persons. I want to stress a twofold sense of body. Body stands for an aggregation of all the people in their physical dimension. Body also indicates the individual in his/her biochemical make-up. There is a "body" of humanity that pertains to the physical makeup of all persons. There are more physical factors that bind all humans together than there are differences between us. This is illustrated by the art of medicine. If all people did not have the same number of bones, teeth, orifices, and appendages, the practice of medicine would have to differ essentially from place to place and from race to race. Some persons may have slight deviations in their physical makeup, but this is minor when compared with our similarities.

This physical likeness is, technically speaking, the province of biology. However, it has theological implications. The human race is one in the sight of God physically. This physical similarity is expressed in Genesis by the solidarity figure of Adam. The theological unity of all members of the human race is expressed by Paul in Galatians 3:26–29. This relatedness does not overlook the individual distinctiveness, but it does stress that the form of humanity is created by God and valued by God. God is not just interested in or Creator of what is sometimes popularly called "the soul." Our bodies, our shapes and those of all persons, are His handiwork and share in His redemptive concern. When we reenforce creation with Christ's incarnation, we must affirm that we cannot despise the form of any person since God Himself became a person in Jesus Christ.

What this "bodiness" of all humanity means ethically is that (1) all persons are creatures of God, and all are loved by Him; their bodies, their forms, are valued. (2) Therefore, Christians cannot justify any prejudice based on physical characteristics. God loves the world (John 3:16). He made it and pronounced it good (Gen. 1, especially v. 31). He will renew and recreate it, even its physical dimensions (Rev. 21:1; 22:1–5). The creation of the new earth will be a spiritual creation. But that creation is based upon and analogous to our present physical creation, or else we would not recognize it or one another. Considering all of these things we must say that Christians must share God's concern for the physical well being of mankind. We cannot proclaim the good news of the Bread of life without also helping to provide the physical bread which sustains life (Jas. 2:15–17). We must be concerned about the corporate body of humanity in all of its physicalness.

We need also to be concerned about individual bodies, our own and those we love. We need little encouragement at this point. "No one ever hated his own body" (Eph. 5:29). Most of us also value our own loved ones. "Honour your father and your mother" (Ex. 20:12). "Husbands, love your wives" (Eph. 5:25). "Wives, be subject to your husbands" (Eph. 5:22). The admonitions of Scripture about family and intimate relationships are explicit and encouraging.[23]

There is no specific Old Testament word for body. This is surprising in light of all the emphasis the Old Testament gives to the physical. But it is understandable when we realize that the Old Testament so presupposes the body that it uses various parts for the whole. It speaks of the back, the front, the face, the belly, the bones, the fleshly parts.[24]

Sins Against the Body. Our modern society has sinned in two directions when it comes to caring for one's own body. On the one hand, we have "cared" far too much for ourselves. We have done this by providing sophisticated medicine for the affluent few. We have done this by sustaining some individual physical lives at too high a cost for the quality of life they have. It is all right to die. Forestalling the inevitable to perpetuate an existing familiar form in a vegetating state is not necessarily "caring" for the body. It is trying to perpetuate the body at all cost. And, in my opinion, the costs are sometimes too high.[25] The finances of the cult of the burial of the dead, likewise, often put too much "care" on the bodily form of our existence.[26]

Families should have candid and appropriate discussions about the medical care, costs, and procedures for its aging individuals. More often than not, older people do not want to "rob" the young of their "turn," their share of physical existence and well-being.

But this frugality can be taken to extremes, and the aged can suffer needlessly in their body needs. This is a social as well as an individual problem, that is, what percent of a nation's resources are to be used in health care for which age groups? This pressing problem will become worse as we perfect the technological means to prolong the life of the individual but do not have increased production of substance or equitable distribution of what is available. These are family, national, and international concerns about the body, the corporate body of humanity and the individual body of all persons.

The full-length mirror is a very crowded mirror, and it is becoming more so. Christians must bring theological insights, drawn from adequate theological principles, to bear on these population problems. God ordinarily "comes down" on the side of life. To value, protect, and promote life as it comes to us and to contribute to it through perpetuating it and sustaining its quality is a godly thing to do. To hold on to the body at all cost, to expend unconscionable amounts of wealth ornamenting it, or giving full reign to its pleasures, or to expend lavish amounts in disposing of a biologically dead body can be a selfish form of idolatry.[27]

The second problem our society has in its undue attention to the body is the abuse of the body. Physical abuse takes many forms. I am referring now to self-induced physical abuse. This is the opposite number of too much and too costly care for the body. Body abuse may be *substance abuse.* The dependency on any substance that ruins the body and confuses, disorients, or permanently damages the mind is bad abuse indeed. Narcotics, even the gentle addiction of the aging who take just one more pill than necessary, is one form of substance abuse. Alcohol, nicotine, and so forth, may be other forms of abuse. *Types and quantities of food* also may constitute body abuse. Sugar to the diabetic or a whole loaf of bread to the overweight glutton is abuse. Various segments of the Christian community have become frightfully indignant over the social abuse of the body by others. It is an old and unfortunate way of defining sin by what we do or like and what we do not do or like. One characteristic all forms of body abuse share is that they are expensive. Usually, they are expensive to sustain, and always they are expensive in every way to cure. "Know ye not that your body is the temple of the Holy Ghost? (1 Cor. 6:19, KJV). "I beseech you therefore, brethren, by the mercies of God, that ye present your bodies as a living sacrifice, holy, acceptable unto God, which is your reasonable service" (Rom. 12:1, KJV).

Diminution of the Body. There is a gradual mourning process that occurs with aging and/or illness and physical traumas of the body. Aging is an elusive term. In our world one can, because of physical and social conditions, be old at thirty and young at eighty. The premature aging of the underprivileged is a problem with which the body of Christ ought also to be concerned. The actual aging and diminution of strength is a personal dilemma with which you cannot help but be concerned. Surgery is a law of diminishing returns for the aging. The question is not only does one have enough strength to survive serious surgery, but will one ever have comparable strength or use of the body after surgery? It is the same with all major illnesses and malfunctions of our various organs and systems. The first question one asks is of survival. The subsequent question is of sustenance, strength, and freedom for mobility and from pain.

There is a mourning process for the gradual death of the body. We need to marshal all of our resources to face this process. In addition to our spiritual resources, here are a few suggestions for survivors: (1) Don't panic. Either you will or you won't survive. If the situation is life threatening, your chances are better if you and everyone else remains ACAP (as calm as possible). (2) Be informed. One source may be prejudiced or guided by self-interest! Find out all you can about your problem, its cause, symptoms, prognosis, and possible cure. Trust your physician, but don't force him to play God. (3) Be courageous. If your chances for survival are not good, you should be the first to know. We all have unfinished business. Our most important business is with God. (4) Be realistic. (5) Be patient in recovery. Impatience in patients makes for difficulties for everyone. (6) Try not to plea bargain with God. We all have made hasty vows. Divine healing is possible, but it isn't permanent in this life. A wise friend once said, "You must trust your body even when it is failing you." He is right. Most aging people come to a realization of these obvious tips on their own. For some, giving in is harder than for others. Do not torment yourself about your own pain threshold. It is usually a part of your original equipment. It does help when strong inner will and trust in God at the spiritual dimension come to the aid of an ailing body.

Death of the Body and Dynamics of Grief. There is always a trauma when the body dies.

Why do we fear the trauma of death? (1) Because death is unknown and unexperienced. (2) Because death cuts us off from the familiar and the usual. (3) Because death may be violent or lingering, involving trauma at the moment of death. (4) Because death is final in matters of this life.

Let me give you some things to think about: (1) We can experience dying. (2) We cannot "experience death." Death is the moment of nonbeing, of transition between the closing of consciousness in this life and the awakening in consciousness in the eternal dimension. (3) We cannot choose our time and way to die, unless we are suicides. Acceptance of what life brings even to the end of life is the better part of wisdom. (4) If our lives should end tragically or by violence, the experience of dying is quickly over, and we are with the Lord. (5) We may each appropriate the promise of God to be with us at death and to receive us after death. (6) The way in which one dies is not as important as the faith and the practice of our lives. Not all Christians die triumphantly. Do not grieve unnecessarily if a relative has died "struggling with death." None of us know what we will do in the terminal moment. But what we do then cannot undo a life of commitment or a previous confession of faith.

There are things to think about as all of us face death. Seldom are we ready to die, but unpreparedness does not stop the inevitability of our death. There is one thing we all can do and ought to do. Do not leave unfinished business in personal relationships, especially family relationships. Even aging people today have aging parents. Make peace. Do not carry grudges to the grave. Unforgiveness and unacceptance reach beyond death in that they torment the living and diminish the capacity of those who have gone on to be as mature in grace as they should be in our Father's house. Ultimately, we need fear nothing absolutely. "Perfect love casteth out fear" (1 John 4:18, KJV). We need only fear (reverence) Him (God) who is able to destroy both body and soul (Matt. 10:28). And we shall not fear Him, if He is our Father who is in heaven, for He desires to give us all good things in Jesus Christ, our elder brother.

Let me share a pastoral word about grief. Well-intentioned friends try to assuage the grief of the immediate family by saying, "That is not really your wife." "That is not your father. He is actually in heaven with our Heavenly Father." And the intention is sometimes: "Therefore, do not cry. Stop mourning!" The statements are correct in one sense. But this route of advice is "cold comfort." We do mourn but not as those "who have no hope" (1 Thess. 4:13). We do affirm the resurrection of the body. We do believe that we shall see God and one another in the world to come. *But* we are missing what we actually knew of a person. This tangible form in its energized, living state is the basis on which all of our experiences were formed. How can we say that form is not the "them" we knew? And we are intensely aware that that form is not as it was, and it will not continue to be with us any more in any actual way we can perceive. Therefore mourn. Let grief have its full and awful expression in the shock of nonbeing, in the loss of a familiar form.

The full-length mirror, the central panel of the three-way mirror, gives a long and realistic look at the physical body. We have seen in this mirror: the corporate and the individual bodies, two ways of abusing the body, suggestions about how to look at death and how to grieve at the death of the body of a loved one, and suggestions for handling the gradual diminution of one's own body.

A Two-Way Mirror

A second panel in the three-way mirror of who we are as complete persons is what I would like to style a two-way mirror. Two-way mirrors are those in which you can see out, but others cannot see in. On one side of the mirror we see only the reflection we want to project. But on the other side of a two-way mirror, we have more of a window that can look out on the reflected self and on others. We cannot be seen as we look through this window side of the mirror. This mirror is an analogy for the self, the inner person. We are aware and are self-aware, but others really cannot see through to the inner us, at least we would like to think they cannot.

There are several Bible words to describe the inner person and its consciousness, but before I elaborate on them I would like to remind you that this second panel of the mirror is hinged to the first one as long as we have earthly existence. As we know ourselves in this world, and that is the only experienced knowledge we have at this point, there is no inner reflection without the outer person. However it is that we think, we use our physical brain as a tool and vehicle for thought. Keeping this in mind, we can go on to explore the biblical terms.

Biblical Terms. The first and very significant term for the inner person is *psyche.* We usually translate the word as *soul.* And when we do, this conjures up notions of a part of us that is separable, self-contained and self-sufficient. I refer to this notion as the angel-in-the-slot-machine view. This dualistic view does not do justice to the biblical meaning of the term. This view that we come in two parts, soul and body, is an unfortunate gift of the Greeks. It is, in particular, the notion of some groups called Gnostics. Combined with this separate-part view was the idea that the inside part was a divine part and the outside part was a sinful part. This was further refined so that the sinful part was sinful just because it was physical. This led to the denial of the goodness of physical existence. The Gnostics left the impression that we are sinful because we have bodies. This unwarranted downplaying of the physical side of our existence, the body, is not biblical. Strict logic would require that if you wanted to get rid of your problem you would commit suicide and escape the body by releasing the divine soul within you. Life is not that uncomplicated. Whatever is wrong with us is wrong with us both inside and out.

We can avoid this strict dichotomy (dividing into two parts) if we realize the biblical word for *soul* is best translated "self." *Psuche* is the self which reflects on *soma,* the New Testament word for body. The body is the shape a self is. The modern combination of the Greek terms yields the compound word *psychosomatic.* Unfortunately, that phrase is usually used to refer to an illness which is all in one's mind. Some illnesses can be related more to the mind, and some can be related more to the body. Usually, all illness is, technically speaking, psychosomatic because of the interaction of the inner and the outer person. Let me clear up one point. It is sometimes supposed that Christians can be ill physically, but they cannot be ill psychologically. That is not so. All of us can and do suffer in the inner and outer being because they are intrinsically bound together. When your body is sick, you should see a physician who treats the chemical dimension of you. When your mind and emotions are distressed, you should see a qualified person who treats the psychological dimension of you. Every wise physician will work with fellow physicians in helping the total healing process.

The confusion of the psyche of psychology and the "soul" of religion has created considerable difficulty. In my opinion, the two are not the same. They both treat of the inner person, but there are elements peculiar to each. It is not appropriate for the minister to suppose that his comments and proclamation on the soul take the place of or do the same thing as the work of the psychologist. But conversely, it is not appropriate for the psychologist/psychiatrist to suppose that his treatment can substitute or make dispensable the task of the minister.

There are, however, biblical terms which express what goes wrong with the inner person which affects the outer person. Those terms should be explained. One of the words is flesh (*basar* Heb., *sarx* Gr.). Many times in Scripture the term *flesh* just means the physical part of existence. Flesh is sometimes used as a synonym for *body*. Sometimes the word *flesh* means ourselves in their physical manifestation which is prone to creaturely weakness. Paul had a theological use of the term *flesh* which is highlighted in Romans 7 and 8. In this particular use, flesh means that capacity we have to follow after evil (the evil one) and order all of life in that direction. This is what Paul meant by walking after the flesh.

The other biblical term which has to do with the inner dimension is *spirit*. Spirit means a great many things. It can refer simply to the wind, breath, or power of any living thing. It can refer to those experiences and the capacity for them in persons which is most like God, or enables us to relate to Him. Paul had a special theological use of spirit, and it, like flesh, is best described by Romans 7 and 8. In those chapters Paul's idea of spirit may be defined as that capacity which seeks self-transcendence and which, when energized by the Spirit of God, enables us to cooperate with God's Spirit and to order all of life in that direction. This battle of the flesh and spirit is not so much between the outer and the inner person as it is a struggle between warring capacities and desires within the total self. The preferred state is to walk after the spirit. The warring state, which is our usual state, is to be torn between flesh and spirit. To walk after the flesh happens every time flesh is predominant. To walk after the spirit happens every time spirit predominates. The black spiritual says it well: "I'm sometimes up and sometimes down, yes, my Lord."

Corporate Use of Self. There is a collective consciousness just as there is a corporate body. There is also a universal sameness about the composition of all humanity and of individuals. Just as there are individual idiosyncrasies of the body, there are idiosyncrasies of the mind. But there are more similarities between the psychological makeup of the human communities than there are differences. All persons have elation and depression although the cultural causes and manifestations of it may differ. We are related biologically, and we are related psychologically. And it is God who is the Creator of us all. His concern is with our physical well-being and with our psychical well-being. He meant us to be whole and healthy. And He is moving to make us that way eventually. In the meanwhile, all of those things which contribute to the wholeness and health of God's world are godly.

There is a collective psyche which groups and nations have. It is a cultural, contextual way of looking at things. The Germans call it *Zeitgeist* (spirit of the time). This climate of thought can become selfish, destructive, and harmful to the human community. The *Zeitgeist* of Hitler's Nazi Germany has been a classic example of this in the twentieth century. A more recent example of a destructive cultural spirit is found in the policies of fundamentalist Islam in the latter portion of our century. Christians are a part of some culture, and this culture helps to shape who they are and what their collective psyche is. But Christians have an ultimate allegiance to God through Christ to bear the responsibility of shaping their culture and their context.[28] Christians cannot afford the luxury of destructive prejudice, hate, and bitterness. The result of these attitudes to the psyche of the group and of the individual is too costly. This is true even when, and especially when, these attitudes are promulgated in the name of religion and are propagated by powerful personalities.

There are forms of sin which I mentioned above that are special problems for the psyche, corporate and individual. These are the pride and grasping which brings everything into the self. In the individual it results in egocentrism. In the group it results in chauvinism. Among nations and people it results in hypernationalism or visions of superior ethnicity. The other forms of sin which affect the psyche of individuals and of corporate bodies are the rebellion which holds everything out of the self. And there is the sloth which refuses to help the other(s) in distress. Elitism, isolationism, and indifference are the corporate sins of groups.

The Diminution of the Self. Just as the body weakens in the aging process, so does the psychological dimension of our being. And this causes many serious problems. A few words of obvious advice may help older people at this point. (1) Do not be unduly anxious about psychological problems over which you have no control. (I used to worry about "losing" my mind. Then it occurred to me that I would not know it if I did. When I confessed this to a group of students, one of them quipped, "How do we know you have not lost it already?" I assured him that when his grade report came out, he would know I had not lost my memory.) (2) Memory loss and a slowness to recall are the psychological counterparts of slowness of reflexes. Expect it. Our anxiety comes at the point of fearing to lose dignity and control. (3) Be patient with the evidences of psychical aging in others. We will all need it ourselves. One is reminded of the forgetful old gentleman who is always accusing his mate of forgetfulness. (4) Limit the scope of your expectations of your own performance. (5) Try to adapt routines that will provide less strain on the psyche than totally new and foreign experiences do. (6) Strive to do things that will "exercise" the mind. It needs activity just as our physical bodies do. All spectator sports are bad for the body. All spectator activities for the inner person are equally unproductive. It is often said that television is a "blessing" for the aged. I would want to suggest that it is mixed blessing. Unreflective, unchallenging watching can soothe us into an artificial world and make us considerably less interested and mentally active in the real world.

It is difficult to look into, or out of, the two-way mirror. There is always a reserve about revealing too much of the self. There is even some hesitancy in knowing too much about the self or admitting to the self that what we know of ourselves is true. There are haunting looks to be had from and about the inner self. Eventually these anxieties can overwhelm us, if we do not look away to the third mirror. This third mirror is in one sense a magic mirror. It will help us to cope with, balance out, and find promise for the other two dimensions of our existence.

The Magic Mirror

Do you remember Walt Disney's wonderful production of *Snow White and the Seven Dwarfs?* There was a magic mirror owned by the wicked queen. It always told the truth, even when the queen did not want to hear it. We have a magic mirror like that, and we, too, are not always pleased at the reports. The third panel of the three-way mirror is a magic mirror, in the best sense of the word *magic.* It is not theological sleight of hand or a trick mirror that can be explained by a certain knowledge of optics.

The magic mirror is the spiritual dimension of our existence. It, too, is hinged to the other panels. As I have said, *spirit* is a biblical word that means life, breath, energizing power. Spirit is the dynamic element of the self. It is the capacity for God. The spirit of a person is interdependent in our earthly existence with the form (body) we are and the soul (self) we are. It may be analogous to what Paul called the law of conscience. It certainly is our capacity to want to go beyond the merely physical or the isolated psychological dimension of who we are. Spirit seeks the "other." This is true of relationships with other people. There is a relationship we call the spirit of friendship. There is spiritual love, and it does not necessarily exclude physical love. The spirit of a person especially seeks and is created for a relationship with God. This highest/deepest, best relationship is realized in our physical bodies and with the use of our psyches.

But the redemptive relationship with God cannot be equated with these two dimensions. The spirit of a person is the integrating and wholesome factor in any life. Scripture expresses that it is also the most satisfying and appropriate relationship of a group or a nation. "Happy is the nation whose God is the Lord" (Ps. 33:12). The proper and appropriate use of our spiritual dimension will start with our realization that we are finite. We as individuals do not last forever in our present state. There is an awareness of our dependency, not just on others but also on something beyond ourselves. We will not last forever. We did not call ourselves into being. We are both finite and contingent, temporal and dependent. The awareness of our impermanence and our smallness in the midst of a vast cosmos is a collective, corporate, and cultural feeling as well as an individual one.[29]

This spiritual awareness is at the same time the vacuum which calls out for God. It is the juncture where we relate to and are led by God. Ordinarily we undergo these experiences with God in a bodily, psychological way that is like other experiences of life. But we realize that the spiritual experiences are not just like other experiences. The referents or objects of our other experiences are physical, visible, tangible. The experiences we have in prayer, reflection, Bible study—our deepest interiority—are not just physical or psychic. The stream of Christian experience that has witnessed best to this inner reality is called mysticism.[30] Mysticism is common to all religions. And, in my opinion, mysticism has received a very bad press in recent days. Mysticism is not the cheap God-told-me claim of a too-fervent, nonreflective religionist. Mysticism is at the end of our thinking, not at its beginning. Mysticism does not outrage reason, but it does sometimes outrun it. I hope I have convinced you that there is a spiritual dimension to your life. I imagine I did not have to convince you, but I hope this description of the undescribable resonates with your deepest experiences with God.

Spiritual guidance and growth are very sensitive things. They are, in one sense, highly individual. Yet, on the other hand, they may be given some form and direction from classical[31] and contemporary Christianity.[32] There are spiritual manuals to assist in the expression and formation of the spiritual life. Corporate Christian worship is the major arena for the development of our spiritual life and its manifold possibilities.

A word needs to be said about the misuse of our spiritual impulses. In my description of the image of God, I chose the position which holds that all persons everywhere have a capacity for God and a longing for God. The reason this does not seem apparent in some is because they are trying to fill the spiritual vacuum with something other than God. This is idolatry. It is the primary sin of the spiritual life. There are overtly harmful pursuits such as sexual promiscuity, alcoholism, or substance abuse that some use to fill the spiritual yearnings of life. There are less blatant and supposedly "beneficial" pursuits that some use to fill the spiritual vacuum. Acquisition of wealth, obsession with the health of the body, and pursuit of academic learning, can also be idolatrous. God does not forbid idolatry because He is jealous of our "good times." Idolatry is wrong because it does not work. Nothing can adequately fill the life of a nation, a group, or an individual but the ultimate, the absolute, the ground of our being—God. A divorce from our ultimate roots is apparent in every arena of life and takes its toll in all of the forms of sin and estrangement discussed above.[33]

The magic mirror reflects the truth of where we came from and where we are going. It shows us the original outline of the purpose and wholeness of the way life ought to be. God has not left Himself without a witness. Paul describes its twofold forms as the world about us and conscience, the world within us (Rom. 1). Our problem is that we have not read the witness rightly. We must return to the "true mirror" image of Jesus Christ before we can see the "magic mirror" properly. The image in the "true mirror" can assist us to put all of the other mirror images into place. The image of the true mirror invites us to a journey "through the looking glass."

Through the Looking Glass

The actual title of Lewis Carroll's classic includes *Through the Looking Glass.*[34] We usually know it by the short name *Alice in Wonderland.*[35] When Alice steps through the looking glass, she is in another world, an exciting world of imaginative possibilities. Rabbits are not just ordinary animals. The pictures on a deck of cards come to life. There is delight. There is threat. Most of all, there is a different way of looking at reality. We may write all of this off as pure fantasy. We may want to stick with the stern, no-nonsense physical way of looking at all reality. We may. But such a reduction of all reality to the observable dimension of what we can see, taste, touch, smell, or feel is "hard on God." That is, such a physicalist view makes it very difficult for us to talk about and relate to God, the object and source of our faith.

The spiritual life is no fantasy world. But it is an exciting, imaginative other kind of reality than the world of everyday life. When you step through the looking glass of faith, you do not leave the ordinary world; you enlarge it. The reality of the spiritual dimension is not a fantasy, but it does require imaginativeness and a willingness to be open to things other than the ordinary in order to explore the realm of the spirit to the fullest. There is in the Bible and in our lives a place for dreams, visions, and the internal guidance of God in ways other than typed memos.[36] God's spiritual world is not just a future, physical structure on some remote planet. The reality of God's own dimension, Spirit, and the fullness of our apprehension of God are related to realities and realms about us and within us. John's revelation is a looking up to an open heaven where ultimate reality is seen. God fights for and with His people in an ongoing struggle, the outcome of which is sure. In the meanwhile, the reality of the struggle of the spiritual world is reflected in the historical actualities of what goes on around us.

An invitation to believe in God, to receive Jesus as Savior, to commit the self to God is an invitation to another dimension of life, another way of looking at reality, another enlargement of the meaning and possibilities of life than we have otherwise.

Some have feared that this talk of a spiritual realm would make us lose touch with the reality of our world. The old charge of pie in the sky by-and-by always surfaces when one introduces the spiritual realm. Let me respond to those charges in two very specific ways: I am not talking just about, or even primarily about, the future when I am speaking of the spiritual pilgrimage. I am talking about an interpretation of this life which faces historical actuality and difficult ethical decisions with courage and an enlarged way of perceiving all of life and its experiences. As I have suggested in the opening chapter, we must leave the future to God. But the God of the future has not left us alone with the stark realities of this world. Through Jesus Christ, He has come to us bringing the power and the hope of the future into the present. "Faith is the substance of things hoped for" (Heb. 11:1, KJV), and it is substantial, both the faith and the hope. And one reason we are assured of the future is because of the effective working of these gifts of God in the present.

There is the charge that this talk of imagination, a world beyond and within us, will become subjective only. Maybe we are talking of a world of make-believe conjured up by our imaginations and our wishful thinking.[37] If we step through the looking glass, will we lose our hold on reality and enter a world where everyone's imagination is king? No. Not if our guide and norm in relating to the spiritual dimension of life is the Bible. Scripture is firmly embedded in history.

The practical, ethical implications of the Ten Commandments, the Sermon on the Mount, and the down-to-earth advice of Paul will provide an adequate check against uncharted spirituality. When imagination and interpretation run counter to Scripture, we are seeking things through the looking glass that are not true images. There is a great new outlook through the looking glass. It is the satisfying world of the Spirit.

Conclusion

We have labored long and lovingly over our analogy of mirror looking. I hope the images are not too blurred. There is the distant mirror which shows us what we all are. We are related to the race. We have solidarity in humanity and its weaknesses. The cracked mirror gave us a view of ourselves as those who see a shattered picture of what we were intended to be, creatures made in the image of God. The mirror of distortion gave a view and description of sin and of ourselves as sinners. Having seen the dark image, we needed a true mirror to image what humanity is intended to be. The face in the true mirror is Jesus. He gives us perspective and hope. These preliminary mirrors are necessary looking glasses on the way to discovering who we are.

The three-way mirror gave us the full picture of ourselves as total beings. We need to see the image of who we are altogether. Then we took a careful look into each panel of our reflected selves. There was the full-length mirror symbolizing our physical aspect. It was the mirror of the body and our embodiment. The second panel was the two-way mirror of the soul, the self. We looked behind the mirror to the reflections of ourselves that lay behind the surface. The third panel symbolized the spiritual dimension of who we are. This panel reflects the other two, but it cannot be reduced to the sum of the others. It has its own authentic and absolute image to present. Last, and by no means least, is the invitation to faith to step through the looking glass. The how of that step, the description of life in that realm, and the conclusion of a life lived in the realm beyond the looking glass have all been described in previous chapters. Now, in our working backward from the last things to the first, we leave the world of mirrors, the analogy for humankind and sin, and take a look in the kaleidoscope. It is under that image we will explore the doctrines of creation and providence.

Notes

1. I have intentionally duplicated the mirror image for this chapter from *A Theology for Children* because a concern for the self and a fascination with images of the self is a lifelong preoccupation and provides a good metaphor for our discussion. See Alexander Miller, *The Man in the Mirror: Studies in the Christian Understanding of Selfhood* (Garden City, N.Y.: Doubleday, 1958) which also uses this metaphor for a theological discussion of mankind.

2. Barbara Tuchman, *A Distant Mirror: The Calamitous 14th Century* (New York: Knopf, 1978).

3. She has continued this line of reasoning in a more recent book, *The March of Folly: From Troy to Vietnam* (Boston: G. K. Hall, 1984) which points out the similarities and futilities involved in a series of wars in Western civilization.

4. For a fuller explication of the corporate nature of mankind see Reinhold Niebuhr, *The Nature and Destiny of Man: A Christian Interpretation,* 2 vols. (New York: C. Scribner's Sons, 1941-1943); Jurgen Moltmann's *Man: Christian Anthropology in the Conflicts of the Present,* trans. John Starch (Philadelphia: Fortress Press, 1974); Wolfhart Pannenberg's *What is Man? Contemporary Anthropology in Theological Perspective,* trans. Duane A. Porebe (Philadelphia: Fortress Press, 1970) and my *The Doctrine of Man* (Nashville: Convention Press, 1977).

5. See James B. Pritchard's *Ancient Near Eastern Texts Relating to the Old Testament* (Princeton: Princeton University Press, 1955).

6. This is not precisely what P. Tillich has in mind by the phrase "dreaming innocence," but I would like to use his familiar phrase as a double *entendre* and thereby also incorporate some of his meaning in this discussion. See P. Tillich, *Systematic Theology,* vol. 2, *Existence and the Christ* (Chicago: University of Chicago Press, 1957), pp. 33-36.

7. Compare K. Barth *The Epistle to the Romans,* trans. E. Hoskyns (London: Oxford University Press, 1933), pp. 149–187. Also, *Christ and Adam, Man and Humanity in Romans 5,* trans. T. A. Smail (New York: The Macmillan Company, 1957).

8. This analogy is not new. J. Calvin uses it to describe the status of mankind after the fall. See *Institutes of The Christian Religion,* ed. John T. McNeill, trans. Ford Lewis Battles, 2 vols. (London: SCM Press, 1960), book #3 , ch. 2:6, vol. 1, p. 549. Also see *Calvin: Commentaries on the First Twenty Chapters of the Book of the Prophet Ezekiel,* 13:19 (trans. Thomas Myers, 2 vols. [Grand Rapids, Mich.: Eerdmans, 1948], vol. 2, p. 32). For a good secondary discussion of Calvin's complex use of the mirror analogy, see T. F. Torrance, *Calvin's Doctrine of Man* (London: Lutterworth Press, 1949), pp. 35–51, 95–97.

9. Isaac Watts, "Joy to the world! The Lord is come," 1719,

10. See George Hendry, *Theology of Nature* (Philadelphia: Westminster Press, 1980) for a good treatment of how Christians have looked and should look at nature.

11. On these shifts and their physical and psychological consequences for humanity see Alvin Toffler's works: *Future Shock* (New York: Random House, 1970) and *The Third Wave* (New York: Morrow, 1980).

12. See James Smart, *The Interpretation of Scripture* (Philadelphia: Westminster Press,

1961), pp. 134–159; see also Mary Frances Thelen, *Man as Sinner in Contemporary American Realistic Theology* (New York: King's Crown Press, 1946), especially pp. 11–32, 61–163.

13. Reread the section in chapter 1 on death. You will realize that this definition of image is also my definition of human life which involves three levels of existence: the biological, the psychosocial, and the spiritual. This definition is very similar to the thought of Reinhold Niebuhr, *The Nature and Destiny of Man: A Christian Interpretation,* 2 vols. (New York: C. Scribner's Sons, 1941–43), vol. 1, pp. 150–177; and H. Richard Niebuhr, *The Responsible Self: An Essay in Christian Moral Philosophy* (New York: Harper & Row, 1963), especially pp. 47–68.

14. John K. Ryan (trans.), *The Confessions of St. Augustine* (Garden City, N.Y.: Image Books [Doubleday], 1960), book 1, chap. 1, p. 43.

15. Alexander Pope, "An Essay on Man," Epistle II (1733), 11.217–220, in Henry W. Boynton (ed.), *The Complete Poetical Works of Pope* (Boston: Houghton Mifflin Co., 1931), p. 144.

16. See Paul Ricoeur, *The Symbolism of Evil,* trans. Emerson Buchanan (New York: Harper & Row, 1967).

17. Karl Barth, *Church Dogmatics,* vol. 1, 2, trans. G. T. Thompson and Harold Knight (New York: Scribner's, 1956), chap. 2, Part 2, § 15 "The Mystery of Revelation," Section 3, "The Miracle of Christmas," pp. 172–202. Also, see K. Barth, *Evangelical Theology, An Introduction,* trans. Grover Foley (New York: Holt, Rinehart, and Winston, 1963), especially pp. 15–26.

18. See Geoffrey Wainwright's *Doxology: The Praise of God in Worship, Doctrine and Life: A Systematic Theology* (London: Epworth Press, 1980), especially pp. 1–12, 218–283.

19. See Paul Ricoeur, *Main Trends in Philosophy* (New York: Holmes and Meier Publishers, Inc., 1979).

20. See the theological definitions of death above.

21. There has been a long argument in Western philosophy as to whether or how abstract concepts exist. See the above discussion on truth. I tend to agree with those thinkers who say that everything, including abstract ideas, exists only in some tangible way and in some embodiment. The Old Testament knew God because He used "bodies" to express Himself. The incarnation of Jesus is not just to get God on the scene. It is to express that even God, who is Spirit, comes to us specifically in some shape. See F. C. Copleston, *A History of Philosophy,* 8 vols. (London: Burns, Oates, & Washbourne, 1946–66).

22. Philosophers have argued heatedly since the sixteenth-century philosopher Descartes as to what precisely constitutes the self and its consciousness. They have not agreed. But most disagree, and I certainly would, with behavioral psychology which is willing to define the self solely in terms of physical actions and reactions. See "self" in Dagobert D. Runes (ed.), *Dictionary of Philosophy* (New York: Philosophical Library, 1983), pp. 304–305, or Anthony Flew (ed.) *A Dictionary of Philosophy,* revised 2nd ed. (New York: St. Martin's Press, 1984), p. 322.

23. Compare James B. Nelson, *Embodiment: An Approach to Sexuality and Christian Theology* (Minneapolis: Augsburg Publishing Co., 1978) for a good discussion of the personalistic, physical relationships of Christians.

24. See C. Ryder Smith, *The Bible Doctrine of Man* (London: Epworth Press, 1951) for a good discussion of biblical words for mankind.

25. Compare Aldous Huxley's novel *After Many a Summer Dies the Swan* (New York: Harper & Brothers, 1939).

26. Compare Jessica Mitford's *The American Way of Death* (New York: Simon and Schuster, 1963) for examples of the overcost of attention to dead bodies.

27. Compare my "Life-style: A Theological Base" in the 1978 Christian Life Commission Seminar Proceedings.

28. See H. Richard Niebuhr, *Christ and Culture* (New York: Harper & Row, 1956), especially pp. 1–44, 190–256.

29. Compare Langdon Gilkey, *Naming the Whirlwind: The Renewal of God-Language* (Indianapolis: Bobbs-Merrill, 1969) and *Reaping the Whirlwind: A Christian Interpretation of History* (New York: Seabury Press, 1976) for good descriptions of how these "feelings" are evidenced in our contemporary world.

30. Compare Evelyn Underhill, *The Mystics of the Church* (London: J. Clarke & Co., 1925).

31. Compare Bro. Lawrence, [that is, Nicholas Herman] *The Practice of the Presence of God,* trans. John J. Delaney (Garden City, N.Y.: Image Books, 1977); and Thomas a Kempis, *The Imitation of Christ* (for example, ed. Thomas S. Kepler [Cleveland: World Publishing Co., 1952]) as classical examples of spiritual exercises.

32. See the records of the spiritual pilgrimage of Thomas Merton, *The Seven Storey Mountain* (Garden City, N.Y.: Image Books, 1970) and the suggestions for spirituality in the writings of Henri Nouwen: *Making All Things New: An Invitation to Life in the Spirit* (New York: Harper & Row, 1981); *Out of Solitude* (Notre Dame, Ind.: Ave Maria Press, 1974); *The Way of the Heart: Desert Spirituality and Contemporary Ministry* (New York: Seabury Press, 1981); *With Open Hands* (Notre Dame, Ind.: Ave Maria Press, 1972); *Reaching Out: The Three Movements of the Spiritual Life* (Garden City, N.Y.: Doubleday, 1975); and also especially (with Walter Gaffney) *Aging* (Garden City, N.Y.: Doubleday, 1974). For an example of more specific and programmed instruction for Christian discipleship see MasterLife (Avery T. Willis, Jr., *MasterLife: Discipleship Training for Leaders,* rev. ed. [Nashville: Convention Press (The Sunday School Board of the Southern Baptist Convention), 1982]).

33. For a philosophical discussion of this understanding of the sin of idolatry, see Paul Tillich, *Systematic Theology,* vol. 2, *Existence and the Christ* (Chicago: University of Chicago Press, 1957), especially pp. 44–78.

34. Lewis Carroll [pseud.], *Alice's Adventures in Wonderland and Through the Looking-Glass, and What Alice Found There* (Philadelphia: It. Altemus, 1895).

35. A book for children by C. S. Lewis, *The Lion, the Witch and the Wardrobe* is another way of inviting the imagination to reckon with the spiritual dimension of life. This is the first volume of Lewis's *The Chronicles of Narnia,* 7 vols. (New York: Macmillan, 1983). I perceive J. R. R. Tolkien's trilogy, *The Lord of the Rings,* 2nd ed. (Boston: Houghton-Mifflin, 1965) this way. Also see Calvin Miller's *The Singer Trilogy* (Downer's Grove, Ill.: Inter-Varsity Press, 1980).

36. On the place of dreams in Scripture see Morton Kelsey, *God, Dreams and Revelation: A Christian Interpretation of Dreams,* rev. ed. (Minneapolis: Augsburg Publishing House, 1974). On the significance of dreams for the Christian community see *Dreams and Spiritual Growth: A Christian Approach to Dreamwork,* edited by Louis M. Savary, Patricia H. Berne, and Strephon Kaplan Williams (New York: Paulist Press, 1985).

37. The charge of inventing God as our "wish-fulfiller" is often leveled against Christians. See Sigmund Freud, *Moses and Monotheism,* trans. Kathrine James (New York: A. A. Knopf, 1939); and *The Future of an Illusion,* trans. W. D. Robson-Scott (New York: Liveright, 1949).

5

The Kaleidoscope

Home entertainment today means VCRs and professional shows on prime-time television. In other days there was a small world that turned in one's hand and had the capacity to delight old folks no less than children with an ever-changing no-commercials program. This small entertainment device was known as a kaleidoscope. A kaleidoscope is a tube in which a person looks through a small hole. The other end of the tube has a clear glass and a frosted glass. Between these retaining glasses is placed an assortment of colored bits of glass which falls into a variety of patterns when the kaleidoscope is turned. It was hard to keep track, but it seemed as though the same pattern never appeared twice. Perhaps older people can remember and still be warmed by the memory of this delightful toy. My wife recently gave me a small kaleidoscope with a musical attachment which plays when the tube is turned. It is, after all these years, even more delightful than I remembered it.

I want to use this metaphor drawn from a long-ago experience of childhood as an analogy for the doctrines of creation and providence and for the topics which cluster around those doctrines. The multiple possibilities of the kaleidoscope serve as an analogy to the marvels of creation. Extraordinary patterns speak of the extraordinary events of angels and miracles. The given framework of the kaleidoscope is comparable to the bounds of providence. Irritatingly and devastatingly, there is a fragment out of place, and it often spoils the picture; this is a metaphor for the evil one. There are those times when we turn our world and there seems to be no pattern at all. This analogy is an apt one for the problem of evil. Come turning with me through the world of the kaleidoscope.

Multiple Possibilities

There is an old argument for God based on the beauty and intricate designs we see in nature. It was reasoned that something as elaborate and full of patterns and purpose as the construction of our world could not have just happened. Someone had to make the kaleidoscope.[1] The English poet Wordsworth put the gist of the argument in his own romantic way. "One impulse from a vernal wood/May teach you more of man,/Of moral evil and of good,/Than all the sages can."[2] This sentiment may also be applied to God. Addison's hymn "The Spacious Firmament" (taken from "The Heavens Are Telling" in Haydn's *Creation*) recalls Psalms 8 and 19 and Job 38.

Any gardener among you readers could add your own version and testimony to these. Today our appreciation for the "beauties of nature" is more secondhand and nostalgic than it is primary and actual. Urban settings may have their well-ordered rows of high-rise apartments, and traffic patterns may yield some night photographs on a rainy evening. But more often we can appreciate Ogden Nash's parody on Joyce Kilmer's poem: "Trees."

> I think that I shall never see
> A billboard lovely as a tree.
> Indeed, unless the billboards fall
> I'll never see a tree at all.[3]

I would like to emphasize that our technological, industrial, computerized world is as dependent on God as the world of nature is. For although we made the machines, God made the people who made the machines and the basic matter of which the machines are made. God is the initiator. God is He who ultimately causes to be. God is He who lets be.[4] A good theological overview of Genesis 1 and 2 will provide a fresh appreciation for what we mean when we repeat an old phrase of the early Christian community, "I believe in God, the Maker of heaven and earth."[5]

A theological view of creation is exactly what the Bible gives. If we try to make the biblical account of creation a scientific account, we are reading back into the Bible modern views and modern perspectives. There is no conflict between religion and science when each one does its own work and does not preempt the tools, methods, and results of the other.[6]

"In the beginning" (Gen. 1:1) has an absolute ring. It is not so much a temporal as a qualitative phrase. The stress is on nothingness. Then something is created. Finally, step by step, all things are created, and it is God who does it. The early Christians expressed the absolute dependence and coming into beingness by the old phrase *creatio ex nihilo* (creation out of nothing). Nothingness is an important idea. It is the black backdrop against which the light of creation shines (Gen. 1:2). Chaos, the void, no-thingness are both physical and psychological categories. Raging chaos must be held back and blown away by the mighty breath of God. This is a constant and continuing process, or else our world and we would collapse if God withdrew His breath or permitted the destructive chaos to rush in and overwhelm us.[7] On days when we feel our world crumbling about us we understand Genesis 1:2 very well. On nearly any day as we read the newspaper, which seems to report predominantly bad news, we can visualize the whole world crashing in on us, and we fear this very much. In such times, the Christian message in all its fullness should pertain. By this I mean that we should run forward to our hope in God's deliverance, but we should also run backward to our confidence and faith in His creative, sustaining power.

The separation of light and darkness is an act that is, at the same time, physical, psychological, and moral. It is ironic that we do not try more than we do to apply the account of God's creative acts to the full implications of our universe and its existence. To see the Genesis account of creation as only a chronological, physical expression is, in my opinion, to miss the richness of the meaning of Genesis which is picked up and expanded by such later biblical materials as the Gospel of John.[8]

With the banishing of chaos there comes cosmos, order and design. The separation of light and darkness constitutes the first day. The Jewish way of reckoning days from evening to morning is used to count off the periods of creation. The division of water from land is a second period. The theological intent is that God is in charge. It is God who creates and controls time. It is God who makes and masters the elements. It is God who is the God of place, all places. Day two and day three are concerned with the division of place. There is heaven. There is earth. And on the earth is growth, vegetation, which is the first type of life. God's good green earth has priority of time and place. Humanity will have preeminence in God's affections. One evidence of God's favor is the trust God gives humanity over His green, good world and all that is in it. It was a trust betrayed, a confidence not kept. We have not done well by God's earth which was given to us for comfort, provision, and as pride of place. Ecology is a religious responsibility from the first, a responsibility in which we were not responsible.

Time and seasons as we know them were the gifts of the fourth period of creation (Gen. 1:14–19). What is being stressed is not so much chronology as consolidation. Light and darkness (day one) take on their distinctive normative patterns in the sun and moon (day four). Heaven and the boundaries of earth (day two) are consolidated in the land and the waters under the heavens (day three). The fifth period of creation brings life to inhabit the places of days two and three. There are birds for the heavens. There are fish for the waters (Gen. 1:20–23). And on day six there are the first creatures of the land (Gen. 1:24–28). And on the sixth period there is a profound awareness that all which God made is part of an interacting whole (Gen. 1:29–31). Creation is an interacting, interconnected, interrelated whole. The light and darkness, the sun and moon, are required to nourish the life of the heavens, the sea and the land. The fruit of the land, vegetation, is given for the nourishment of the creatures of the land, the animals.

And, as the conclusion of the sixth day, God created humanity as crown and custodian of God's creation. Humanity is both male and female. God creates the complementary counterpart of woman with and for man (Gen. 1:26; 2:20–25). It is God's world and His work, and God has pronounced it good. But we and the evil one have tried to ruin it (Gen. 3). Nevertheless, God will make provision for its reclamation (John 3). His is the last word, and God's renewed creation will end where it all began, in the Garden of God (Gen. 2; Rev. 22).

This is the theological story of creation, the complete scenario, and we who know the end from the beginning and the beginning from the end can and should proclaim the whole story; for it is cut from a single cloth. We should read the Bible forward in a historical framework one section at a time. This is the first way of reading Scripture. Any good commentary can help you. And we should also read the Bible backward from a theological assessment of the whole.

Any layman will recognize the story, and every theologian should have some elemental grasp of it.[9]

Why does God do it? Why is there something rather than nothing? Several answers have been given to this question.

1. Some say because He was lonely and wanted company.[10] This view is from a very human and anthropocentric (man-centered) argument. A deeper reflection on the nature of God might well suggest that God was never lonely. For in His threeness, there was an original fellowship of loving one another which is indeed demonstrated in the earthly manifestations of the Father, the Son, and the Spirit.[11]

2. A prevalent interpretation today as to why God created the world is that God is realizing Himself through the world.[12] God does radically introduce Himself into our world in the incarnation of Jesus Christ.[13] Yet I do not take this historical enlargement of the incarnation to place other, internal limitations on God so that He does not "know" or guide the direction of His creation in prospect and in the present. It does not seem to me compatible with the basic biblical view of God that He must wait and see how things are going to turn out (Job 39–41; Matt. 4–7; 10 [especially verses 16–24]).

3. A third view as to why God created the world follows the old philosophical principle of determining the purpose of a thing from its end or its conclusion. This view suggests that God created the world in order to redeem it. This suggestion, when followed through on a chronological or priority scale, gets bogged down in a nonbiblical way of talking about predestination. Such a discussion includes all of the "lapsarian" controversies—supra, infra, sub, and so forth.[14] This whole discussion evolved around such questions as: Did God first decree to save the elect? Did He first agree to permit all to fall? Did He decide to permit the fall and to provide salvation at the same time? To these kinds of questions God's questions to Job seem pertinent. "Where were you when I laid the earth's foundations?" (Job 38:4) "Who is this that darkeneth counsel by words without knowledge?" (v. 2, KJV). God created the world good. It did not originally need saving. But since evil has distorted and attempted to destroy the world, we may be glad that God does move to save it through Jesus Christ.

4. A fourth answer to the question as to why God created the world seems more appropriate than the previous three. Creation is an

act of sheer grace.[15] In other words, without being irreverent to the seriousness of the question, He wanted to. I am thoroughly convinced that the Bible is less concerned with the why of things than with the that of things. As I heard an old gentleman in his eighties say to the county clerk when asked for his birth certificate, "I am here, ain't I?" Creation, like life, is to be enjoyed. Creation is life. It is here. We must make the best of it. God is certainly working on doing just that.

A more fruitful discussion will bring us back to the kaleidoscope. How many possibilities are there? And as the telescopes, gyroscopes, and bathyscopes turn, the number enlarges. We who look through the small aperture of our limited vantage point should be very glad about that. For it is our affirmation that however many natural, fabricated, hybrid, invented new things there are, it is God who brings the possibilities into being. The God of creation is the God of new beginnings. His bringing to be and His letting be are accompanied by the mysteries of His calling into being the new and the not yet. The words above the Library of Congress are true: "The past is prologue." And the Washington cab driver's interpretation of that ancient motto is well spoken: "You ain't seen nothin' yet."

The achievements and accomplishments of civilization up to this point are not "nothin'." But the possibilities of God with His world loom large on the horizon. Our age of apocalyptic doom sayings looks too much for an easy way out and, above all, for a quick way out. Biblical faith usually leads the people of God through problems, not around them. There is positive encouragement to be gained from the multiple possibilities of creation. When we have become stuck or bored with one picture in the kaleidoscope, it is time to turn the whole thing around. New patterns can emerge. Other options are available to us as the human community and as individuals. Creation, no less than consummation, is a basis for lively hope. Different pictures can emerge.[16] The world of the Bible had extraordinary patterns that our closed philosophical and theological systems seem to disallow. Related to the multiple possibilities of creation in Scripture were the extraordinary patterns of angels and miracles.

Extraordinary Patterns

Western technological man suffers from a terrible disease. It is the inability to believe in anything but his ability. If we didn't do it or make it or see it, we don't believe it. So much the pity. For the biblical world, the primitive world, and most of Asia and Africa believe intensely in things unseen. In our technological societies, we can have germs, hallucinations, drug-induced mystical experiences, psychoses, neuroses, but no angels.[17] In our modern world it seems that angels, the messengers of God, must always be human, explicable, rationally explained "people." We have a hard time seeing any extraordinary patterns or even supposing that there could be such. Every event must have a logical, physical secondary cause. Imagination and imaginative tales are for children. And the sooner we can get them out of that stage and into a profitable, technological education, the better. So here we are. Caught in our sophistication. Yet there is the haunting possibility that these "signals of transcendence" which could make this a spiritual as well as a physical universe might be being sent.

Lest you be swayed by rhetoric and buy into a bizarre and fantastic mind-set, which you do all the time at the movies, let me review for you the biblical view of angels. There are nearly three long columns of references to angels in a standard concordance, and there would be more than that if we took all of the uses of the word *messenger.* In Scripture, the angels are functional. In later theology and philosophy, they became philosophical abstractions whose existence, number, ranks, and appearance were argued.[18] There are, strictly speaking, no biblical descriptions on angels, per se, only functions. Early Christians put together the cherubim, seraphim, and the apocalyptic creatures to provide visual descriptions of angels which then became popularized in the visual arts of sculpture, painting, drawing, woodcuts, prints, and carvings. Artistic imagination has run riot in Western Christendom, but the cold-sober fact is the Bible speaks only of the functions of angels. They guard, guide, bring messages from God, herald good news, rebuke the arrogant, reassure the faithful, and, chiefly, worship God.

Why didn't God do all of that directly Himself? For the same reason that He uses humankind to do what people can and ought to do toward making this a balanced world where spirit and physicality lead to wholeness. God grants integrity, grace, and usefulness to each portion of His creation. Flowers and angels instinctively and inherently sing the praise of God more readily than humankind, who is so preoccupied with the makeup of the kaleidoscope that we often cannot enjoy the pictures. I am not asking for a suspension of rationality. I am asking for an enlargement of imagination and a willingness to give possibility to scriptural portrayals and potentialities we may not have seen or experienced personally. And it is this last point that bothers us moderns most. We have not seen nor experienced personally a presence of angels, at least in ways we can demonstrate.

As we explore the biblical references more intently, we become aware that the manifestations of messengers were more prevalent in the pre-Pentecostal, early church period and in the Apocalypse than at any other time. The logic of belief would indicate that the Holy Spirit and the Scriptures are the normative ways in which God relates to us today. The Spirit Himself bears witness to the historical Jesus and to the written Word in a more definitive, historical, and sustained way since then. In Acts, the church was in transition from direct, intermittent ways of relating to God toward instrumental normative ones. These normative experiences came through the witness of the prophets and apostles as these became "inscripturated." The remainder of the New Testament references refer to troublesome, idolatrous attachment to angels (Col. 2:18), the witness of angels to our arena of life (all of the four references in 1 Corinthians plus the favorable references in Hebrews 1:7; 13:2; 2 Thess. 1:7), the subordination of angels to God's Son (most of Hebrews references; 1 Peter 3:22; as witness of Christ, 1 Tim. 3:16), and the references of Revelation where they are the agents of God in the struggle of good and evil.

All of this boils down to saying: (1) God used angels to break through to His world; (2) the angels of God perform His work in the world largely through historical circumstances and always by unexplained ways; (3) the angels are less than the Son and less privileged than humanity at the point of participating in the redemptive efficacy of Christ's death (1 Pet. 1:12); (4) the angels lead the worship and work of God in heaven. It is they, apparently, who do His will in heaven as it ought to be done on earth. All of this can put color and panache in the fullness of God's creation without requiring that we see angels, commune with them, or find out the ways in which they serve Him. The angels belong to God. Their praises are toward Him. Their implications for us lie primarily in two things: an awareness of the angels keeps us from being insufferably arrogant; God has other concerns and other creatures to praise Him. An awareness of angels can expand our horizons of belief in what is more than bread . . . and raiment (Matt. 6:25). Angels make us aware of a spiritual dimension of creation. The shadowy traces of beauty and celestial worship can be, indeed, extraordinary and real patterns in the kaleidoscope of creation.

We have a great deal of concern and curiosity about the elusive pattern of God's miracles or mighty works. All I said above about the predisposition of our age not to believe in angels is also true of the mighty works.[19] Yet the pictures through the kaleidoscope would be more somber without those few, purposeful bits of color called miracles.

The Old Testament is not much on abstract nouns. The major way in which miracles are described in the Old Testament is through the descriptions of the events themselves. And these events become the didactic (teaching) wonders to remind Israel of what God has done. The wonders performed for the covenant community center around the Exodus. Prophetic signs are recounted in the ministries of Elijah, Elisha, and Jonah. The wonder of a miracle is to be remembered as an admonition. There is no great Old Testament discussion as to whether miracles are possible. It is assumed that the wonders which bring into being the covenant community of God are done by Him Who performed the wonders of creation. The world, in the eyes of the Old Testament, did not run by some force called "natural law." The world and all that is therein was brought into being, run, and directed by God. All of this—creation, Exodus, the formation and preservation of the nation—was "marvelous" in their eyes.

The New Testament continues the concept of signs and wonders for God's special acts. But it adds the idea of power. The major New Testament word for miracles is *dunamis* (the stem gives us our word dynamite). The New Testament is aware that it is the power of God in Jesus Christ which is responsible for making "the blind see, the lame walk, [and] . . . the deaf hear" (Luke 7:22). The mighty works of Jesus were continued by the earliest church. The Spirit of God, the endowment of God, God's force, wind, breath, energy, is at work in the ministry of Jesus Christ. His mighty works (and I prefer to call them that in order to avoid the miracle mongering of the ancient world and the denial of miracles in the modern world) fall into four broad categories.[20]

There are the healings. Jesus healed blindness, deafness, lameness, hemorrhaging, epilepsy, and leprosy. The impact of these healings brought gratitude from some of the recipients, wonder from the crowds, and incrimination from the religious leaders. Jesus' touch was therapy, and His tones were balm, not blame. The second category of mighty works was exorcism. Exorcism is the casting out of the evil one in all of his manifestations. As we shall see, evil is an involvement of the total person. The people in New Testament days made no such fine lines of distinction as physical, psychical, and spiritual evil. Whatever was contrary to the plan and purpose of God, whatever limited life and led to despair was of the evil one. Jesus shed His light upon the prince of darkness and all forms of bondage were broken. The third category of Jesus' mighty works was the raising of the dead. The one who gave life entered the kingdom of the dead and brought back to life some few persons as tokens of His life-giving ministry to all the world. The miracles involving nature were the final category of His mighty works. This power over nature did not seem incongruous to those who had seen His power over the devil, disease, and death. Those witnesses were they who would become convinced that this special power of the mighty works was an extension of the primordial power of the Logos and the final power of Him Who would conclude the age.

Two questions arise about the special and extraordinary patterns called mighty works. What was their purpose? Do they continue?

It is often suggested that Jesus did miracles to prove He was the Son of God. However, when asked by Herod to do a small wonder, Jesus declined (Luke 23:8–9). He said no sign would be given to His generation except the sign of Jonah—the resurrection (Matt. 16:4; Luke 11:29–32). Jesus' awareness of self and confidence in the Father (John 8:25–59) make this "evidential" explanation of His mighty works implausible to me. Miracles were not used by Jesus as a celestial identification card to prove who He was.

A second suggestion about the purpose is that He performed miracles because of His compassion. There is no doubt that Jesus was compassionate. His sympathy with the human condition was itself extraordinary. He was in touch with suffering and pain, and He was deeply touched by those who underwent these affictions. But Jesus did not heal all who were sick. He did not raise all who died in His day. There were natural calamities and disasters in His time which He did not prevent or make right. Jesus Himself forfeited His life in mortal combat with evil. We must look for another reason.

It seems to me that Jesus' mighty works were tokens of what God would ultimately do in redeeming His creation. These were examples of what redemption would finally and completely accomplish. The Book of Revelation gives the full picture of what God will do through Christ in the final miracle of restoration and recreation. The evil one will be closed away to keep harm away from God's good world (Rev. 20:1–3). The tree of life will bear fruit which will heal whole nations (Rev. 22:2). God will adequately and completely recreate the natural world. There will be a new heaven and a new earth (Rev. 21:1). And the final enemy, death, will be overcome as well as all pain and tears (Rev. 21:4). What Jesus began, He is coming to complete. His mighty works are the down payment of what is finally to be realized. These extraordinary patterns of the kaleidoscope bear the outline and tracings of God's final picture which is both similar to and built upon the lovely designs we see here and now.

Do miracles happen today? Technology and research claim they do. But these, of course, are man-made miracles. Are people still healed by the power and the strong name of Jesus? Is evil still cast out by the "finger of God"? Many believers would answer yes. Do natural phenomena still obey the voice that stilled the storms in Galilee? Dramatic, unexplained, fortuitous rescues, and relief from natural peril are not unknown in our time. And the initial impulse of the rescued ones is to say it was a miracle of God.

It is death, to be sure, that remains the greatest problem. There have been dramatic reversals of unconsciousness, comatose states, and rescues from some clinical symptoms of death. But the incident of those raised after three days in the tomb is nonexistent. Why is death exempt from the continuity of mighty works? Possibly because it is the last, fiercest, and least reversible of all of the enemies of humanity. Possibly because Jesus is the only One who has been resurrected with all of the full implications of what that means.

There are three views about mighty works and their possibility today that bear mentioning. There is the perspective that miracles were confined to New Testament days. This argument cannot, of course, be proved or disproved from Scripture since it is by definition a postbiblical idea. The confined-to-the-first-century view is a convenient "out" for certain forms of Christian rationalism that cannot reconcile biblical mighty works with the sporadic and often ineffective efforts of religious miracle claims of today. A second view of miracles seems to imply that miracles are normative. They are available on demand through faith. Not to accept, expect, and live on the current from one miracle to another is a weak walk in Christian experience. This view has no explanation as to why Jesus did not heal all. This view makes the extraordinary pattern of the kaleidoscope the norm. All of the glass pieces in the patterns of this view are bright, intense, and lack any shading necessary to balance and beauty. Last, but not least, this view has no explanation to give and only cold comfort to give for the dead and to the irreversible dying. The claim of lack of faith is cruel in the case of many suffering saints. A word needs to be said about faith healing before I shake the kaleidoscope for a third, and for me, much preferred view as to the possibility of the miraculous today.

"Faith healing" is a misleading term. All healing is divine. Not all who have faith are healed. Paul was not (2 Cor. 12:7–10). The mistaken notion of faith healers is, in my opinion, threefold. They are wrong in the assumption that God intended for everyone to have perfect health, whatever that is, in this life. Faith healers are not able to establish from Scripture that only certain members of the body of Christ have the gift of healing and that these should live "so well" from the gifts of others as a result of God's gift to them. They overlook the fact that even medically indisputable healing, whatever that means, is not permanent. It is, like the lives of the unhealed, concluded by death. I am especially strong in these suggestions in this book, for I feel that the ill and the elderly—and they are often one and the same—are most susceptible to the encouragements and inducements of faith healers. It is the old and ill who cannot expect permanent remission who often seek desperately and expensively temporary remission. In many instances the price is too high, both economically and in the return(s) of health problems, some one of which will prove fatal.

The third position regarding the possibility of miracles today I call the faith, love, and hope view. There is faith in God and in His power that what He wants accomplished can be accomplished. There is a loving trust which can accept what comes and yet reply, in bane or blessing, "Blessed be the name of the Lord" (Job 1:21). There is always hope, for God is the Guarantor of all our aspirations. If what we hope for is realized, it is occasion for rejoicing. If it is not, there is yet a final hope, the "blessed hope" (Titus 2:13). It seems to me that this is the view of Christian realism. It does not lack faith. Neither does it presume on providence.

Anyone who feels himself/herself a recipient of a mighty work from God must ask serious questions: Why me, Lord? To what purpose? And the answer, to be acceptable among the unhealed members of the body of Christ and to the wounded head of the body, must be for some special redemptive purpose. Divine healing is not about favorites. It is about having special obligations, if special favors seem to have been granted.

I would want to hold that the kaleidoscope of creation and its multiple possibilities can have extraordinary patterns. In seeing these especially bright-colored bits of glass among the more somber tones, some have "entertained angels unawares" (Heb. 13:2), and some have become special recipients and instruments of His peace.

Staying in the Framework Makes the Pattern

The colored bits of glass have a bounded freedom in order to make a large variety of patterns. The pieces fall into place within the framework of the instrument. They are held in a circle and between the protecting round glass covers. The God who made the world has set more pattern possibilities than any generation of the human community has imagined,[21] and the patterns happen only because they are possible within the given structure of the kaleidoscope. What may seem like a tight, restrictive holding of things together is, in reality, the rules by which things work. And we may see in the regular, patterned elements of life a comforting and enabling structure. It might be inconvenient for the sun to rise in the east because that is the direction of your bedroom windows. Might it not be better, for you, if the sun rose in the south so as not to waken you? The suggestion is absurd. If the sun rose in the south, your comfort might be secured, but the rest of the world would be in pandemonium. A grieving parent said to me, after his teenaged son was killed in an automobile accident in which a car traveling at high speed hit a stalled truck, "I know God could not have suspended gravity that night in that place without killing several other folks." This was a wise, even if a grieving, view of providence.

Providence was defined by A. H. Strong in a classic, memorable way. "Providence is that continuous agency of God by which he makes all the events of the physical and moral universe fulfill the original design with which he created it."[22] The roundedness and the boundedness of our existence may seem aggravating. At times these bounds have the making of the tragic. Yet, all in all, it is important that the world works as it does. The dependent regularity of what some call the laws of nature provide the possibility of our continuing existence. If some same-old patterns keep cropping up, it is a blessing —not an occasion for boredom. God has set the parameters. Within them "we live, and move, and have our being."

Yet the Christian will see in these continuing patterns something more than "laws of nature" or dependable and routine occurrences. The Christian will discern the personal, purposive guidance of God in the way all things work. In the smallest organisms, there is a microscopic evidence that God makes very little things very well and very beautiful. In the macroscopic patterns of the galaxies and the universe we can hear His music of the spheres.

Naturally, we understand the secondary causes by which things work. We have, in our day, broken open some of the secrets of nature. We have split the atom and planted satellite stars. This could lead us to a god-almighty complex in which we can harness nature, rule the world, and replicate the created order by clones of our own "creation." It could, and in some instances it has.[23] This is the sin of Titanism. The Titans were those in Greek mythology who stole gifts from the gods to help humanity. They were severely punished. A ship that was supposedly unsinkable was called the *Titanic.* She sank, as you know, on her maiden voyage.

In our Titanism we have become so smart that we may have made ourselves sick. There is no need that we should steal gifts from the true God. For He is more than willing that we should have all of the blessings that exist within the possibility of the kaleidoscope. But there is every reason that we should not presume on providence by restructuring, retreading, and rearranging God's world purely for our own convenience and selfish indulgence. The weapons we make can destroy us, and the energy we consume can leave our children's children in a cold and barren world. It is God who made the world. It is we who have tried to destroy it. Nevertheless, this is still our Father's world, and He continues to guide it.

There are many lovely biblical expressions of appreciation for and confidence in the providence of God. In Genesis we read of the declaration of God that what He made is good (Gen. 1:1 to 2:3). In creation, the patterns and regularity of providence are discernible. What Genesis conveys is something of a plan rather than the particulars and details of a method. From the first turning, the kaleidoscope shows a world that brings forth fruit after its own kind. And the world has continued to turn and to survive because of that pattern and that design. We rejoice in the so-called nature Psalms such as Psalms 8 and 19. But we should be quick to note that these are not songs of praise for nature so much as they are hymns of confidence in the God who made the world and blesses people with special tokens of His presence. The Bible is not "into" romantic naturalism. It is "into" natural contextualism. I mean by this that all of God's ways with His world are held together in Scripture. This holding together of God's ways is seen especially in God's answer to Job. Chapters 38—41 of Job could be seen as an assessment of God's wonderful world. These chapters are far more. They are the revelation of God to a hurting human. And the central message of that revelation is that the God who does the wonders is the God who heals the woes of His suffering servants.

Jesus' teachings about God's providence are instructive. The Father sends the rain on the just and the unjust (Matt. 5:45). The Father knows every sparrow's fall and the number of the hairs of our head (Matt. 10:29–31; Luke 12:6–7). The Father knows what we have need of (Matt. 6:31–32; Luke 12:29–30), and Paul would quickly add that He supplies all of our needs in Christ Jesus (Phil. 4:19). The Father takes time for the lilies of the field (Matt. 6:28; Luke 12:27), small blossoms that grow out of the dust and are short-lived. How much more is the Father concerned for us! The pride and place of providence in the teaching of Jesus wraps up the details of "all things great and small" and delivers them in a package inscribed as a gift from "the Father."

The providing of God comes about in His foreseeing (*pro videre*) the needs of the world and moving faithfully to supply them. We do not stand alone. God stands with us. Providence is not an isolated doctrine. It is built on creation, fully expressed in redemption, and finally realized in eschatology. Providence is a connecting link. It connects creation (the beginning) with eschatology (the end). Providence works its way out between God's sovereignty and human freedom. Providence must be affirmed on the basis of the goodness of God and in the face of the reality of evil.[24]

Musical affirmations about God's providence abound. They range from Mendelssohn's *Elijah* to Ethel Waters' rendition of "His Eye Is on the Sparrow." The experience of American blacks affirms that "He's Got the Whole World in His Hand." The blindness of Fanny Crosby prayed, "All the way my Savior leads me." Augustus Toplady requested that God would provide a crevice in the "Rock of Ages." Henry Lyte asked that God would "Abide with me." All appearances to the contrary, "This is my father's world." Providence says that God cares for the world He made. If we should ask how to differentiate creation from providence and vice versa, it might be said that creation is crafting the world and providence is caring for it. Creation says beginning. Providence speaks of continuing. They belong together. And they combine to provide an arena and an attitude for redemption. They are consummated and coalesce in eschatology. The pieces of the kaleidoscope stick together. They touch. It is only in this way that the pictures can be produced, and the patterns can be seen. But these pleasant sounding truisms of faith seem to fall apart when a piece of the pattern breaks loose or the glass is smashed so that no patterns seem to appear at all.

A Piece Is Loose

The patterns on the kaleidoscope depend on all of the parts being in place. I remember one kaleidoscope from my youth in which one piece of glass became loose and moved in an unpredictable way across the glass cylinder ends. It spoiled the entire picture. In fact, when the one piece came loose, it was the beginning of the end of that kaleidoscope and its usefulness. The one loose piece soon began to push other pieces out of the way and to disturb their way of fitting into the pattern of the picture. It wasn't long before the entire kaleidoscope was ruined and had to be discarded. This loose piece seems to me a powerful analogy for the evil one.

Scripture expresses and experience confirms that there is something out of place in the beauty and pattern of God's kaleidoscope: His creation. There is no systematic chapter or book about how this is so or why this is so. But there is a loose piece that runs through the whole. As early as chapter 3 in Genesis there is a dissident, insinuating voice. It occurs through the serpent. It raises doubt about the divine purpose: you surely will not die!. It challenges forbidden prerogatives: Can you eat of all the trees? This original pattern, or antipattern, of evil persists in our experience. Forbidden fruit seems sweeter. Consequences of disobedience always seem remote and related to others.

The serpent figure gives way to the phrase "sons of God." That name is even more insidious. It is as one of the "sons of God" that the evil one appears in Job 1. This time, reversing the Genesis circumstances, the ancient enemy raises questions about man to God. Does Job serve God for nothing? The irritating loose piece is once more intent on disrupting the divine pattern. A third Old Testament passage (Zech. 3:1) illustrates another peculiarly demonic trait, cynical criticism. "Is this the best, O God, you can find to serve you? This high priest who represents you looks like a brand plucked from the fire" (vv. 1–2, my paraphrase). Whether in heaven or on earth, the insidious and insinuating presence of evil takes its toll. Pride of place and the desire to displace others, even God, is the occasion. Later interpreters would see in Isaiah's proverb against the king of Babylon (Isa. 14:4–23) a parabolic description of Lucifer, the daystar, the angel of light, who defied God and had to suffer the consequences. This interpretation of the origin of evil was also applied to the prophetic description of the prideful prince of Tyre (Ezek. 27) and his downfall. A displaced piece of glass, lodged against the purpose of God, is ruining the pattern of God's creation.

The New Testament intensifies the picture. *Satan,* the Old Testament word for "adversary," becomes the *devil.* The term *devil* means accuser or one who throws something against another. As the fullness of God's revelation comes to its zenith, in Jesus Christ—its high point, the opposite number—the evil one—is at its nadir, the lowest point. And that is an appropriate analogy for good and evil. In the life of the Son of God, a "fallen" son of God seeks, through Herod to have the child killed. Some early church interpreters elaborated beyond the biblical accounts. They portrayed the evil one as the younger son of God who fell because of his jealousy of his elder, perfect brother.

There is more than sibling rivalry in the interaction of Jesus and the evil one. The temptation was a time when Jesus was encouraged to do God's will the devil's way.[25] Jesus heard the tempter all through His earthly ministry. And near its close, there was the familiar "you must not go to Jerusalem and die" suggestion on the lips of a trusted friend (Matt. 16:22–23). Another trusted "friend" had walked with Jesus but was not really with Him. This friend, Judas, was described by a third friend of Jesus, John, as one who was devillike from the beginning of his discipleship (John 6:70–71). Judas was also portrayed by John as being invaded by Satan (John 13:2, 27). Behind Judas and the arresting party at Gethsemane, Jesus saw the evil one coming (John 18:1–12).

The very pattern of Jesus' ministry was, according to John, to destroy the works of the devil (1 John 3:8). Evil was most intense when good was most present. And at the end it seemed that evil had won. It was finished (John 19:30). The serpent had bruised the heel of the seed of woman (Gen. 3:15). But the resurrection revealed that the head of the serpent was mortally wounded. Granted, there was strength enough and enough other manifestations of evil to create havoc in the war between heaven and earth (the Book of Revelation); nevertheless, the Spirit whom Jesus sent ensured His followers that "greater is he who is in you [the Spirit], than he that is in the world" (the evil one whose doom is already ensured by Jesus' resurrection) (1 John 4:4, KJV). Paul certainly knew of the injured and doubly dangerous manifestation of evil whose final appearance as "a man of sin" (2 Thess. 2:3–4) presages Jesus' own final coming. In the interim, the deceptive appearance of the evil one is as an angel of light (2 Cor. 11:14–15). He is divisive of churches. And the "principalities" and "powers" of earth (Rom. 8:38) are assisted in evil by the spiritual darkness that lies behind them.[26] The serpent of the beginnings (Gen. 3) has become the dragon of the earth's ending (Rev. 12:3–17; 13:2,4, 11; 16:13, and especially 20:2). The "whole world lieth in wickedness" (1 John 5:19, KJV) in such a way that the errant piece of glass seems to have spoiled all of the pattern of God.

But this is not the way things really are. The way things really are is the way they are seen from God's viewpoint. And in that perspective the cry of Jesus that "it is finished" referred to God's plan and purpose in overcoming evil. The displaced sliver of glass is neutralized by the power of the Spirit (1 John 4:4). And He who made the kaleidoscope will ultimately shut away this loose piece, so that it can no longer disturb the patterns of God's purpose (Rev. 20). That is the way it *really* is. Granted, it often seems different from the perspective of those who are looking through a mirror darkly.

Older people know that there is more to evil than any easy description can capture. We do not fear the popular pictures of evil (the horns, the hoofs, the pitchfork). What is to be regarded with anxiety and awe is the demonic way in which we and others can cooperate with the evil one to destroy the patterns of God's intended beauty in our own lives and in the lives of others. We have also read enough history and seen enough social and corporate examples of disturbed patterns to recognize that the impact of evil can and does displace the patterns of what God intends in the world.

I have spoken of evil in a personified way. The evil one is the designation I have chosen. Is this merely a personification? What advantage is there in suggesting a personal devil? Is evil not just the absence of good? Do we not conjure up all the evil that is in our own lives and in the world around us? If we have lived long enough, read Scripture often enough, and reflected deeply on the destroyed patterns of life, there are four things I believe we would want to affirm. (1) The Bible speaks of evil in personalistic terms even as it does of God. We cannot have a Hebrew (personal) God and a Greek (impersonal) devil. (2) Personhood is the highest and lowest categories in which we can think of good and evil. (3) The personification we give to both good and evil, God and the devil, are expressions of function (what they do), not descriptions of existence (how they look). (4) All of us have had "help" in doing the good and in undoing the good with the bad.

We are sure of two additional things. We cannot blame our problems and disclaim our responsibilities solely because of God or the evil one. God did not make you do it. And the devil did not make you do it. Good and evil are joint ventures between God and the self and the evil one and the self. We also know that if evil really is to be shut away and the devil, finally, is to receive his due, that it will have to be God who does it. God only can withdraw and remove the offending piece of glass that wreaks havoc in our world and disturbs the patterns of our cosmic and personal kaleidoscope. There is, however, a worse condition. That comes when the glass cracks or explodes, and all of the pieces of the kaleidoscope fall out, and we cannot see any pattern at all.

When No Pattern Appears

It is too academic and philosophical to say that we are discussing the problem of evil. Our analogy of the kaleidoscope is very helpful at this point. Evil is the crisis which occurs when the glass is shattered, the pieces fall out, and there is no more pattern. Evil is not just an intellectual problem to be solved (incidentally, no one has ever done that satisfactorily). Even if we had logical and rational answers to the dilemma of evil, they would not help. Rational answers and explanations do not solve emotional crises. To know why pain hurts does not remove pain. To know that all must die does not diminish the grieving process when we lose a loved one or face death ourselves. Older people need no lengthy persuasion that evil is real. The clear glass of our youthful kaleidoscope has been scuffed and scarred too often to deny evil. It may help to talk about the perfect will of God versus the permissive will of God. The books distinguish between moral evil (that which humanity as a moral agent causes) and natural evil (that which the insurance people unfortunately call "an act of God").

Yet, in the last analysis these are only words, unclear distinctions designed to give us something to say so that we can face the trauma of evil, the harsh realities of life, and the Father whom we must believe still cares for us. It is that love and care of the Father which most concerns us. For it is the love and goodness of God which is most powerfully called into question when there are no patterns discernible. The problem of evil arises most acutely for those who believe that "God is great, and God is good," and that evil is real. Those who limit the power of God can ascribe evil to His weakness. Those who limit the love and goodness of God can suggest that evil is a result of God's unconcern or His ambiguous or double-natured character—a God who is both good and evil. Those who deny that evil is real can astonishingly declare that there is no problem. But we who cling to the power of God, the goodness of God, and the reality of evil, must make peace with the Father and with our pain.

Perhaps this is an appropriate place to acknowledge old resentments. Some of us have never expressed resentment we have felt toward loved ones who died and left us. Pain is often followed by anger. When anger is acknowledged and expressed, it can more quickly be resolved. It is absurd and illogical to hold resentment and anger toward those who have died. In most instances they could not help it and did not want it. Evil is absurd and irrational. Evil results in unsolvable riddles and nonrational responses. It has no right to exist. But it does. Our anger toward the loss of loved ones is a self-protective measure which asks, "What happens to me now?"

But the more difficult crisis of faith is our anger at God. If God is ultimately responsible, we will hold Him so. If He could have helped, why didn't He? If He is good, how could He let "bad things happen to good people"?[27] This is our religious crisis. The One who made our kaleidoscope has permitted it to be broken. Or perhaps we assume, denying all human responsibility, that He has broken it Himself. These are the dilemmas of people of faith. Perhaps this is our penalty for belief. If we had not affirmed pattern and purpose in the kaleidoscope of our life, we would not have missed it when it fell apart. If we had not affirmed providence (God's loving care), we would not have to have a theodicy (an explanation for evil). Is faith worth the risk? I want to answer with a strong yes. But how can it ever be the same, this broken existence of ours in which pattern and purpose are gone?

Let me try to answer that probing question as honestly as I can with four suggestions:

1. Things never are the same. Life is a process. There can be some constant factors, some predictable outcomes. But nothing is ever the

same. If this is true of the minor experiences and the good times in our life, it is even more exaggerated and prevalent in crises. The first shattering word of reality about a crisis in life is that crisis will change us and our circumstances. That is one constant truth in our changing scene.

2. We need to be careful when we define good and evil. These terms should refer to more than our personal desires and conveniences. Using good and evil too cheaply, ascribing direct actions to God and the evil one too quickly, can lead to a passel of problems. We need not suggest that the devil made it rain at Sunday School time so that we cannot get out. The rain may be the blessing of God on the farmers' crops. Immediate, unambiguous interpretations of what is good and what is bad for ourselves and for everybody else is not a blessing. Such ready pronouncements may rise up to haunt us. The supercilious "it serves them right for acting that way" may choke in our throats later when similar circumstances such as ill health and adversity come to us who were not "acting that way."

3. Do not interpret other people's sufferings for them; you will have enough trouble with your own. Job's comforters are not comforting. People who have it all figured out for others often do not have all the parts and figures in the problem of others. And calculations of their own tragedies do not always add up quickly or correctly. When asked by a friend the why of sorrow and suffering, the best and most honest answer is, "I do not know."

4. Try, if you can, to help yourself and others to transform the question "Why has this happened?" to "What now is my path, O God?" This converted question accepts the inevitable. It avoids the unanswerable. It points toward the future. I hope these suggestions help. It is easier to make them than it is to practice them.

Let me give some partial reasons others have suggested as to why we suffer. They are partial indeed, for they do not fit every occasion, and no one of them is capable of fully answering the problem of evil. (1) Evil and tragedy in life may be a punishment for personal wrongdoing. That may be, but there are many instances where the innocent suffer. (2) Suffering can teach us valuable lessons. It can, but what is an infant to learn from painful, terminal cancer? (3) Suffering is a trial from God which He will explain later. Possibly, but what kind of relationship is based on a friendship that deliberately causes grief so that it can make the other happier later on?[28] (4) Suffering may be vicarious, helpful to others. Surely this is so, yet there are a lot of senseless tragic deaths and sufferings that serve no purpose and help no one.

What then is the resolution? Shall we give up our kaleidoscope toy with its pretty colors and its enchanting patterns? I am not willing to do so. Let me make a final suggestion. When our kaleidoscope is shattered nationally, socially, or personally, what may we do? The only resolution is to turn to the maker of it and ask for repairs. Why not a whole new one? Because then we would not be ourselves, and our world would not be our same world. Whatever we will have to work with will be reconstituted on the basis of the former pieces. But perhaps when we are broken and no pattern seems to emerge for us, a wonderful thing can happen. Perhaps in these periods of brokenness we can see Him who fashions the kaleidoscope as at no other time. And in those clearer glimpses of the Father in times of tragedy, we will discover His sorrow with our brokenness. And it may be that through our tears we will catch a glimpse of His ultimate pattern. That pattern features a cross (symbolic of His suffering) and a crown (suggesting that through His pain He is remaking our ultimate, good destiny). If, when the kaleidoscope is broken, we can catch some visions of His suffering and our salvation, then maybe we can content ourselves with the temporary, restored instruments through which we have to look until that time when the glass finally shatters and we see His final pattern, which is more beautiful than anything we could have imagined.

Notes

1. This was called the argument from design or the cosmological argument. See "Cosmological argument" in Antony Flew (ed.), *A Dictionary of Philosophy,* rev. 2nd ed., (New York: St. Martin's Press, 1984), pp. 77–78. The argument was weakened, according to some, because of our awareness of secondary causes and because design could not prove a personal, loving God. The argument is undergoing a revival today due to such sciences as astrophysics and the awareness of an expanding universe.

2. William Wordsworth, "The Tables Turned" [1798], stanza 6 in Emily Morison Beck (ed.), *Familiar Quotations by John Bartlett,* 14th ed. (Boston: Little, Brown and Co., 1968), p. 509a.

3. Ogden Nash, "Song of the Open Road," in *Many Long Years Ago* (Boston: Little, Brown and Co., 1945), p. 139.

4. Compare John Macquarrie, *Principles of Christian Theology,* 2nd ed. (New York: Scribner, 1977), pp. 104–122 for a good discussion of God as He who lets be.

5. See Langdon Gilkey, *The Maker of Heaven and Earth* (Garden City, N.Y.: Doubleday, 1965) for a good account of how the Christian community has looked at creation and what this doctrine means.

6. On the relation of religion to science, see Arthur Peacock, *Creation and the World of Science* (New York: Oxford University Press, 1979); *Intimations of Reality: Critical Realism in Science and Religion* (Notre Dame, Ind.: University of Notre Dame Press, 1984); and *Science and the Christian Experiment* (New York: Oxford University Press, 1971); Ian Barbour, *Issues in Science and Religion* (Englewood Cliffs, N.J.: Prentice-Hall, 1966) and *Myths, Models, and Paradigms: A Comparative Study in Science and Religion* (New York: Harper & Row, 1974); and Langdon Gilkey, *Religion and the Scientific Future: Reflections on Myth, Science and Theology* (New York: Harper & Row, 1970). For an attempt to express science in a theological mold see Henry Morris, *Biblical Cosmology and Modern Science* (Grand Rapids, Mich.: Baker Book House, 1970); *The Biblical Base for Modern Science* (Grand Rapids, Mich.: Baker Book House, 1984); *Science, Scripture, and the Young Earth: An Answer to the Current Argument Against the Biblical Doctrine of Recent Creation* (El Cajon, Calif.: Institute for Creation Research, 1983); and (with Gary Parker) *What is Creation Science?* (San Diego, Calif.: Creation-Life Publishers, 1982). For a prejudicial work that represents religious teachings from the viewpoint of science, see Andrew Dickson White, *A History of the Warfare of Science with Theology in Christendom,* 2 vols. (New York: D. Appleton & Co., 1908).

7. See Karl Barth, *Church Dogmatics,* vol. 3, pt. 1, trans. J. W. Edwards, O. Bussey; and Harold Knight (Edinburgh: T. & T. Clark, 1958), § 41 "Creation and Covenant," section 2, pp. 101–117. Also, vol. 3, pt. 3, trans. G. W. Bromiley and R. J. Ehrlich (Edinburgh: T. & T. Clark, 1961), § 50 "God and Nothingness," pp. 289–368, especially pp. 352–353.

8. Compare the understanding of John as the new Genesis, Raymond Brown, *The Gospel According to John,* The Anchor Bible, 2 vols. (New York: Doubleday, 1966–1970) especially pp. 1ix-1x, 4–6, 26–30.

9. For an introduction and demonstration of this pattern of biblical theology, see Robert Dentan, *The Design of the Scriptures: A First Reader in Biblical Theology* (New York: McGraw-Hill, 1961).

10. This is presented in poetic fashion in the lovely expression of American black lore in *God's Trombones* (James Welden Johnson, *God's Trombones: Seven Negro Sermons in Verse* [New York: The Viking Press, 1927]).

11. See Leonard Hodgson's social view of the Trinity, *The Doctrine of the Trinity* (New York: Charles Scribner's Sons, 1944); also *For Faith and Freedom,* 2 vols. (Oxford: Basil Blackwell, 1957), Vol. 2, pp. 37–46, 225–233.

12. See John Cobb and David Griffin, *Process Theology: An Introductory Exposition* (Philadelphia: Westminster Press, 1976) and Ewert Cousins, (ed.), *Process Theology: Basic Writings* (New York: Newman Press, 1971).

13. See chapter 7 below.

14. For a resumé of these issues and their answers in Calvinism, see A. H. Strong, *Systematic Theology* (Philadelphia: The Judson Press, 1951), pp. 777–793.

15. Compare Jurgen Moltmann's *Theology of Play,* trans. Reinhard Ulrich (New York: Harper and Row, 1972), pp. 15–24.

16. It is regrettable that the Christian community has not followed some social trends and theories into more optimistic evaluations. See John Naisbitt, *Megatrends: Ten*

New Directions Transforming Our Lives (New York: Warner Books, 1982) and Kenneth H. Blanchard & Spencer Johnson, *The One Minute Manager* (New York: Morrow, 1982).

17. Compare Joseph Haroutunian's "Demons, Demonic, and the Devil," in Marvin Halverson and Arthur Cohen, *A Handbook of Christian Theology* (New York: New American Library, 1974), pp. 74–77 and from a sociological viewpoint Peter Berger's *A Rumor of Angels* (Garden City, N.Y.: Doubleday, 1970).

18. For an interesting contemporary argument on behalf of angels and the possibility of their existence from a philosophical view without recourse to Scripture or faith presuppositions, see Mortimer J. Adler's *The Angels and Us* (New York: Macmillan, 1982).

19. For a discussion of the logic of belief about miracles see C. S. Lewis *Miracles: A Preliminary Study* (New York: Macmillan, 1947).

20. See Howard Clark Kee and Franklin W. Young, *An Introduction to the New Testament* (Englewood Cliffs, N.J.: Prentice-Hall, 1957), pp. 98–103.

21. On the wonders of the "expanding universe" see Loren Eiseley *The Immense Journey* (New York: Random House, 1957); *The Invisible Pyramid* (New York: Scribner's, 1972); *The Star Thrower* (New York: Harcourt, Brace, & Jovanovich, 1979); *The Unexpected Universe* (New York: Harcourt, Brace, & Jovanovich, 1972); *et al.*, and Immanuel Velikovsky, *Worlds in Collision* (New York: Doubleday, 1950); *Earth in Upheaval* (New York: Doubleday, 1955); and *Ages in Chaos* (New York: Doubleday, 1952).

22. A. H. Strong, *Systematic Theology* (Philadelphia: The Judson Press, 1907), p. 419.

23. See B. F. Skinner's frank and candid request that we turn over the "engineering" and control of the human community to the social scientists: *Beyond Freedom and Dignity* (New York: Knopf, 1971).

24. For theological discussion of providence, see M. J. Langford, "Providence," in Alan Richardson and John Bowden (eds.), *The Westminster Dictionary of Christian Theology* (Philadelphia: Westminster Press, 1983); "Providence" in Karl Rahner and Herbert Vergrimler, *Dictionary of Theology*, 2nd ed. (New York: Crossroad, 1981); Albert Outler, *Who Trusts in God: Musings on the Meanings of Providence* (New York: Oxford University Press, 1968); Karl Barth, *Church Dogmatics*, vol. 3, pt. 3, trans. G. W. Bromiley and T. F. Torrance (Edinburgh: T. & T. Clark, 1961), chapter 11, § 48, "The Doctrine of Providence. Its Basis and Form," pp. 3–57.

25. See chapter 7 on the temptation of Jesus, pp. 195–96. On the idea of the demonic in Scripture see my "The Concept of Satan: A Biblical and Historical Approach and its Relevance to the Christian Life." (Th.D. Thesis, Southwestern Baptist Theological Seminary, 1958).

26. Compare Jer. 13:18; Rom. 13:1–4; Eph. 1:21; 3:10; 6:12; Col. 1:16; 2:10; 2:15; Titus 3:1.

27. Compare the title of Rabbi Harold Kushner's book, *When Bad Things Happen to Good People* (New York: Shocken Books, 1981). Kushner's discussions are very helpful. His answers lean toward human responsibility and the self-limitation of the power of God.

28. See John Hick, *Evil and the God of Love*, 2nd ed. (London: Macmillan, 1977) and David Stewart (ed.), *Exploring The Philosophy of Religion* (Englewood Cliffs, N.J.: Prentice-Hall, 1980), pp. 243–297.

6

Breathing

We are working up to God. The first chapter, "Last Things First," took us on a doctrinal survey of what we anticipate—eschatology. There was a "Pilgrim's Progress" as we used the analogy of traveling to express the Christian life. The "Identifying Marks" of the church helped us to describe and to strive for a definition of what it means to be the people of God. We used the analogy of "A Look in the Mirror" in chapter 4 as a metaphor for discussing the doctrines of mankind and sin. A nostalgic toy, "The Kaleidoscope," provided a focus through which to see important insights about creation and providence. The first five chapters are topics that usually would be discussed in the second half of a formal theology. We have discussed them first, however, because they reflect on our expectations (eschatology), the arena of our own religious life and service (the church), an expression of who we actually are (humanity and sin), and the context of our lives (creation and providence). These are the areas in which we have our experiences. We know what it is to be human. Personal experience interacts with biblical affirmation in these areas.

We now come to the more important doctrines theologically. They deal with God and revelation. We have experiences with God. Some people's attitudes notwithstanding, we have had no experience being God. Therefore, what we will talk about in the last four chapters of the book are really the foundations and the groundwork of what has been discussed above. I have tried to choose the analogies for the "experienced" doctrines of chapters 1 to 5 carefully so that the metaphor would provoke thought[1] and facilitate understanding.

It will be even more important to use metaphors of life and experience to help us understand these concluding chapters which deal in an arena in which we have had no experience, the areas of being God and of receiving primary revelation (such as the biblical authors) from God. I feel that the metaphors and figures by which we discuss God need to be clearer and more related to our experience, if possible, than the metaphors we use to discuss ourselves and our world. I have chosen three metaphors to use as windows or illustrations for talking about God. These are: breathing, for the Spirit; children, for Jesus, the Son of God; and singing, for God the Father. The rules and guidelines for all of the discussion will be put in the final chapter. This midpoint of theology seemed a good place to pause and refresh the reader's mind as to this method of working up to God by working back from our expectations and involvements as Christians.

This sixth chapter is about breathing. Breathing is an experience we all share. If we are going to keep on living, we must keep on breathing. What could be more natural or more necessary than breathing? This metaphor is especially appropriate to discuss the Spirit of God because the words for *spirit* and *breath* in the Bible are the same and carry a close and parallel meaning. The reader doesn't have to be reminded of, introduced to, or encouraged to breathe. If you are reading, you are breathing. It is not possible for it to be otherwise. It is that naturalness that nonreflective, necessary experience—breathing—which provides a good metaphor for discussing the Spirit.

Likewise, the metaphor of breathing is significant for seniors. We, more than younger people, have had to learn to pay attention to the process of breathing. We hear the expressions and display the symptoms of "labored breathing," "shortness of breath," "lung and respiratory infections and problems." Modern medical expertise has made us acutely aware and conscious of breathing. These two reasons, the aptness of the word similarities and the reality and sensitivity of our involvement with breathing, make the analogy helpful.

Anyone can define big words. The standard dictionaries are helpful in giving us precise origins and meanings of unfamiliar terms. It is the little words that give us trouble. One of those little words is *spirit.* No dictionary has space enough to define and illustrate all of the different nuances of that word. Let me remind you of a few uses of spirit that you already know. Spirit may mean attitude. You will hear a person say, "Our civic club has a good spirit." This usually means a harmonious attitude, a genial relationship between the members. Spirit may be used in a social, broad sense to apply to the culture of an age, or an intellectual movement. The spirit of the Enlightenment stressed the worth of the individual.

Neither of these modern, cultural, or psychological uses is used in the Bible. The biblical uses of the term *spirit* are more elemental. They are related to the root meaning of the words.[2] Both the Old Testament and the New Testament terms for spirit mean: wind, breath, force, power, or energizing principle. Ancient people were not dull. They knew what every person can observe by long and painful experience. When the breath leaves a thing, when a person quits breathing, she or he is dead. Spirit is the force of life. When Jesus breathed out His spirit, He committed Himself into the hands of God, and His earthly life was over. In this elementary sense spirit or breath has an almost quasi-physical meaning.

This stress on the physical aspect of breathing gives rise to what I will call the animistic view of spirit. This early view is found in all world religions and is certainly present in the Bible. The animistic (from *animus,* a Latin word which means energizing force) view gives the idea that when one is full of the spirit, it is almost as though something is being poured into the individual. In order for this to happen and for the outside spirit to come in, there must be an emptying of the spirit of the person filled or possessed. The process is almost a kind of standing outside of the self, an ecstasy. The term *ecstasy* comes from two Greek words which mean "to stand outside." This animistic model is primarily an emotional model. The early prophets in Israel (for example, 1 Sam. 19:23–24; 2 Kings 2:1–17) were ecstatics and seemed to have lost control of the self. Many would argue that when Paul speaks of such gifts of the Spirit as speaking in tongues (1 Cor. 12—15) that he is referring to an ecstatic gift. Some charismatics and revivalists of the Pentecostal type speak of one who has lost emotional control and seems to be invaded by another Presence as "having the Spirit" or "being in the Spirit."

Another biblical use of spirit deals with a rational view of spirit. In expressions such as "having the mind/Spirit of Christ" or "discerning (that is, making a critical judgment about) the spirits" this meaning stresses the mental and rational actions of the individual. It seems to me that it is a mistake to identify the Spirit of God and His work with any one faculty of the human personality. A spiritual person is not, in my opinion, one who is at the mercy of invading physical forces either divine or demonic. A spiritual person is not one who is either emotionally or exceptionally gifted intellectually. A spiritual person is one who, in every area of life, seeks and follows God and the direction of God in all phases of one's existence. In the last analysis, I would define *spirit* as God's dimension. This means that there is through, around, and beyond our natural, physical existence another dimension of existence. That domain or area or quality of existence involves us and our world, but it also goes beyond and becomes the ultimate meaning and center of life itself. When we define *spirit* this way, we are able to talk about Spirit as the Breath of God.

The Breath of God

This section of the chapter is about the Old Testament insights concerning the Spirit of God. And this particular paragraph is about the Spirit of God in and through creation. It is as natural as breathing. The breath of God is the life of the world. Spirit is God's dimension. God is everywhere. Spirit is God's energizing power, the Source of all life. All life has life because God breathes into it. I am not talking about a method. I am talking about a mode of being. Life is associated with the Spirit of God. The Author of life and the Source of life invests His creation with His life. These are strange words. It is important to say what I do not mean by them. I do not mean that God is in everything in such a way that you could add up the total of all living things, and they would be God or equal God. The view that God is the sum of all living things is pantheism. By making everything God, pantheism can have no God in particular.

God differs from His creation. There are two basic orders of existence: Creator and created. And the created order exists because the Creator brings it into being, energizes it with His breath, and continues to uphold all things by His power (Spirit). God is the ground of all actual being, whatever has life. God is the possibility of everything which will come into being, whatever will have life. God is the preserver of whatever has ceased to live, of whatever has had life. This energizing principle of life is the divine Spirit. This is the Creator Spirit which brooded over primeval chaos. And the Breath of God (the wind) blew chaos into cosmos, God's ordered world. Everything that is is because God lets it be.[3] Creation expresses beginning, and it expresses dependence. The world would crumble if God withdrew His breath. The threatening chaos of nothingness would overwhelm whatever is and collapse being into nonbeing. This is a theological statement that deals with ultimate reality. This is not a how of creation. It is a rationale for existence.

All of the above statements may sound strange, poetic, even unrelated to the Spirit. What theologians mean by all of these curious expressions is: (1) God is the Source and Giver of life. (2) God's presence calls everything into being, sustains it, and conserves it. (3) The realm in which this principle of God's creativeness takes place is Spirit. (4) Spirit, or God's breath, is the agent and energizer of all life. These four conclusions mean that life is ultimately good because God declared it to be so. These conclusions also mean that all existence is graced by God through His first gift: life. If we understand that life is the gift of God, we must respect life and place life, the breath of God, above death and destruction. All of these things mean that the Spirit of God is everywhere, and it is by this Breath of God that everything has its own existence. The breath of God, of life, of the Spirit grants integrity to everything. That is, each thing has its own existence alongside of its existence from God. This means that God works through the "natural" to perform His acts in His created order. Life is as natural as breathing. Life as the gift of God comes with and through the natural "breathing" of the world. This is the first gift of the Spirit.

But not all of life is of an equal value in God's sight. When God specifically breathed into humanity, the crown of creation, there was a special recognition of the worth of mankind. Physicians tell us what midwives have known for centuries, birth is a trauma for the child and for the mother. The lusty squall from a newborn child, freshly slapped on the bottom, is a cry of outrage. The coming into being of a new human is a welcome trauma; nevertheless, it is a trauma. And there is a traumatic counterpart in the birth of the human race. God's Spirit especially fulfills and enables human life to be, in God's sight, different from other forms of life. With human birth there is the risk, which God takes, that this inbreathed (inspirited) creature will rebel against the Creator, will thwart and waste the breath of life so wondrously given.

There is another gift of life—everlasting life. A great deal of love and special care is required to undo the trauma of birth. In the Old Testament the Spirit gives life to all living things, gives a special meaning to the life of persons, and draws together an elected community: Israel. The Spirit is active in the promise to Abraham and Moses and in bringing into being the covenant community Israel (for example, Gen. 15 and Ex. 3). There was trauma in the birth of Israel through the Red Sea. In the traumatic birth of Israel and her receiving special divine love and care God is beginning to breathe in a special way to accomplish His redemptive purpose. There are not two Spirits of God, One active in creation and One active in redemption. But these are two ways in which we perceive the work of God's Spirit. In a general way God's Spirit is active in all life, giving it being. And in a special way God's breath, the Holy Spirit, is the active principle of redemption. This "second sending" of the breath of God works through special events. The beginning of the redemption of life by God's Spirit starts with the formation of a special community.

To sustain and guide this special community, God's Holy Spirit came upon her leaders, the kings of Israel who were considered annointed of God. The Holy Spirit also breathed in this special redemptive way through the judges, prophets, and the psalmists (Judg. 3:10; 6:21–24; 1 Sam. 11:6; 16:13; Ps. 51:11–12). We might well say that in these special acts God is teaching some to breathe more deeply. And last, but certainly not least, the Holy Spirit of God gave a promise of a fresh and sustaining breath of air in the promise of a coming Messiah (Ps. 31:5; Isa. 11:2; 61:1–3; Joel 2:28). In these general and special ways, the breath of God is celebrated in the Old Testament. To help review the work of the Spirit in the Old Testament, let me make a brief list of a more traditional nature and add to it my analogies about breathing.

General Uses:	Bringing cosmos out of chaos, breathing life into all things	As natural as breathing
Special Uses:	The creation of humanity	
	The bringing into being of Israel, the covenant community	Traumatic births
	The special breath of inspiration and aspiration to prophets, the leaders, the psalmists	Teaching some to breathe more deeply

	The promise of the Messiah	The promise of a fresh breath

In the New Testament the deepest and most sustaining breathing of God upon and through His creation comes to pass. This happens in two ways. Jesus is the fresh breath of God bringing salvation. The Spirit, by His gifts, enables the church as the body of Christ to breathe, to be sustained, and to become an agent of God's reconciliation.

A Breath of Fresh Air

Jesus was a breath of fresh air from God. The Holy Spirit is a breath of fresh air to bear witness to Jesus. In the gifts of the Son and the Spirit, the Father ensures not only the survival but also the salvation of His world. Why did the world need a breath of fresh air if God created it and pronounced it good? Because humanity, the special recipient of the Breath of God, fouled the air of God's good world, and the pollution is fatal (see ch. 3). God does not give up on His world. He blows fresh air into His polluted creation, and the pollution will not overcome it. He breathes the redemptive breath of life, and the pollution will not be able to nullify or contaminate this fresh breath of God (see John 1:5).

Before Pentecost the Holy Spirit of God is distinctly and especially concerned with Jesus who embodies historically the life of God. Jesus was conceived by the Holy Spirit (Matt. 1:18–25). His ministry was performed by the power of the Spirit, God's power (Matt. 3:11). Jesus was driven by the Spirit into the wilderness to be tempted (Mark 1:12). After He was baptized, the Spirit came and remained upon Him[4] (see John 1:32–34).

Jesus returned from the wilderness to Galilee at the leadership of the Spirit (Luke 4:14). In the synagogue at Nazareth, His ministry was begun and blessed by the Spirit (Luke 4:14–16). Jesus' mighty works were done in the power of the Spirit (Matt. 12:28). He promised the gift of the Spirit to those who ask (Luke 11:13) and particularly to His disciples. Jesus yielded up His spirit to the Father (Luke 23:46). This was a fresh breath of air. Here is One who was foretold, was conceived, was led, was empowered, and Who died in the power (Spirit) of God. His was a spiritual life in that He, as no other, knew and felt a dependence on God and lived in the power of God. And the most effective and encouraging evidence of the power of God in and upon Jesus was the resurrection (Rom. 8:11). I like to say, in poetic fashion, that Jesus' empty tomb is the opening through which God breathes the fresh air of His new life into our stifling world.

After Jesus' earthly life and from His position and power as the resurrected One He sends the Holy Spirit, Who continues to be the fresh air supply of the people of God. Pentecost was the occasion of the coming of the Holy Spirit in a full and normative way. That is, it is normal and natural since Pentecost for persons to approach the Son, because the Spirit has born witness to Him, and to come to the Father because of the Spirit's power to enable people to believe. If we were doing theology in a logical order, we would discuss Father, Son, Spirit. But we are coming at the doctrine of God just as we came to God in our Christian experience. We were led by the Spirit to accept the Son who pointed us to the Father.[5] The breath of God takes a new, redemptive freshness in Jesus. And it takes a powerful, continuing presence through the Holy Spirit.

Pentecost began the full redemptive era of the Holy Spirit in history, just as Bethlehem began the fresh breath of Jesus in history. Both the Son and the Spirit were in the beginning with the Father. But both the Son and the Spirit had a specific definitive entry point in our history. Pentecost was the coming of the Spirit to give us a sustained breath of God. The Jewish festival of Pentecost was fifty (*pente*) days after Passover. This initial, historic coming of the Spirit was accompanied by a rushing wind (power), tongues of fire (cleansing), and tongues (both other languages, *dialektoi,* and ecstatic utterances, *glossa*).[6] The power of God, the Holy Spirit, breathed life into the church, the body of Christ.

Ever since that occasion, the Spirit is the breath that renews the church by the adding of new parts (persons) to the body of Christ and by giving vitality (gifts) to the body. There may be times in which certain parts of the body of Christ are energized to a greater extent—the periods throughout history of the renewal of the church. And there may be periods in the lives of individuals when they are more open to the Breath of God. But there has not been a time since Pentecost when the body of Christ has been without the Breath of the Spirit. The fresh breath begun in Jesus is continued by the Spirit, and this is the life of the people of God. Just as the world could not exist if God withdrew His creative/sustaining breath, even so, the church could not exist if God withdrew the Holy Spirit, His redemptive/consummating breath.

Pentecost began the happy, traumatic life of the infant church that set that body to breathing. And the mature completed body of Christ will be the bride of Christ (Eph. 5). These mixed metaphors mean that God channels His redemptive witness through the church (as carefully defined in chapter 2) even as He channels the creative, sustaining power of His life through the natural world. As one has rightly said, the inner life of the people of God is parallel to the outer life of the history of the world.[7] It is the Breath of God that permits both the world and the church to live. It is the fresh Breath of God in Jesus Christ through the Spirit that permits the church to live in a world like this. Pentecost is about breathing, God breathing into life His redemptive community.

There is much discussion in the life of the church today as to whether the traumatic gasps of fresh air with which the church began is the way in which the church should continue to breathe. That is, should we expect the unusual acts of the Spirit in the Book of Acts of the Apostles to be the norm for the church's breathing? Are the special gifts of healing, casting out the evil one, and raising the dead the gifts of breathing that are the regular and permanent way that the church should breathe? As I suggested above, God's power can empower the church in any way; but the remainder of the New Testament and of the life of the church in history would lead us to believe that the first traumatic breathing of the church is not the sustained pattern of breathing by which the church ordinarily lives. For the automatic, regular breathing of the body of Christ we need to look at the writings of Paul and John. Chapter 8 of Romans gives us a capsule digest of Paul's understanding of the formative work of the Spirit in bringing to life the body of Christ. A detailed sketch of that chapter will help us to see the regular breathing of God's life into His people.

The "life-giving law of the Spirit has set you [us] free from the law of sin and death" (Rom. 8:2). And our "conduct [is] no longer under the control of our lower nature, [it] is directed by the Spirit" (v. 4). Life and peace is the outlook of those living "on the level of the spirit" (v. 6). God's Spirit must dwell in God's people. "If a man does not possess the Spirit of Christ, he is no Christian" (v. 9). And this Spirit who possesses and empowers us is the same Spirit (power of God) that raised Jesus from the dead and gives "new life to [our] mortal bodies" (v. 11). "For all who are moved by the Spirit of God are sons of God" (v. 14). It is the Spirit who leads us to call upon God the Father with the same familiar "Abba" that Jesus used (v. 16). This is the breath of freedom, not slavery. By it we become members of God's family, His heirs (vv. 15, 17). The Spirit of God helps the children of God in their weakness by aiding us in prayer (vv. 26–28). Many times we begin our reading of Romans 8 with the familiar and comforting promise of "All things work together for good" (v. 28). It should be noted that the breath and basis of that promise is the normal breathing of the Spirit's work in verses 1–27.

Chapters 12—14 of 1 Corinthians give Paul's understanding of how God's Spirit sustains the body of Christ through the gifts of the Spirit. In the listing of the gifts of the energizing Spirit, Paul names structural gifts and dynamic gifts (1 Cor. 12:27–31). These gifts are to be used as different parts of the body of Christ (1 Cor. 12:14–26). Each Christian does not have all of the gifts of the Spirit. But every Christian has the essential gifts of the Spirit: faith, hope, and love (13:1–13). Secondary gifts come after that and can be ranked in order of their usefulness. Those gifts which build up the individual (for example, tongues) are subservient to those gifts that build up the whole body of Christ (for example, clear proclamation, prophetic preaching). All gifts ultimately are to promote the welfare of the whole body, and all gifts must be used in an orderly way, for the "God who inspires them is not a God of disorder but of peace" (14:33). The gifts of the Spirit issue into the fruits of the Spirit (Gal. 5:22–26). So it is that individuals are born of the breath of the Spirit, added to the body of Christ, and enabled to live by the gifts of the life-giving Spirit. Birth and nurture require breathing. God gives the air.

John's Gospel is written about events before Pentecost; but it is written from a post-Pentecostal perspective. The historical life and death of Jesus are seen in the power and remembrance of the Spirit. John, as well as Paul, parallels the spiritual breath with the natural act of breathing in the creation. John's Gospel is the new Genesis.[8]

The light of creation is paralleled by the light of redemptive shining in Jesus Christ. The creative act of the Spirit who came on chaos is paralleled by the redemptive act of the Spirit who comes upon Jesus (John 1:32–33). The breath which gave life to the first Adam is a parallel to the spiritual birth in Christ (3:5–8). The Creator God who formed the world by His breath is the spiritual God whose worship is life for the redeemed (see 4:23–24). The promise of a Messiah (Gen. 3:15) is extended by the Messiah's promise of the Spirit (John 14—16). This Spirit of truth, of remembrance, is the Convicter of the world (16:8–11) even as the Spirit in Genesis was the creating agent of the world.

Paul and John speak the fullest words about the Spirit in the New Testament. Their words speak of a regular pattern of breathing that brings into being and sustains the people of God. The ecstatic, traumatic birth of the church brought the fresh gasps of air the infant church needed. This breathing pattern may occur again when healing and renewal are needed in the body of Christ. But, for the most part, the breathing pattern of the church is a well regulated breathing that incorporates and enables the body of Christ to have the life of God in the power of the Spirit. In Scripture the life of the world and the life of the church are as natural as breathing. The first breath for all the world is life, the deepest breath for the world is eternal life. It is natural to breathe in order to survive physically. It is normal to breathe God's fresh breath of air in Jesus—to exist spiritually. When we separate the breath of God from the natural and the normal, we concentrate too much on the act of breathing. When we concentrate too much on how we are breathing, we do not breathe well. Paying too much attention to natural and normal processes can produce irregular and strained breathing. It is good to accept the breath God gives in our day-to-day living. It is appropriate to receive the redemptive fresh breath of God in our renewal and resourcefulness as the people of God.

Various Breathing Techniques

In the full course of life there are a variety of breathing techniques. When born, we gasp for air. When overexerted, we pant; when ill, we breathe shallow breaths. Sometimes we hyperventilate. On certain occasions special breathing devices are used to promote breathing. There is easy breathing and labored breathing. I want to select four breathing techniques to use as analogies for the four ways in which the Christian community has felt it has breathed the breath of God, received the Holy Spirit.

Some Christians feel that the Spirit comes through the Christian community by special rites or rituals. These acts are called sacraments, and this is the sacramental view. This view is somewhat like an oxygen mask. Pure oxygen is available to help breathing. The theory is that the human organism requires, almost daily, special assistance. Special and extraordinary help is needed. This oxygen mask approach is generally and primarily related to sacramental communities. Yet Protestants who insist on certain rituals as required for salvation—making one's profession in a certain way, being baptized only after a special kind of religious experience, and so forth—can be viewed as using the oxygen-mask model to a certain extent. This mode of understanding as the only model usually requires special assistance. Just as special medical personnel are required to supervise oxygen breathing, so licensed spiritual personnel are required to administer spiritual oxygen. This spiritual "oxygen" is available only from certain sources, and it is breathed only at particular times. Oxygen-mask breathing is designed to help one out of trouble or to make it easier to breathe in time of crisis.

A second breathing technique as a model for understanding the reception of the Spirit is hyperventilation. In the experience of hyperventilating, one breathes rapidly. The system is flushed with excitement. The whole pace of the breathing apparatus is accelerated. It seems to me that charismatic Christians who require the excitement and rapid pace of some special gift of the Spirit use the spiritual breathing technique of hyperventilation. It is not generally possible to sustain this technique of hyperventilation without throwing the system into some abnormal condition. When there are breath-denying conditions present, a person may need to breathe extraordinarily fast and with a sense of excitement. Hyperventilation is a condition that can give a surcharge of energy, most of which is spent upon breathing itself.

Mysticism is like holding one's breath. The mystic is one who, by great concentration and discipline, comes to a special experience with God. Paul was given, as a special gift, a vision of God which placed him in the immediate presence of God (2 Cor. 12:1–5). There is much debate as to whether mysticism is a direct gift of God or whether the mystical state can be induced by the individual. Ordinary people can't hold their breath, or at least are not practiced enough in doing so, until they lose consciousness. The mystic model of holding one's breath seems certainly reserved for special occasions and possibly only for special people.

A fourth breathing technique is the nonreflective, spontaneous breathing we all do in the process of living. I relate this "natural" breathing technique to the Spirit breathing life-through-the-Word-of-God model. By this I mean that one ordinarily receives the Spirit by hearing and accepting the biblical message of salvation and of spiritual growth. It is as natural for Christians to live out of Scripture as it is for persons to breathe. Obviously, I seem to have "stacked the deck" so that the breathing technique my tradition ordinarily uses receives the best model. But I would want also to indicate that all four of these breathing techniques, when adequately defined, could be seen as inclusive rather than exclusive. While not sacramental in a technical way, baptism and the Lord's Supper are special moments in the life of the Christian. And the oxygen-use model is not altogether an unhappy one. Too much oxygen, an excess of the Spirit, can be a peculiar and occasional circumstance in which special gifts of the Spirit are "aired." The deep-breathing techniques of holding or regulating the breath can produce "altered states of consciousness," and it is, in my opinion, still possible to be given a special vision of God we could style mystical. It should be obvious that I feel that the church lives out of the Bible. This is the normative way we breathe regularly. It may be that the wisdom of the Spirit has given Himself in all of these models so that at all times and in many ways the body of Christ may breathe deeply and be kept vital and alive.

Breathing is something we seniors want very much to keep doing. Until some special problem arises, we do not think much about it. God has given us His breath, first in the creative act of life itself and finally in eternal life through Jesus Christ, our Lord, in the power of the Spirit. Spirit is the dimension of God. Spirit is the breath of God. Spirit is as personal, intimate, and necessary as breathing. Through the Spirit's witness to Jesus Christ the idea of Spirit takes on "personhood." Spirit is God's way of being God. Spirit is God's way of blowing His cosmos together. And the Holy Spirit is God's way of supplying the fresh breath of air the world requires to be redeemed. The poet said:

> Speak to Him, thou, for He hears,
> And Spirit with Spirit can meet—
> Closer is He than breathing,
> And nearer than hands and feet.[9]

God said, "I will pour out my spirit on all mankind" (Joel 2:28). At Bethlehem He began His fresh breath, at Pentecost He confirmed it, in the breath of the body of Christ He continues it, and at the last day He will rebreathe a new heaven and a new earth. Two words of advice are in order. Keep breathing! Relax and breathe deeply of the Spirit!

Notes

1. Compare Paul Ricoeur's well-known dictum, "The symbol gives rise to thought" in *The Symbolism of Evil,* trans. Emerson Buchanan (New York: Harper & Row, 1967), "Conclusion," pp. 347–357. Also see *Freud and Philosophy: An Essay on Interpretation,* trans. Denis Savage (New Haven: Yale University Press, 1970), p. 38.

2. For good but very technical discussion of the Greek New Testament idea of Spirit, see Eduard Schweizer's article in *Theological Dictionary of the New Testament,* vol. 6, eds. Gerhard Friedrich and Gerhard Kittel, trans. G. W. Bromiley (Grand Rapids, Mich.: Eerdmans, 1968), pp. 332–455.

3. For a more extended, philosophical discussion of these points, see John Macquarrie, *Principles of Christian Theology,* 2nd ed. (New York: Scribner, 1977), pp. 211–238; *Contemporary Religious Thinkers: From Idealist Metaphysicians to Existential Theologians* (New York: Harper & Row, 1968); and *Twentieth Century Religious Thought: The Frontiers of Philosophy and Theology, 1900–1980* (New York: Charles Scribner's, 1981).

4. This should not be taken to mean that Jesus received it for the first time or was adopted by the Spirit. Rather we should see this as a special empowering for ministry and a further clarification of Jesus' earthly growth in the Spirit. See Luke 2:52.

5. For an entire book using this approach to God, see Henry Pitney Van Dusen, *Spirit, Son, and Father: Christian Faith in the Light of the Holy Spirit* (New York: Scribner, 1958).

6. For a more detailed discussion of Acts 2 and of the meaning of speaking in tongues see my *Theology for Children,* Appendix C, and my article, "Glossolalia in the New Testament," in Watson Mills (ed.), *Speaking in Tongues: Let's Talk About It* (Waco: Word Books, 1973), pp. 48–60.

7. Karl Barth, *Church Dogmatics,* vol. 3, pt. 1., trans. G. W. Bromiley and T. F. Torrance (Edinburgh: T. & T. Clark, 1958), § 41 "Creation and Covenant," especially section 3,

"The Covenant and the Internal Basis of Creation," pp. 228–329.

8. Compare Raymond Brown, *The Gospel According to John,* The Anchor Bible, 2 vols. (Garden City, N.Y.: Doubleday, 1966, 1970), vol. 1, pp. 4–8,23–27.

9. Alfred Lord Tennyson, "The Higher Pantheism" [1869], stanza 6, in *The Poems and Plays of Alfred Lord Tennyson* (New York: Modern Library, 1938), p. 720.

7

Children

Where would the world be without children? It would be without a future. "Children" is a subject that engenders its own enthusiasm. All of us used to be children. Many of us are returning more often to childhood memories, and, unfortunately, some of us are returning to childish ways. Every senior is an "expert" on children. Those who have the fewest or none at all often offer the most advice. And as to grandchildren, they are a class unto themselves. One bumper sticker says, "Let me tell you about my grandchildren." Most grandparents do not wait for permission. They usually proceed at full speed. It does, however, need to be acknowledged that as we grow older, children seem to grow noisier. I have often said, especially to middle-aged parents of young children, the Lord knew what He was doing when He gave children to young people. We need to acknowledge also that those who have never had children of their own, nevertheless, can and do have fulfilled lives. It is necessary to recognize that children can turn out badly. Parenting is ambiguous. It is a risk. Sometimes we lose, and the losses are painful and permanent. Despite these exceptions, children are worth having. They invite loving. They light up our lives.

It seems particularly appropriate that we discuss Jesus Christ, God's Son, under the metaphor of children. All of the warmth, the promise, the joys associated with childhood are truly analogous to our relationships and experiences with Him. It is traditional, in books of theology, to discuss the person of Christ and then the work of Christ. I am not going to do that. People are what they do. It is artificial to separate person and work. Christ is a whole person, and He brings the resources of who He is to bear on what He does. And He does what He does because He is who He is.[1] His person and His performance constitute one unified divine event. His eventful life, death, and resurrection comprise our planet's biggest event. An event is composed of what happened, how what happened was interpreted, and how the happening and the interpretation influence and shape what comes after them. A stone thrown into a pond makes waves throughout the entire body of water. The "rock of Zion," cast into the waters of our world, has created ripples and reverberations that reach eternity. With the birth of each child the world is changed. With the birth of this Child all of heaven and earth are affected.

Most of the traditional topics found in books about the person and work of Jesus Christ are included in terms we draw from childhood.

1. Children are usually eagerly expected and fervently hoped for (the prophecy of His coming and the purpose He fulfills).

2. The birth of a child is a time of celebration (Bethlehem was no exception).

3. Every child born has a birthright to be loved. (Jesus gave up this birthright to accomplish the Father's purpose.)

4. Children are dependent and innocent. (Jesus as the child of God drew His resources from the Father. His innocence, while being greatly tested, did not waver—sinlessness.)

5. We celebrate the growing up and the achievements of our children. (We remember the mighty works and the teachings of Jesus.)

6. There are tragic possibilities inherent in having children. (Jesus' suffering and death involve the sorrow of the Father.)

7. Most children who are loved by their parents assume that they can depend on their parents in crises. Their parents will see them through (what better phrase to describe the resurrection of Christ!).

8. Parents are justly proud of the honest, legitimate accomplishments of their children.

9. "Look what my son did!" (In the great accomplishment of Jesus, providing our salvation, the Father rejoices and is glorified.)

10. Some eager parents want "many children." (The Father has purposed a family circle as wide as humanity with Christ as elder brother.)

11. Since the invention of photography, parents have kept the makers of film for cameras in business. "We have lots of pictures!" (There are many assessments, snapshots, full-length portraits, and so forth, of the Son; beginning with the Gospels, His followers ever since have been presenting His picture in a variety of ways.)

These eleven experiences associated with childhood can be related to a description of God's child, Jesus.

A Long-Expected Unexpected Child

Children today are big business. In developed countries, many markets are aimed at them: food, clothing, education, entertainment, and so forth. Having children is a complex issue. Shall we, shall we not? When? How many? The distribution of children seems unequitable, to say the least. In some countries and societies they seem cheaper by the dozen. Elsewhere, having children for someone else threatens to become a business. It is a mark of our developed technological society that we have put the production of human life on an economic, technological basis. The most populous country in the world has limited each family to one child. And the culture of that country prefers that the one child be a male. In that country—China—abortions are legal and encouraged. A perceptive Chinese asked, "What will it mean in fifty years when spoiled, male, only children are running the country?" In the wealthiest country in the world, America, more families are having fewer children. More couples are preferring to have no children. More couples who cannot have children are using every avenue to acquire a child.

We have become, in the matter of having children very clever but not necessarily wise. Is it a natural, inherent inclination of couples to desire children? Do all women want to be mothers? The polls are still out, and the specialists disagree. We cannot read all experiences from our own experience. We can suggest that there are some children who are much expected and dearly loved. We must conclude that it is the birthright of every child who is born to be loved. In the light of God's incarnate life among us, we can affirm the goodness of life that God, the giver of life, comes down on the side of life in ethical decisions. Life, as God's first gift, is to be cherished, nourished, and made abundant. All of these things the baby Jesus teaches us.

He was a "long-awaited child" by all the world and a nonexpected child by his "parents." By this I mean that the appointment (Eph. 1:3–12) and promise (Gen. 3:16) of God were from eternity and from the first history of the race. But Mary and Joseph had not expected a child at that time in their engagement. This long-awaited, yet immediately unexpected, paradox of Christmas speaks of both planning and spontaneity. In the history of God's planning, certain promises and prophecies were important. They came to focus in this unexpected child. The promises and prophecies of a long-awaited child spoke of good overcoming evil (Gen. 3:15). There was a promise to the father of faith, Abraham, that his seed would bless the earth (Gen. 12:1–3). There was the promise to David, a shepherd/psalmist, who became king, that there should always be an heir to his throne (2 Sam. 7:16). To people who walked in darkness there was the promise of light (Isa. 9:2). Those weary of war were promised that swords should be turned into plows (Isa. 2:4; Mic. 4:3). Persons who felt the estrangement in the world of nature were told of a time when the wolf and the lamb would lie down together (Isa. 11:6). The cold and sick were assured that "the sun of righteousness [would] arise with healing in his wings" (Mal. 4:2). There was good news for the lame, the mute, the blind, and for prisoners (Isa. 61:1–2). There was the promise of a child whose name would be "Wonderful, Counselor, The mighty God, The everlasting Father, The Prince of Peace" (Isa. 9:6, KJV).

Great expectations! God's expectations. Were they too much to be placed on one small child? An unexpected child in one sense and the most-expected child in another. And then, in the fullness of time, the child was announced to the unexpecting parents: a young maiden who did not understand but who gathered up in one song (Luke 1:46–55, we call it the Magnificat) all of the expectations and promises of the people of God. She was overshadowed by God's Spirit and informed by angelic messenger of the coming of her child. The father, who knew he was not the father, was reassured by an angel. And the child was on the way. His parents were on their way to an appointment with the Roman government. And the whole world was on the way toward its redemption. Once the child is on the way, the theoretical questions with which we started this section pale into insignificance. But the paradox of a long-expected yet unexpected child grows larger.

The Celebration of His Birth

What was there to celebrate? There was the embarrassment of a not-yet married couple who were expecting a child. There was the arduous trip to Bethlehem. There was poverty. There was no appropriate place for a child to be born. But there was more to those who would take the time to hear and be available to hear. There were the announcements of God. Did they fade in the midst of the problems? It would certainly have been natural. It would not be blameworthy. Keep the visions and announcements of God bright. Sometimes that is all the light there is. When it happened, the birth, the painful natural birth, there was joy. It was the conception of Jesus that was virginal. The birth was really like every other actual birth. There was at least a manger. Thank God for some shelter. There were linen strips used to bind the newborn and to wind the dead. There was a star.[2] Stars help dark nights.

To the shepherds, there were angels. To Mary, there was wonder and the intrusion of curious guests with talk of angel song. To Joseph, who knows? Relief, delight, renewed determination. In a palace there was a cruel king. In a faraway place there were Magi, the legends about them would grow longer than their journey. The marvel of Christmas is in its simplicity. The beauty of Christmas is in the determination that it shall happen.

The purpose of Christmas is as complex and complete as the plan of God. This child was to save His people from their sins (Luke 1:77; see Matt. 1:21). This child was purposed to be God with us, Emmanuel (Matt. 1:23). This child, visited by shepherds, was to become the Good Shepherd (John 10:11). He came in order to increase the quality of life (John 10:10). His first and foremost purpose was to do the will of God (Heb. 10:7–9). Evil would complicate His purpose if it could, for He came to destroy the work of the devil (1 John 3:7–8). What is the purpose of a child? To live and to continue the line of life. Mary had much to ponder in her heart (Luke 2:51). The Father had purpose and pain in His heart. But for the moment, it was celebration. Both mother and child were well.

Later we began to see that the cry of the newborn was the melody line for God's symphony. We would count back forty days and start to march to the cradle. Each year His people would move toward His birth, even as He moved toward (Advent) them and the possibility of rebirth. We celebrate at His birth the worth of every child. And we celebrate at His birth the decision of God to unite Himself with His world in the frailty of a human child. We celebrate at Christmas the humanity of God, the humanizing of God, the willingness of God to become one with us by becoming one of us. Ideologically and philosophically, all of this rhapsodic poetry does not seem very impressive. But to all who rejoice and celebrate the wonder of the birth of a child, it seems like the best way in the world for God to express Himself.

A Birthright of Love

Every child born has a birthright of love. This is so because God, the Author of life, delights in His creation. Since God loves His world and has invested each human life with worth, every child has a right to be loved. Unfortunately, it is not the case that every child born is loved. There are many unwanted, unloved, abused children. These have been deprived of their birthright by selfish and sinful conditions in our world. Jesus identifies with and represents all of the unwanted and underprivileged children. There was acceptance and nurture by His own family. There was an eternal and never-faltering love from His eternal Father. But in most other quarters there was hatred, misunderstanding, and betrayal. The birthright of love begins at birth and continues throughout life. This means that each person, throughout life, has the right to be loved and affirmed. By being born, you are worthy in God's sight. I stress this privilege which begins at birth, in order to emphasize the love of God, which does not wait upon our accomplishments before it is given. Even the birth of Jesus teaches us something about the love of God and something about the nature of our world.

This child of destiny, the second Adam (Rom. 5:12–19), had to suffer the results of the mistakes of the first Adam and all of his descendants. In starting a new "race," Jesus had to cope with and overcome the evils of an old "race." There was no room for Him at birth. He was a fugitive child marked for death. And what Herod the Great did not accomplish, Herod Antipas was able to help bring about later. Jesus accepted the baptism for sinners although He did not need it. Jesus was thoroughly tempted (Heb. 4:15) by the evil one (Luke 4:1–13; Matt. 4:1–11; Mark 1:12–13), by crowds who wanted Him to be a bread Messiah (John 6:15), and by a friend who sounded like the devil (Matt. 16:21–23). Jesus' earliest friends and followers unintentionally misunderstood Him. The religious leaders of His day intentionally and persistently misunderstood Him. His immediate family sought to deter Him from ministry in order to save them embarrassment. He had a very hostile environment. Finally, His own people handed Him over to foreigners. And His reward for being a man who went around doing good (Acts 10:38) was to be hanged on a Roman cross.[3] His birthright of love became, to all appearances, a legacy of hate.

It is a travesty and an outrage for individuals or society to subvert or prevent the birthright of love for any child. It was a cosmic crime that Jesus' birthright of love became a legacy of hate. There is, however, an even more astonishing fact. There is a sense in which the infant Jesus, grown to manhood, surrendered His birthright for the sake of others. Most of us remember and condemn the hasty sale of Esau's birthright for a mess of pottage (Gen. 25:29–34). Jesus' forfeiture of the world's love was for a larger reason (Mark 10:45). It was for the redemption of the world. Jesus did not invite the hostility He faced in childhood. But He did accept and encourage what He suffered as a man.

It was the love of God which made Him do it. For, according to the plan of God, it was the will of God that by the surrender of Jesus' birthright of love to the hatred of the world the world could be saved (John 3:16). His life was not just taken from Him, He surrendered it (John 10:17–18). This man child in the Promised Land secured the birthright of love for the human race. Crimes against childhood are special crimes against the love of God. They violate the birthright of every child for which Jesus gave up His own birthright. It is true. "Jesus loves the little children,/All the children of the world." And because He faced hostility as a child, He can identify with injustices to them. And because He faced a legacy of hate as a man, He can redeem them.

Dependent

One indisputable fact about all children is that they are dependent. The human young are dependent longer than any other creature. It is the helplessness of childhood that brings out the best and the worst in people who care for children. Parental instincts are some of our highest and holiest impulses. It is the absolute dependence of children that brings out the protective impulses in us. Jesus' dependence on the Father was complete. It is hard for American independent adolescents to relate to the sayings of Jesus as a grown man that He always did the will of His Father. Two things need to be remembered. In ancient cultures and in many modern ones, relations between fathers and sons are different than they are in "liberated" Western cultures. Second, Jesus was dependent on God as Father. God is the only Father Whose love expresses itself always and only on behalf of the other. God's unconditional love and complete trust in the Son made it possible for Jesus to be completely dependent on Him.

The dependency of childhood is touchingly expressed in innocence. Innocence is characterized not so much by not knowing things. Innocence is characterized by complete trust. Children, who have had no reason to learn otherwise, believe what they are told, do what they are asked, and expect to be given what is promised. In these ways God's "holy child Jesus" (Acts 4:27, 30, KJV) was always innocent in His relationship with God the Father.[4] Jesus was also innocent in His relation to the world. This means that He put trust in people, expected and practiced honesty and candor, and committed himself and His unswerving principles even to those He knew would not keep faith with Him. This was not naiveté. "He knew what was in man" (John 2:25, KJV). This kind of innocence expresses itself without guile because that is the only way in which such a person can act. His dependency on the Father was self-fulfilling. The innocence of His relationship with God is foolish to the cynics, but it is salvation for the sinners. His innocence in relation to the world would occasion His death.

He was innocent also in relation to any personal guilt or wrongdoing (Heb. 4:15). The temptations of Jesus, like our own, were tailor-made. The "in all points tempted like as we are" in Hebrews does not mean that He underwent every specific trial, testing, wicked impulse or particular sinful inclination which each person in the world undergoes. The sinlessness of Jesus does mean that He was as thoroughly tested at His level and by whatever would be for Him as genuine a test as anyone can have. His sinlessness was not just the result of His divine nature. His innocence, expressed in His sinlessness, was the result of His complete resistance to evil and of the total determination of His entire person not go give in. His sinlessness was accomplished because of His absolute dependence upon God. He trusted in God, even when tempted. And His temptations had to do with His relationship to God, even as ours do. He would be God's "child" in the way in which God wanted Him to be; for only in this way could He accomplish the Father's will and be fulfilled in His own mission. His path lay in being a suffering servant, not a bread messiah, or a spectacular messiah, or a compromising messiah (Matt. 4:1–11; Luke 4:1–13).

His baptism and His temptations were integrally connected. His baptism was an act of obedience, and through that experience God clarified Jesus' messianic task. "Thou are my beloved Son" is a rendering of Psalm 2. It was a Psalm of exalted messianic expectation. "In whom I am well pleased" is a quote from the Suffering Servant passage of Isaiah 42. The divine voice gave guidance to Jesus as to the shape of His messianic task. The first period of temptation placed great strain upon doing God's task some other way than by suffering and death. Jesus was dependent on the Father for the guidance in what kind of Messiah He would be (the baptism), and He was dependent on the Father to hold fast to His determination to follow the will of God (the temptation).

Jesus was dependent on the Father in His innocence, His sinlessness, and His temptations. He was also dependent on the Father through His experience of prayer. "He went away to a lonely spot and remained there in prayer" (Mark 1:35). "He departed into a mountain to pray" (Mark 6:46, KJV). When He taught His disciples to pray (Matt. 6:9–13), He taught them to depend on God for the future ("thy kingdom come"), for daily necessities (daily bread), for spiritual sustenance ("lead us not into temptation," KJV), for deliverance from evil ("Save us from the evil one"). All of this is because all power, all rights, and all fulfillment are from God. In the moment of His greatest crisis (Gethsemane) He prayed His greatest prayer of petition and intercession (John 17). His petition that the cup might pass from Him was denied so that His intercession on our behalf might be accomplished. And at the last He trusted in God and commended His spirit into the Father's hands (Luke 23:46). For Jesus that was where matters always lay, in His Father's hands. His life of dependence ended in dependence to the end in order that God's creation could be independent of sin and death. Part of the charm and drawing power of Jesus lay in His innocence, His dependence, and

His commitment to God. These are childlike traits. And through them He effected the adoption of the children of God.

Growing Up

Let me give you a word of advice about family reunions. The old love them because old people have a long family narrative and many memories. The young tolerate family reunions because they do want to belong and to relate to their peer groups. But the young feel very awkward when Great Aunt Martha, who has not seen them for ten years, keeps exclaiming, "My, how you have grown!" Unless there is some physical abnormality, that is the way it should be. Children do grow up. At least they grow up physically. There is little a parent can do to stop that. Unfortunately, spiritual, mental, and psychological development are not automatic. There are ways parents can block these phases of growth. Even aged parents of middle-aged people can stunt some phases of their children's growth.

Jesus grew "in wisdom and stature, and in favour with God and man" (Luke 2:52, KJV). Those ancient words are the best description I know of what we mean today by a well-rounded, healthy growing person. It is possible to draw a picture of what a Jewish boy in Israel, in the time of Jesus, may have experienced.[5] But it is not possible to know with any degree of certainty what Jesus specifically underwent as He was growing up. It is likely that Joseph would have been considerably older than Mary, if theirs was an average match of the period. It is also probable that Joseph died before the beginning of Jesus' ministry because we hear nothing about Joseph in the Gospels. Jesus, as oldest son, would have had the major responsibility for the family after Joseph's death. There may have been a period as carpenter's apprenticeship reflected in the invitation: "Take my yoke upon you, . . . for my yoke is easy, and my burden is light" (Matt. 11:29–30, KJV).

There certainly must have been trauma when Jesus decided to leave home and wander as a well-known prophet. His one attempt to bring family and friends together ended in an embarrassing situation. It is probable that His unexpected disciples occasioned the wine shortage at Cana's wedding feast. And there were spirited words (John 2:1–11). The one attempt of His family to persuade Him to forego His prophetic calling must have ended in what seemed to them like a rebuke (Matt. 12:46–50). There was no permanent estrangement. Mary was, as we shall see, at the cross. But there was definitely a time of "growing up." Part of His growth came through adversity and suffering (Heb. 2:18; 5:7–9).

The fruits and proofs of His growth were dramatically illustrated in His miracles and His teachings. His miracles were signs of the presence of God with Him. In His process of growth Jesus learned how to use the power of God in a redemptive way. There was no miracle mongering. There was no use of the gift of God in a showy, selfish way. Miracles were evidences of God's power. And Jesus was always quick to affirm that His power came from God (Matt. 9:6–8; 28:18). Miracles were evidence also of Christ's great compassion (Matt. 9:36; 14:14; 15:32; 18:27; 20:34). But His maturity helped Him to know when He must feed them no more bread. The primary purpose of Jesus' mighty works (This is a more accurate translation than the philosophically overfreighted term *miracle.*) was to show what God would ultimately do for all of His people when He finally and completely redeemed them. Were God's people oppressed by the evil one? Jesus' exorcisms (for example, Mark 1:23-28; 3:11–12; 5:1–20; 6:7; 7:24–30) were preludes to the time when God would finally shut away the evil one (Rev. 20:1–5). Were there sickness and sorrow? Always! Jesus healed some and alleviated their sorrow as a token of what God would do when He wipes "every tear from their eyes" (Rev. 21:4). Was not humanity always prey to the last enemy, death? Yes! But by raising the dead, Jesus gave a prelude of His own resurrection as the firstfruits of that time when God will do away with the last enemy, death (1 Cor. 15:12–28; especially v. 26; Rev. 20:1–8; 21:4). Even the world of nature could threaten God's people and God's Son. Yet He could still the waves as a preview of a new heaven and a new earth (Rev. 21:1) in which all the former things were passed away.

We cannot leave Jesus at Bethlehem. The baby had to grow, for He had to "work the works of him" who sent Him, while it was yet day (John 9:4). Too often Christians have reveled in the Christ child and have denied Him the growth that was necessary. The Christ child does not threaten us. The grown-up Jesus can drive money changers from the Temple, call hypocrites to account, and can hold before us the radical demands of the kingdom of God. There is among us a kind of theological stifling of Jesus' growth, so that He cannot really meet us with His demands. This backfires. It is not the "real" Jesus we have. It is a dangerous picture, made from our own expectations. It is a chilling thought that the innocent, youthful, innocuous Jesus of our own tailoring will be replaced at the time of accounting by the authentic full-grown Jesus of the Gospels.

The mighty works were one evidence of God's power through the growing Jesus. Jesus' teaching about God was a second legacy of the full-grown Son of God. Jesus' teachings reflected wisdom. He taught by precept and example. He taught by parables and by direct injunction. He was not always tactful in His rebuke of religious hypocrisy (Matt. 16). But He was always patient with those whom others would not acknowledge, the tax collectors, women of ill repute, children, Gentiles, even Romans. His teaching could be baffling. "It is easier for a camel to pass through the eye of a needle, than for a rich man to enter the Kingdom of God" (Matt. 19:24; Mark 10:25; Luke 18:25). His teaching could dramatically portray the concern of God as a waiting Father, as a distraught woman who had lost her "engagement ring," or as a searching shepherd seeking one lost sheep (Luke 15). He likened the requisite faith of the Kingdom to the faith of a child (Matt. 18:2–4). He taught His disciples to love one another (John 15:11–17). And He taught one of them so well that his letter would measure discipleship in terms of loving action (1 John 4:7–21). Even "the opposition" recognized that He was a teacher come from God (John 3:2). His content and His method demonstrated that He had grown in God and with God.[6]

Just as we cannot attribute His sinlessness only to His divine nature, so we cannot attribute His teachings only to directly revealed divine content. The revelation of the divine content came along with His growth and the powers of observation He used as the total person He was and is. Bethlehem was not just a stage setting to get Him on the scene so He could die. Growing up in Nazareth was not just a marking of time until He could do miracles and teach. There was, in the growing up, grace and guidance on God's part and commitment and learning on Jesus' part. He became obedient (and knowledgeable) by the things He suffered (Heb. 2:9–18; 5:8). And He became aware in His dependence on the will and the way of God. He became a man who went around doing good (Acts 10:38) because He had a good relationship with the God who was absolute goodness (10:14–30). He taught as one having authority (Matt. 7:29) because God was His authority (Gr. *exousia*), the essence out of which He lived.

Before you know it, the children grow up and make their contributions. Do not despise the little ones. Do not downgrade the fledgling achievements of young people. Do not suppose that because you "knew them when" and are neighbors that they cannot surprise you with what they can do (Mark 6:3). Remember Jesus. He grew up, and the world has never been the same. Just be sure you do not regard Him only at the stage of the infant of Christmas. Do not neutralize His lordship by conceiving of Him as a "nice young man." It is true that He died relatively young. But from Him came the knowledge of eternity, and in Him there was the knowledge of the years. In His growing up He never outgrew His dependence on God. And we should not outgrow our necessary dependence on them both, this Father who sent a dependable Son and this Son who had an utter dependence on the Father.

Tragic Possibilities

Children are to be "worried over." It is their dependence and our responsibility which causes us concern about them. I once knew a deacon whose wife was a classic worrier about their grandchildren. He once said jokingly, "Grandmother is going to be terribly disappointed if those children live to grow up." He meant by this that she was exceptionally anxious about the children and about what might harm them. There are tragic possibilities for children. Some of them do not live to grow up. It seems particularly bad when a childhood sickness leaves a child permanently damaged. Accidents which maim a child have lifelong implications. A play called *Twentieth Century Lullaby*[7] is a tragedy. Its setting is a time in which war, crime, and all kinds of threatening possibilities pertain. The young mother begins to brood over all these potential threats. The tragic climax of the play is that she finally takes the life of her own child rather than have him grow up in a world in which so much pain and problems might be his fate. This is an exaggerated situation. Good will prevail. These are our affirmations. When we read the life story of Jesus, however, we can understand Mary's anxiety. And as we reflect on the cross that is always in God's heart, we can believe that His pain has enduring consequences.

One of the Old Testament phrases which was applied to Jesus was that He was "a man of sorrows, and acquainted with grief" (Isa. 53:3, KJV). This does not mean that Jesus himself was a sad or depressed person. It does mean that at the purely human level things did not turn out well for Him. Jesus was an essentially positive person. He refused to give in to the carping criticism of those who viewed His ministry with suspicion and hostility. It is hard living in a climate of anger and deliberate misunderstanding. Jesus' public ministry was not pleasant from the viewpoint of what people thought about Him. It is particularly vexing to suffer ill for doing good. It is obvious that Jesus was sensitive. This is demonstrated by His acts and attitude of compassion. He must have felt keenly the obvious, necessary estrangement from His immediate family. Jesus makes a wonderful older brother (Rom. 8:29). There is every reason to suppose that the brothers and sisters who grew up in His home had a lively, kind, and helpful older brother. Their inability to understand His prophetic calling must have grieved Him deeply.

Mark's Gospel represents Jesus' disciples as slow to understand His purpose. They doubtless were. The loneliness of espousing a misunderstood cause and doing what one has to do, despite the criticism of friends and foes, must have been enormous. It took all of who He was and the resource of His total person to remain positive, confident, and outgoing. He was all of that. The common people heard Him gladly. The outcasts sought Him, especially. His grief was compounded when He saw the unacceptance of all of God's children by those of God's children who had been given special privileges (Matt. 5:24–26). He was grieved when His disciples did not follow His example of complete dependence on God (Matt. 17:21, KJV). It is a mistake to suppose that Jesus suffered only six hours on Good Friday. In many ways, His was a tragic, lonely life. The crescendo of His anxiety came in Gethsemane. But the dark dirge of impending tragedy was being composed throughout all of His life.

The deepest physical and spiritual anxiety occurred, of course, at His death. The death itself was an execution in agony. But the circumstances surrounding His death were heartbreaking. He was executed as a political criminal on trumped-up charges. He was handed over to a foreign, occupying power by His own people. He was "rejected of men" (Isa. 53:3, KJV), by His own kind of men, whom He had come to seek and to save. He had been faithful to Israel. It was not mutual. And the betrayal was accomplished by one of His own disciples. Treachery among friends is one of life's most embittering experiences. At last, He was deserted by His followers. He was illegally tried, unmercifully tortured, and forced to carry, as long as His strength could endure, the instrument of His execution. The final hours of anguish were compounded by taunting, being forced to see His mother's suffering, and being publicly displayed without clothing before a curious crowd. In death, as in life, His deep dependence on the Father was His comfort. In the power of God He could pray for the forgiveness of all who had a part in His death, and that is all of us. He rejected a narcotic despite His thirst. He forgave a robber. He took the place of another robber, Barabbas. He made provision for His mother, expressed His dismay to God, and realized His task was finished. Then He died, commending His Spirit to God. All of the tragic possibilities of life came crashing in at that awful death. There could be no immediate talk of a divine plan. There was too much pain, too much loss. Too much tragic waste. Injustice had claimed another victim. It was dark, really dark.

Some few of you may have suffered some painful tragic circumstances through the life and death of a child. You are in a position to be especially close to God if you have not been overwhelmed by your experience. It is not just a pious platitude to say to you, "God understands and cares." It took time for the shattered followers of Christ to regroup and seek the guidance of God in making sense out of this event.

Nor was death the end of it. First Peter 3:19–22 is a much-disputed passage.[8] This passage about Jesus preaching to the spirits in prison does not have a simple resolution. I believe that it has to do with the complete, thorough routing of evil on its own territory. John Calvin gave it another, plausible interpretation. Calvin's primary interpretation of the death of Christ was that it was a substitution of what sinful humanity should have endured.[9] The 1 Peter 3:19 passage was given considerable attention in the ancient churches because of the clause which referred to it in what came to be called the "Apostles' Creed." That expression is: "He descended into hell." Calvin's position was that Jesus descended into hell to suffer what sinful humanity ought to have suffered. Taking this interpretation, one could add to the suffering of Christ on the basis of this highly symbolic expression.

One thing seems plain. His sufferings, in every respect, were as complete as His temptation. The suffering prayer of Jonah (Jonah 2:1–9) formed a psalm that the Suffering Servant of the Lord, who gave His generation the sign of Jonah, could relate to. The tragic possibilities were realized in Jesus' suffering, death, and descent. He reached the depths. And from the depths, the lowest point of His story, God heard. The ancient Psalm, "Out of the depths have I called to thee, O Lord" (130:1) was a sad song Jesus could sing. Even in death and the depths "He trusted in God; let him deliver him now" (Matt. 27:43, KJV). This cruel taunt of His oppressors would become the key to His release.

My Father Will See Me Through

"For thou wilt not abandon me to Sheol nor suffer thy faithful servant to see the pit" (Ps. 16:10). This aspiration of the psalmist became the only hope of God's Son. Many years ago, a missionary physician gave his testimony to some college students. His credentials had been accepted for medical school. He was having the all-important interview with the dean. The student was economically poor and did not have the resources for his expensive training. The crucial question was asked: "How do you plan to finance your education?" The student replied: "My Father will see me through." The missionary doctor relied on God and his own work to finish medical training. That student's response is especially appropriate in the ultimate circumstances of Christ's death.

There is no other answer to death except that one which God effected in Jesus Christ. Wishing for immortality is a hope of all humanity. Ancient Pharaohs prepared for life after death as soon as they took the throne. Hindu sages hope for reincarnation that will continue until they have earned absorption into the great world soul. Buddhists try to suppress all desire in order to attain enlightenment. Many, including Chinese and Jews, hope for a life through the filial piety and remembrance of their descendants. But resurrection is the only answer to death. The overcoming of death must be accomplished by the One who gave life. Only by the creation of a new and permanent kind of life can we see the resolution of death. Resurrection is not mere resuscitation. It is a new kind of life. It is life out of death, beyond death, in spite of death. Resurrection is God's victorious answer to the defeat of death. If God does not bring us back, we shall not survive. But God did bring His Holy Child back. Therefore, we too shall live.

It is one thing to hope for life after death. It is quite another thing to be able to point to an exemplar of that universal hope. In the Old Testament Bathsheba's child had died. David was distraught. His only comfort was that he, the king and grieving father, could go to the child when David's turn for death came (2 Sam. 12:23). God, too, grieved because of Jesus' death. We must not separate the Godhead in their united purpose of seeking salvation for humanity. "God was in Christ reconciling the world to himself" (2 Cor. 5:19). Whereas David could only go to his son in death, God, the Father, could and did call His Son to life with Him. The triumphant cry of the early Christians was: "The Jesus we speak of has been raised by God, as we can all bear witness" (Acts 2:32). An event like that needed witnesses. There were adequate and reliable ones: Mary Magdalene, the other women, Peter and John, the ten, one week later the ten plus Thomas, seven by the seaside, two on the way to Emmaus, James (the brother), the 500, the ascension, Stephen, Paul, and quaking Roman soldiers. These are the witnesses. So are we. We have not seen Him like they did, but we have "seen" Him through them and by their testimony.

Some modern scholarship speaks of a resurrection without an empty tomb.[10] The New Testament speaks of both. There may be problems with modern science as to how a corpse can be revitalized. There certainly are problems with faith healers who try to raise the dead. But there would be a major problem with first-century, pragmatic fishermen if they had not checked out the grave. Objective visions, mass hysteria, and spiritual visions may provide placating answers to modern sensibilities. But the glowing reality of an empty tomb is all that could persuade fisherfolk, tax collectors, and grieving relatives. How Jesus appeared to them is quite beyond our reckoning. But that He appeared to them and that it was He, this same Jesus, who appeared to them is the only answer that can explain what happened to them. Jesus' resurrected body was a miracle of God. It was one of the "properties" of resurrection. The meaning of resurrection, our hope of resurrection, the proclamation of resurrection, and the growth of the people of God which grew out of all of these are also "properties" of the resurrection. They belong on the "stage of Easter."

The hope of a Child was actualized. His Father saw Him through. And in the process, God saw through to the end of things, all things. It is by the resurrection of Jesus that God gives hope to the world. It is through the resurrection of Jesus that God shows His love for the Son and for all the world. It is in the resurrection of Jesus that the faith of the children of God is born.

The resurrection of Jesus of Nazareth is the primary miracle of the Gospel. From the resurrection of Jesus one works back to virgin birth and preexistence. From the resurrection of Jesus one works forward to the resurrection of all of God's creation and the future of the world.[11] God raised Him up. And this resurrection, like all of the other acts of God in Christ, was on behalf of God's creation. Jesus' resurrection is not the return of a formless figure so that grieving relatives could see Him a little longer. Jesus' resurrection was a restitution to earth that the world might see and know that God had made this Jesus "both Lord and Messiah" (Acts 2:36). The dependence of the Son, even to death, gave an independent possibility to God's fallen world. We are healed by His stripes. And by His resurrection we are sealed for ultimate redemption. The Father and the Brother had the whole family in mind.

God could have taken Christ directly home. But He didn't. A continuing implication of Christ's resurrection is the "forty days."[12] The symbol of forty days is a continuing, complementary part of the ministry of Christ. The beginning of His ministry was spent in a period of clarification of the type and performance of ministry, the forty days of temptation. The end of His earthly ministry was given over to clarifying and fortifying of others as to what His ministry was all about. "He showed Himself to these men after his death, and gave ample proof that he was alive: over a period of forty days he appeared to them and taught them about the kingdom of God" (Acts 1:3). Jesus, during this interim, was the best proof of the resurrection and the basic interpreter of all that this Child of God meant. The appearances were in diverse places (a garden, an upper room, a well-traveled road, a seashore, and a hillside). The effects were electric (a regrouping of dispirited and grieving followers, an "authorized interpretation" of what it all meant, and a promise of continued presence through the Spirit).

There was a final, necessary act, the return to the Father. Ascension was homegoing. The necessity of the ascension from our side was His removal from our time and place, so there could be a way in which He could become universal to all times and all places. The joy of the ascension, from the Father's view, was homecoming. Some would suggest that resurrection and ascension were one event. There is no theological reason why they should be seen as one. There is a theological purpose that we should learn from the interval. The completion of what He came to do was rounded out in the forty days. The period of His physical incarnation was ended by the ascension. It was, as He said (John 14), necessary that He go away. And in the going He gave further witness of His resurrection, further clarification of His future coming (Acts 1:1–11), and further instruction to His people (Matt. 28:19–20). The Father had seen Him through. This was the beloved Son, in whom He was well pleased. The statement which came at the beginning of Christ's ministry, as an indication as to His type of messiahship, could well have been repeated at ascension as an assessment of His accomplishment. The implications and details of the homecoming and the seating at the right hand are Trinitarian private property. But the meaning of the ministry and the evaluation of Christ's accomplishments are to be shared with all the world . . . they really are meant to be shared with all the world!

Look What My Son Did!

Small-town athletic events are great occasions. Favored is the father who has an athletic son. Bragging knows no bounds. Some such fathers are avoided on Saturday mornings. One and all know of the accomplishments of the star quarterback. If you have achieving grandchildren, you well understand. There is, however, something both parents and grandparents should understand. That is that all achievements are not athletic. There are many kinds of accomplishments. Wise parents will learn to value all types of achievements. In some young people one will have to look hard for the positive. But is it all right to fail? The death of Jesus was a great sorrow to God, but it was no disappointment to God. There are many standards by which Jesus' life might have seemed a failure. He was considered by some to be a prophet, an itinerant miracle worker, one who ran foul of both civil and religious laws. Was this a record of which to be proud?

The affirmation, acceptance, and approval of the Father were always present. Even when pain and the burden of cosmic sin weighed heaviest on Jesus, there was no permanent sense of despair. The cry of dereliction, "My God, my God, why hast thou forsaken me?" is the first line of a psalm whose ending is a strong affirmation.

The latest Gospel, John, gives the deepest clues as to the relationship of the Father and the Son. There are at least 125 references to "Father" in John's Gospel and another 16 in the first two epistles. Some few of these references are to earthly fathers. Most are references of the evangelist's reports of Jesus' expressions about God. The reference which plumbs the deepest relationship is the simple claim of Jesus: "My Father and I are one" (John 10:30). This oneness is not to be seen as sameness. The Father sends; the Son is sent. This oneness is the solidarity of purpose, which Jesus shares with His disciples. As the Father sent the Son, so the Son sends the disciples (John 20:21). If God is good and true and right, so is the Son who represents Him, who obeys Him, and who loves Him. Whatever others may say, God is committed to Jesus in an unqualified way. The contention of Jesus against the "best religious people" had the support of the Father who was trying to fulfill the old and project something new through the Son. Jesus' signs, there are seven of them in the Gospel, are designed to point to God. The last sign, the cross, is an eternal emblem which becomes a covenant between God and man.

God was pleased with what Jesus did. The Father's love says to all: Look what my Son did. It was a joint venture, this act of Christ's self-sacrificing cross and God's redeeming, sending love. Jesus' ministry seemed, by the standards of His day, a failure. But the Father did not think so. It is my intention not only to point out the singleness of purpose which existed between that Father and that Son. I would also like to encourage all fathers to look for signs of success in their sons and daughters. I would like to suggest to mothers with too high expectations of daughters and sons that they evaluate realistically the standards by which they judge.

So much of the Father was shared in Jesus that He could, for the sake of their common cause, risk unpopularity, persecution, and death for the convictions He gained from the Father. In the first blush of Jesus' tragic death, there seemed to be no cause for boasting. But the Father saw further than the trauma of rejection. The Father saw the why of this death. For they had covenanted together, this Father and this Son, that what they had to do they did for others. And the way of the cross was the means of accomplishing what had to be done. In John's Gospel there is an ingrained sense of divine destiny. Jesus' destiny is the way and work of God, which is determined by divine appointment. Jesus did His part. And God was very pleased. "Look what my Son did!" It was several years before others could see the picture. Then, with the confidence of faith and the clarity of hindsight, these followers began also to see and to be very pleased with what God's Holy Child had done.

We Have Many Pictures

Where would the camera companies be without parents and grandparents? Much poorer! One almost wonders what else are children, and especially grandchildren, for except to take pictures? There is something satisfying and permanent about catching a child in a charming pose and recording that in a permanent way. Remember those photographers' specials which take special poses? They send you wonderful proofs in a variety of poses and ask you to choose which one you want. The sales psychology is clever. You are offered special prices for several pictures, and for a very special rate you can have a composite photo showing several different poses. If the proofs are good and you can afford them at all, you are hooked. There is something irresistible about preserving a visual record of the activities and stages of childhood.

We have many pictures of Jesus, God's Holy Child. The pictures are verbal. And they are all undeniably of the same subject: Jesus. Yet each likeness captures something different about Him. The Gospels are four remarkable photos which contribute complete and satisfying pictures of Jesus. The first three, Matthew, Mark, and Luke, have remarkable similarities. John paints a full-face portrait in black and white. Paul's letters give us a whole folio of lovely oil paintings done with a full palette of colors. It might be said that Paul provides an official Christological portrait in color. The Book of Hebrews gives a picture of Jesus in which He is the central figure in a crowded scene. The Book of Revelation provides a picture of the overcoming Christ in full regalia. The New Testament provides the earliest and the definitive pictures of Jesus. But the twenty centuries from His time to ours have been filled with other likenesses, snapshots, paintings, and portrayals in a variety of media. We have many pictures. Leaf through the album. His is the face that changes history. He is the "image" we all should learn to recognize as embodying the likeness of God (Heb. 1:3).[13]

Mark, a Basic Sketch. A historical sketch of Marie Antoinette, by Georges Carn, depicts the young Queen on the way to her execution. Her bearing is regal, and the face is composed and resolute. This hurried sketch of a queen en route to execution is an apt analogy of Mark's basic sketch of Jesus. Mark shows us the picture of a young man in a hurry to do His Father's will. Mark's Jesus is sketched against the hills of Galilee. He is busy being the Son of God. The miracles or mighty works loom large in the scenes. The proclamation of the Kingdom comes in active staccato beats.

The center of the picture and the turning point of the story is in Mark 8:27–33, Peter's confession and the first prediction of crucifixion. All of the brief acts lead up to this turning point. All of the short scenes remaining point to the drama of the cross. Misunderstanding clouds the picture. The misunderstanding of Jesus' enemies and especially the misunderstanding of His own disciples. The clarity of focus and the intense brightness of the picture reside in Jesus, the central figure. He strides quickly, purposefully, as the Son of God moving toward the cross. It is a good historical sketch of a King going to His death. The teachings are abbreviated; the encounters with friends and foes are sharp; the power of God as seen in His mighty works is unmistakable. And almost before one knows it, the scene is done. He has died. And just as quickly, He is raised and has commissioned fearful disciples. This is the basic sketch. His person is captured in Mark's strong, forceful, verb-filled language. All of the details are not filled in as they will appear in other pictures. But because of Mark's swift, inspired strokes we can recognize Him anywhere.

Matthew, a Careful Study. Two British portrait painters of the seventeenth and eighteenth centuries were Thomas Gainsborough and Sir Joshua Reynolds. They painted with great attention to detail and put their subjects in a setting drawn from the life of the time and circumstance of the individual. The character of their subjects was clearly stamped in the face, the clothes, and the background of these portraits. Their portraits were often life-sized and rich in color and effect.

Matthew's Gospel provides a Gainsborough/Reynolds type of careful study of Jesus. Matthew's painting is of a royal heir. This prince is of David's line and can be traced back to Abraham (Matt. 1). This Jewish prince brings a teaching which calls to mind the fivefold books of Moses (Matt. 5—7; 10; 13; 18; 24—25). Not only Galilee but also Jerusalem figures large in the background of this noble figure whose words and works are carefully portrayed so as to bring out subtle nuances. The major message of this scion of David is the kingdom of God. His birth was recognized and celebrated by the kings of the East (Matt. 2). It becomes apparent that the earthly kingdom of Jerusalem and the kingdom of heaven are bound together by the fate and the fortune of the Son of man (Matt. 24—25). The royal child escaped the clutches of a wicked king, Herod the Great, and was put to death in the name of the king of Rome as the king of the Jews (Matt. 2; 27). As the risen Lord, He sent forth disciples to proclaim the kingdom of heaven (28:19–20). In his careful portrait, Matthew incorporates the past (the Jewish connection), the present ("the kingdom of Heaven is upon you," 3:2; 10:7), and the future (the mission challenge and the coming Son of man). The basic sketch of Mark has become a careful portrait of the Rabbi, Prophet, Teacher, Son of man.

Luke, the Classic Pose. Every schoolchild "knows" George Washington. Washington is universally recognized primarily through Stuart Adam's classic, unfinished portrait of America's first president. Certain pictures, because of wide distribution and familiar characteristics, become classic poses of a given subject. Certainly this is true of Adam's Washington. A classic is a generally recognized, skillfully executed, and highly valued item. Luke's Gospel is a classic diptych (two-part) picture of Jesus who is concerned with universal causes in Luke and is the cause of a universal proclamation in Acts.

Luke's Jesus cares for Gentiles, women, children, and all the world. He is descended from Adam, as are we all (Luke 3). He is related to John the Baptizer, announced by angels, celebrated in song, and greeted by aged servants of God, both a priest and a prophetess (Luke 2). This "Gentile" portrait includes among its background tax collectors (5:27–28), Roman army men (Luke 7:1–10), a grieving mother (7:11–15), a sinful but repentant woman with an extravagant gift (7:36–50), Mary of Magdala, Joanna, Susanna (8:1–3), and a woman whose hemorrhages were healed (8:43–48). Except for Luke's full painting we would not know of the parables of the lost sheep, the lost coin, or the prodigal son (Luke 15). Luke's two-part work begins in Jerusalem, spreads to Galilee, and returns to Jerusalem, only to spread from there to Judea, Samaria, and the uttermost parts of the world (Acts 1:8). The story of God's Holy Child, the man who went around doing good (Acts 10:38), took on heroic dimensions, and the portrait became a classic. Its well-known implications were given to and provided for all the world. To Mark's sketch and Matthew's careful picture is added a classic two-part portrait of Luke.

John, the Full-Face View. Latest of the Gospel portraits and somewhat different from the first three is John's full-face view of Jesus. Rembrandt painted a marvelous full-face view of Jesus as only Rembrandt could. The work of the renowned seventeenth-century Dutch master is in the Metropolitan Museum of Art in New York City. It is believed that the model was an anonymous Jew of Amsterdam. Rembrandt often employed live models, and the features of this painting are indisputably Jewish. There are deep-set eyes, dark features, and a slight depression of the forehead, as though a stone had left its mark. It is, I believe, my favorite painting of Jesus. He seems to be looking full view at the one who sees the painting. Rembrandt painted in deep, rich, somber tones. The effect is electrifying.

I find this an appropriate illustration of John's picture of Jesus. John sketched in black and white; his is a gospel of contrasts, night and day, darkness and light, life and death. A glimpse of God had been found in Moses, but grace and truth (John 1:17) are found full face in Jesus Christ. John's painting is a gleam of glory, first to all the world (John 1:12), then to His disciples (John 13—20).[14] There are seven signs like Rembrandt's gathering background figures. But the light is all from within; it is a lateral shaft of God's glory which is realized at the cross and fully displayed at the resurrection. Just as Rembrandt, the master of light, depicted his light as radiating in a spreading shaft from left to right, top to bottom, so John portrays the Light of the world whose radiance cannot be put out by the surrounding darkness (1:4–5).

The full face of Jesus sees with penetrating eyes into the very heart of a person: of Nathaniel (1:43–51), of Judas (6:71), of self-righteous religious leaders (8), of all people (1:9; 2:25). The full face of Jesus contains the gaze of God who sent Him (John 3:17), who loves Him (3:35; 5:20), who bears witness to Him (5:37), who is one with Him (10:30), and will give to the Son Jesus whatever He requests (17:1–2). The church fathers referred to the Fourth Gospel as a spiritual gospel. Augustine said it soared like an eagle. And the eagle is the sign of this Gospel. For what we have here are penetrating eyes whose power of love can see what is in the world (1:9). This full face of the man of sorrow who bears on His visage the pain of God can raise a friend from death (11:1–46), can raise His disciples above dissension (21:4–14,20–23), and can be raised on a cross to save the world (3:14–15).

The Gospels are God's composite picture of Jesus. We see Him from different views. Always it is He. We delight that they have captured the scenes and settings of His life. Mark with his basic sketch. Matthew with his careful portrait. Luke with his classic pose. John with his full-face view.

Paul, an Official Portrait. Official portraits always pose a problem. They are commissioned. They are not intended primarily for private, personal enjoyment. They require a special skill in capturing both the realism and the quality of dignity of the subject being painted. There are national portrait galleries in many countries. The Portrait Gallery in London houses paintings of many of the kings and queens of England. The official portrait of Queen Elizabeth II is a good portrait although it was highly criticized at the time of its presentation. The artist did capture her resoluteness, determination of character, and her unfailing regal dignity. Those who were expecting to see the softness and the beauty of the queen were disappointed.

Paul was the first Christian artist to paint Jesus from the viewpoint of the risen Lord. It might be suggested from the number and influence of Paul's letters and the assertive strength of his apostleship that he was commissioned to do the official portrait of Christ in the New Testament. He begins with the Lord of glory, for this is the way in which Paul met Jesus. Paul's favorite title for his subject was Lord or Lord Jesus Christ. The regal bearing is always present in the verbal painting of Paul. Two great hymns which He put into definitive form speak of the grace and grandeur of Jesus (Col. 1:15–23; Phil. 2:5–11). The Ephesian letter adds the heroic demeanor to Christ who broke down all the barriers which arose between God and His world and between all of the divided factions of humanity. The practicality of Jesus' commands are applied to the Christian communities at Corinth and Thessalonica. The full implications of God's plan, Jesus' purpose, and humanity's place in God's plan are spelled out in the grandiose canvas which is the Book of Romans. The direct and simple gaze of the gospel and its saving power are painted with bold strokes for the Galatians. For Timothy and Titus the implications and applications of Christ's lordship and leadership in the life of the churches are painted with clear and incisive colors. There is the tender vignette of Philemon which applies the forgiveness of Christ to the forgiveness Christians should have for one another. The figure of Jesus Christ in Paul is of a Lord striding victoriously over the principalities and powers who oppose Him.

Official portraits are designed to inspire confidence and to provide for the viewers an indication of the inner strength of the subject. Paul's commissioned portrait of Christ was painted in a dozen different contexts over possibly a quarter of a century. The portrait was controversial to those expecting a different kind of Messiah, one domesticated to fit their own tastes. The picture we have from Paul is a pose that brings the cosmic Christ into focus as both a reigning Lord and a personal friend. Something of Paul's portrait works its way into our hearts until looking at Paul's official portrait of Christ one is pleased and appropriately proud to be "in Christ" and to have Christ in the viewer as the "hope of glory" (Col. 1:27).

Hebrews. In Hebrews, Jesus is the central figure in a busy scene. Leonardo da Vinci's *Last Supper* is a great painting for a variety of reasons. The perspective gives balance and harmony to thirteen persons. It is difficult to paint a scene in which so many people can be seen, recognized as to who they are and what their character is. The background provides divided panels of classic proportions which permit the figures to come forward in the viewer's eye. One is aware of the upper room and the table and the inserts which add depth. But one is aware supremely of Jesus as the central figure of the painting. One could quibble over which disciple is which among the figures. Peter, John, and Judas may be easily discerned. But there is no doubt as to which figure is Jesus. This picture is Christocentric in such a way that all attention is drawn to Christ. He is supreme.

One may draw a parallel between da Vinci's *Last Supper* and the Book of Hebrews. Hebrews, with its types and shadows, its elaborate comparisons, its embellished scenes, draws attention to one sole and central figure. It is Jesus. Christ is seen in isolated splendor. He stands above the Law, the Mosaic priesthood, and the sacrificial system. He is above the angels of God. There is no mistaking who is the central figure in Hebrews. Like da Vinci's painting, Christ is in the middle. All of the movement and the action flow towards Him. The portrait of the author of Hebrews has perspective, a kind of divine perspective that puts everyone and everything else in its place around the Son who "learned obedience in the school of suffering" (Heb. 5:8), a Son who is a high priest touched by our human infirmities (4:15). In the midst of the cloud of witnesses (Heb. 12:1) who observe the struggle of our earthly existence, is Jesus, God's Son, who watches most intently and who alone is able to represent us definitively before God.

For every high priest taken from among men is ordained for men in things pertaining to God, that he may offer both gifts and sacrifices for sins:

Who can have compassion on the ignorant, and on them that are out of the way; for that he himself also is compassed with infirmity.

And by reason hereof he ought, as for the people, so also for himself, to offer for sins.

And no man taketh this honour unto himself, but he that is called of God, as was Aaron.

So also Christ glorified not himself to be made an high priest; but he that said unto him, Thou art my Son, to-day have I begotten thee.

As he saith also in another place, Thou art a priest for ever after the order of Melchisedec.

Who in the days of his flesh, when he had offered up prayers and supplications with strong crying and tears unto him that was able to save him from death, and was heard in that he feared;

Though he were a Son, yet learned he obedience by the things which he suffered;

And being made perfect, he became the author of eternal salvation unto all them that obey him;

Called of God an high priest after the order of Melchisedec (5:1–10, KJV).

Revelation—a Portrait in Full Regalia. There is a well-known painting of Louis XIV, king of France, by LeBrun. Louis looks every inch a king, even those inches that are added by his high-heeled shoes. All of the trappings are there. One can well imagine this figure with its aquiline nose and erect posture saying, "L'etat c'est moi!" (I am the state!) The hauteur is unfortunate, but the effect is remarkable. This man who ruled France and rearranged the face and fortunes of Europe for more than fifty years is cloaked in splendor. His robes, his scepter, his medals all constitute the full court regalia. Here is the sun king of France.

There is such a portrait of Jesus in the gallery of New Testament paintings. It is the portrait in the Book of Revelation. The risen Christ, who is the "ruler of the kings of earth" (Rev. 1:5), comes on the clouds with splendor (1:7), and He is gloriously attired (1:12–15). His voice is like "the sound of rushing waters" (1:15). He is sovereign Lord of the churches (chaps. 2—3). Among the heavenly court He alone is worthy to open the sealed document that foretells the future of the world (chaps. 4—5). This magnificent Son is given by God's promise and is kept by God's power (chap. 12). God's risen Christ is victorious and receives the saints' songs of Moses and of the lamb (15:2–4). God's Son is the avenging warrior on the great white horse whose synonymous names are Faithful and True (19:11-20). It is He who shuts away evil and the evil one (20:1–10). And in the end He is seated with God upon the throne of judgment (20:11–15). With His Father, He makes all things new. In the heavenly city He is the temple. The Light of the Lamb provides illumination for the kingdom of God (21:1–8; 21:22 to 22:5). Now that is a portrait in full regalia!

All of these "originals" are the primary pictures of God's Holy Child, Jesus. They range from Mark's basic sketch through Revelation's portrait in full regalia. Whether rejoicing in the smiles of children or facing the hatred of the Roman government, whether walking through wheat fields in Galilee or dying in Jerusalem, whether in Luke's classic picture or in Paul's official portrait, He is the same—yesterday, today, and forever (Heb. 13:8). We have many pictures. The New Testament provides the basic likeness. Every generation of believers and every genre of expression will add their paintings and photographs to the collection that has become the full family album.

The Full Family Album

The portraits of the New Testament are the original and normative likenesses of Jesus, the Child of God. Throughout the centuries there have been many others. All other portraits and all recent photographs may contribute to the family album. They can help us to know more about the likeness of Jesus, who is the likeness of God. Let me list a few ways in which the Christian community has celebrated and given evidence of its love for Jesus by pictures of Him. All of these pictures, to be helpful or correct, need to correspond to the originals. Some persons and groups have given us pictures of Jesus that bear no resemblance to the original. These distortions and misrepresentations we call heresies. Heresy is a split off of the truth. When a split occurs, we need to be particularly concerned to check our drawings with the originals.

There have been thousands of written portraits of Christ in addition to those of the New Testament. Two early representations of Christ had to be taken from the family photograph because they distorted the original, biblical pictures of Jesus. One of the mistaken pictures was drawn by groups of Jewish followers who insisted that Jesus was genuinely human but that He was not really divine. This was the Ebionite picture, and the Christians of the early church wisely decided that this picture should not be placed in the family album. A reverse negative or opposite-number picture was produced by Greek followers of Jesus who insisted that Jesus was divine but that He was not really human. This was the Gnostic picture. It, too, had to be taken from the album because it was not a true likeness of who Jesus is.

During the first four centuries the community of Jesus drew four important pictures of Jesus. They were drawn in reaction and response to distorting views. In 325 a group of Christians meeting at

Nicaea drew a clear sketch which gave evidence that Jesus was divine. This picture was placed in the album instead of the Ebionite pictures and instead of the composite picture of a man named Arius who wanted to portray Christ as being something other than fully divine. A second picture was added at Constantinople in 381 to depict that Jesus was fully human. This picture displeased all of those who suggested that Jesus only seemed (*dokein*) to be human. This picture was drawn against the view of Apollinaris, whose picture of Jesus made Him human in body and soul but not human in mind and spirit.

In 431 a council of Christians met at Ephesus and drew up a likeness of Jesus which portrayed Him as one fully integrated, complete person; this was to correct a picture by Nestorius which could have been seen in such a way that Jesus would look like two persons. The final picture accepted into the family album during those first four centuries was adopted in 451 at Chalcedon. The opposing portrait by Eutyches showed only one nature in Jesus, not two. The picture accepted as being like the Jesus of the New Testament portrayed Him as having two full natures, divine and human in one person.

The composite photograph of these early Christians, as expressed in their belief statements (creeds) showed Jesus as divine and human, one person in two natures.[15] It needs to be noticed that these portraits, while being true to the New Testament pictures of Jesus were of a very different style from New Testament views of Jesus. The New Testament pictures of Jesus were pictures characterized by simplicity and movement. In the New Testament Jesus was active and relating to the scenes in which He appeared. These early philosophical word pictures of Jesus view Him as frozen. They are like the Byzantine mosaics at Ravenna, Italy. They are static pictures expressed in the philosophy of the day.[16]

The full family album of the churches' pictures of Jesus has grown with the centuries. All of the pictures have not been verbal. There have been many other types of paintings. These paintings were on walls (murals), in books (illuminated manuscripts), on board and canvas (paintings), in glass (stained glass art), in music (religious music), in stone (sculpture), in buildings (architecture), and in dramatic form (drama).[17] We have many pictures of God's Holy Child in the full family album. We prize the biblical ones above all others. Every generation of Christ's followers portrays Him in terms of its own understanding, its own culture, its own race. So long as these correspond in likeness to the originals, that is good. For we all need pictures of Jesus to which we can relate. It is the universal Jesus we see. It is the cosmic Christ on whom our gaze is set. We can relate to Him only through the focus of our own viewer's eyes. But we dare not restrict our pictures of Him as the only views we will look at in the full family album. There are indeed many pictures of Jesus. But are we concerned only with God's Holy Child? No, indeed! We cannot be concerned only with God's only begotten Son, because His major concern was with others. He wants a large family.

God Wants Many Children

Did you have several children? You are blessed. Each was different. Each was loved. All were treated equal, I hope. Sometimes this is not true. Sometimes parents play favorites, as one of a famous comedy duo suggests, "Mom always liked you best." Children see it that way. Sometimes it is true that parents prefer or honor one child more than the other. It is not a good thing. The feelings of rejection or unwantedness which people carry with them from childhood to old age are tragic, terrible things. Jesus taught us many things about God, His Father. One of the most important things He taught was that the Father loves us all (John 3:16). He who is God's Son in a unique way was the firstborn among many children (Rom. 8:29; Col. 1:15). It is the basic insight of the only begotten of the Father that we all are equally loved, equally valued, equally cared for. God wants many children. The Elder Brother said so. And He confirmed these sayings by His death on our behalf.

The early Christians drew many pictures about the person of Jesus. Four become classics. But the Christian community has never agreed on just one way to express the work of Jesus. It seems to many today that those distinctions of Jesus' person and work are not the best way to get at who He is and what He does.[18] I have attempted in this chapter to hold together the whole picture of the Son of God. There is, nevertheless, value in expressing what Jesus has done for us. Christians have understood Jesus' death on our behalf, by which He demonstrates and makes evident that the Father loves us all, in three broad streams of interpretation. We call these interpretations views of the atonement (what Jesus does to make us one with God).

One way Jesus shows that God desires many children is called the substitutionary representational view. The views in this group conclude from the New Testament that Christ is our substitute, that His death takes the place of our ultimate death, that He has taken our place and/or represented us in His death.[19] Jesus has done something for us that we could not do for ourselves. This group of interpretations stresses, in my understanding of them, that Jesus brings us ultimate acceptance with God. I discussed above how essential it was that we have and accept God's acceptance of us. Jesus effects and proclaims that God wants and accepts us as His children.

A second group of interpretations is called the example, moral influence, stream.[20] These interpretations say to me that God declares that we are of ultimate worth. Having the assurance that God values us and declares that we are important is important in any life. There is an ability to face adversity when we know God is for us.

A third stream of interpretations about Jesus' death, which effects and declares that God wants many children, stresses the victory of Jesus over those foes we cannot defeat ourselves.[21] What kinds of foes do we face that we cannot, in our own strength, overcome? Ancient Christians answered this question wisely when they listed them as the world, the flesh, and the devil. Paul gave a fourth item: death, the last enemy. There are forces in our environment (the world) which are stronger than we. There are impulses within us (the flesh) which we cannot control without God's help. There is an ancient foe whose craft and power are great (the devil), and we do not always "wrestle against flesh and blood" (Eph. 6:12, KJV). All of these things the Elder Brother will help us handle. He has made possible and knowable that God desires many children. And He has given us the commission to be those who share this good news.

The Child of God, Jesus, has opened for us the way to the Father's house. Christians should be reminded of Christ upon seeing any child. We should remember in our love for our own children and grandchildren God's love for us. This much-longed-for Holy Child traded His birthright of love for a legacy of hate on our behalf. This dependent Child of the Father grew up and actualized the tragic possibilities, which were His lot, in order that our possibility of grace and love might be actualized. His Father saw Him through, all the way through death. There is a justifiable pride in remembering what the Son of God has done. There are many pictures of this Man-Child in the album of the people of God. The earliest of them are from the New Testament itself. And the latest of them are those each of us treasures in our believing hearts. This Child has taught us and freed us all to be the children of God, a God who wants many children. Now we move from the Son to the Father, and as we do, we already know a great deal about the Father from the Son.

Notes

1. See my *Who Is Jesus Christ?* (Nashville: Broadman Press, 1985), especially pp. 9–44.
2. On the historical factors of Jesus' birth, see Ethelbert Stauffer, *Jesus and His Story,* trans. Richard and Clara Winston (New York: Knopf, 1960), pp. 13–42.
3. See E. Schillebeeckx, *Jesus: An Experiment in Christology,* trans. Hubert Hoskins (New York: Seabury, 1979), pp. 17–35, 294–318.
4. See again Schillebeeckx's discussion of Jesus and his *Abba* dependence on the Father. *Jesus,* pp. 256–271.
5. See Stauffer, *Jesus and His Story,* pp. 43–62, and M. S. Enslin, *The Prophet from Nazareth* (New York: McGraw-Hill, 1961). The older work of Alfred Edersheim, *The Life and Times of Jesus, the Messiah,* 8th ed., (New York: Longmans, Green and Co., 1896) is a classic which needs updating to be of maximum help.
6. On Jesus' teachings and mighty works see A. M. Hunter's *The Work and Words of Jesus,* rev. ed. (Philadelphia: Westminster Press, 1973).
7. By Cedric Mount (London: S. French, 1937).
8. See the discussion in chapter 3, p. 112.
9. See John Calvin, *Institutes of the Christian Religion,* ed. John T. McNeill, trans. Lewis Ford Battles (London: SCM Press, 1961), especially Book 2, ch. 17, sections 4–6, vol. 1, pp. 531–534.
10. See Willi Marxsen, *The Resurrection of Jesus of Nazareth,* trans. Margaret Kohl (Philadelphia: Fortress Press, 1970), especially pp. 36–78,112–129.
11. See this strong affirmation in wider and deeper philosophical implications in W. Pannenberg's theology. See, for example: *Jesus, God and Man,* trans. Lewis L. Wilkens & Duane A. Priebe, 2nd ed. (Philadelphia: Westminster Press, 1977), especially pp. 66–88, 378–397. For a good secondary treatment of Pannenberg's theology, see E. Frank Tupper, *The Theology of Wolfhart Pannenberg* (Philadelphia: Westminster Press, 1973), especially pp. 146–164.
12. See Karl Barth, *Church Dogmatics,* IV, 1, trans. G. W. Bromiley (New York: Charles Scribner's Sons, 1956), p. 260; IV, 2, trans. G. W. Bromiley (Edinburgh: T. & T. Clark, 1958), p. 143; IV, 3, 1, trans. G. W. Bromiley (Edinburgh: T. & T. Clark, 1961), pp. 303–305.
13. For more detailed accounts of the descriptions of Jesus according to titles see V. Taylor, *The Names of Jesus* (London: Macmillan, 1953); O. Cullmann, *The Christology of the New Testament,* trans. Shirley C. Guthrie and Charles A. M. Hall (Philadelphia: West-

minster Press, 1959); E. Schillebeeckx, *Jesus: An Experiment in Christology,* trans. Hubert Hoskins (New York: Seabury Press, 1979) and *Christ: The Experience of Jesus as Lord,* trans. John Bowden (New York: Seabury Press, 1980).

14. See Rudolph Bultmann, *The Gospel of John: A Commentary,* trans. G. R. Beasley-Murray (Philadelphia: Fortress Press, 1971); see also Raymond Brown, *The Gospel According to John,* 2 vols. in the Anchor Bible Series (New York: Doubleday, 1966–1970).

15. On the views of Christ in the first four centuries see Aloys Grillmeier, *Christ in Christian Tradition,* trans. J. S. Bowden (New York: Sheed and Ward, 1965).

16. Eric Newton and William Neil, *Two Thousand Years of Christian Art* (New York: Harper & Row, 1966), chap. 2.

17. See Albert Edward Bailey, *Christ and His Gospel in Recent Art* (New York: Charles Scribner's Sons, 1948); Roland Bainton, *Behold the Christ* (New York: Harper & Row, 1974); Frederic William Farrer, *The Life of Christ as Represented in Art* (New York: Macmillan, 1894); Cynthia Mead, *Christ and the Fine Arts,* 5th ed. (New York: Harper & Brothers, 1938); Denis Thomas, *The Face of Christ* (New York: Hamlyn, 1979).

18. *Who Is Jesus Christ?* chapter 1.

19. See Leon Morris, *The Atonement, Its Meaning and Significance* (Downers Grove, Ill.: Inter-Varsity Press, 1983) and *The Cross in the New Testament* (Grand Rapids, Mich.: Eerdmans, 1965); and Vincent Taylor, *The Atonement in New Testament Teaching* (London: The Epworth Press, 1941); *The Cross of Christ: Eight Public Lectures* (New York: St. Martin's Press, 1956); and *Forgiveness and Reconciliation: A Study in New Testament Theology* (London: Macmillan, 1941).

20. See works of Norman Pittenger, especially *The Christian Sacrifice: A Study of the Eucharist in the Life of the Christian Church* (New York: Oxford University Press, 1951); *Christology Reconsidered* (London: SCM Press, 1970); *Cosmic Love and Human Wrong: The Reconception of the Meaning of Sin, in the Light of Process Thinking* (New York: Paulist Press, 1978); *Unbounded Love: God and Man in Process* (New York: Seabury Press, 1976); *The Word Incarnate: A Study of the Doctrine of the Person of Christ* (Welwyn, Herts: J. Nisbet, 1959).

21. See Gustaf Aulen, *Christus Victor: An Historical Study of the Three Main Types of the Idea of Atonement* (New York: Macmillan, 1951).

8

God

The breath of God, the Holy Spirit, leads us to the Holy Child, Jesus, who takes us to God the Father. "It is a fearful thing to fall into the hands of the living God" (Heb. 10:31). We are there. We often do not know it. And when we do know we are in God's hands, we tend to forget His care except in time of trouble. Seniors have heard so much about God. We find it confusing to stop and think about God. Some of us have been living out of His grace so long we have a comfortable presence and a deep relationship that seldom asks what God is like. An aged gentleman had "lost" has wife in a department store. When asked by a helpful clerk what she looked like, the man could only reply, "She looks like my wife." It is humorous. But it is understandable. When we have walked with God, talked about God, and worshiped God for so long, we find it strange to try to analyze God in formal descriptive statements.

Once more we are thrown back onto poetry, music, and analogies. We know we cannot describe God in the same way we describe people. Height, weight, color of eyes and hair are not the descriptive categories we use for God.[1] In some ways it is easier to experience God than to describe God.

In chapter 1 we used some gospel songs to talk about the last things. I find it highly appropriate and very helpful to use ten of the standard hymns of the Christian community to assist in our talking about God. Sometimes in singing we express things in lyrics and tunes that are hard to put into formal logic. I have discovered, after thirty years of teaching theology, that ministerial students do not comprehend or enjoy formal rational theology which leans heavily on argumentation, philosophical definitions, and archaic words.

Our forefathers used to talk about God as having: aseity, immutability, immensity, impassibility, essences, attributes, omniscience, omnipotence, omnipresence, and so forth. Careful definitions and rational explanations and fitting it all together in noncontradictory ways occupied much of their time. There was a twofold division of God that gave rise to talking about what God was within Himself vis-à-vis what God was in relation to His world.[2] All of this was correct and beautifully spelled out. But these kinds of discussions were and are not very exciting or vibrant. We know what God is like by what God does. The picture of God in Scripture is the norm of God in our experience. But in neither Scripture nor experience do we find the God of formal theological discussion. It is better, in my opinion, to let our discussion of God emerge from worship and hymnody than to review for readers of this book the scholastic arguments about God.[3] This does not mean that the more formal and technical discussions of God are wrong, but they are hard to understand, and they are difficult to apply to life.

I want to make an unusual request. If you play the piano and have one at your disposal, play and sing the hymns selected as the introduction of each section before reading that section. It is necessary to talk about God. It is a deeper joy to sing about God.

O God, Our Help in Ages Past

O God, our help in ages past,
Our hope for years to come,
Our shelter from the stormy blast,
And our eternal home!

Under the shadow of thy throne
Thy saints have dwelt secure;
Sufficient is thine arm alone,
And our defense is sure.

Before the hills in order stood,
Or earth received her frame,
From everlasting thou art God,
To endless years the same.

A thousand ages in thy sight
Are like an evening gone;
Short as the watch that ends the night
Before the rising sun.

Time, like an ever-rolling stream,
Bears all its sons away;
They fly, forgotten, as a dream
Dies at the op'ning day.

O God, our help in ages past,
Our hope for years to come,
Be thou our Guard while life shall last,
And our eternal home.

Isaac Watts's lyrics are beautifully matched with William Croft's ST. ANNE tune.[4]

Stability and permanence are important characteristics of life. Change and novelty are exciting. But having something and someone that one can count on is essential. Formal theology spoke of the eternality of God and entered into philosophical discussions about the relation of time and eternity. The psalmist in Psalm 90, upon which this hymn is based, found a wonderful way of speaking about God who has always been "there" and who will always be "here." There is a popular saying that refers to someone or something being as old as the hills. The psalmist and the songwriter refer to God who is older than the mountains, who brought them into being, and with whom a thousand years is as an evening gone.

We, who know the weakness and frailty of all persons, are grateful that God is certain. Calvin's reminder that "the knowledge of God and that of ourselves are connected"[5] is reinforced by Watts's expressions "From everlasting thou art God" in contrast with "Time, like an ever-rolling stream,/Bears all its sons away." Deuteronomy 33:27 is a verse vexed with translation problems, but the King James Version gave a memorable phrase which is hard for many of us to forget. "The Eternal God is thy refuge, and underneath are the everlasting arms." The eternality of God is extended and expressed by John in the gift of eternal life (fifteen references in the Gospel and the First Epistle). Paul concurred. "The gift of God is eternal life through Jesus Christ our Lord" (Rom. 6:23, KJV). First John equates a vital relationship with Jesus Christ with having a sure knowledge of God. His brief conclusion is: "This is the true God, this is eternal life" (1 John 5:20). God's eternality is not so much a way of saying how old God is. It is way of saying how dependable God is. Henry Lyte's hymn "Abide with Me," written over a hundred years later than Watts's lyrics, adds a poetic testimony to the eternality of God. Lyte said: "Change and decay in all around I see,/O Thou who changest not, abide with me."[6]

As our own powers fail, as the familiar is replaced by the new, it is wonderfully comforting to reflect on and rely upon the God who changes not. This stable unchangeableness of God is closely related to God's faithfulness and solidarity.

GREAT IS THY FAITHFULNESS

Great is thy faithfulness, O God my Father,
There is no shadow of turning with thee;
Thou changest not, thy compassions, they fail not;
As thou hast been thou forever wilt be.

Chorus:
Great is thy faithfulness! Great is thy faithfulness!
Morning by morning new mercies I see;
All I have needed thy hand hath provided;
Great is thy faithfulness, Lord, unto me!

Summer and winter, and springtime and harvest,
Sun, moon, and stars in their courses above
Join with all nature in manifold witness
To thy great faithfulness, mercy, and love.

Pardon for sin and a peace that endureth,
Thine own dear presence to cheer and to guide;
Strength for today and bright hope for tomorrow,
Blessings all mine, with ten thousand beside.[7]

In the early part of our century (1923) Thomas Chisholm provided words for which William Runyan contributed his tune, appropriately called FAITHFULNESS. As God's eternity speaks of stability, God's faithfulness speaks of His responsibility to creation. God will not leave us alone. God will not leave the world alone.[8] This is both comforting and disturbing. When we want to rely on God's presence, it is comforting to know "Thine own dear presence to cheer and to guide." But when we do not want to be reminded of His faithfulness to us, the reality of His faithfulness and presence is disturbing. Unfortunately, Chisholm's words only take into account the positive implications. But the negative implications are there as well. Since God will not let creation go, because God is faithful to the creature, there is both heaven and hell. Those who come to grips with the faithfulness of God can sing about "Strength for today and bright hope for tomorrow,/Blessings all mine, and ten thousand beside!" Those who will not exercise faith, nevertheless, are confronted with a faithful God. That has the making of hell. Lack of faith in God or others may breed a distorted faithfulness only to self. Such a self-centered faith seeks no pardon for sin. It cannot, therefore, have a peace that endureth.

Most of the biblical references to faith, God's gift to humans, are in the New Testament. Most of the biblical references to faithfulness, God's own disposition toward the world, are in the Old Testament. And these latter references are primarily to God. The psalmist rejoices that God's faithfulness extends as high as the clouds (36:5). God's faithfulness extends to all generations (119:90). God is the faithful God. God keeps the covenant and extends mercy to a thousand generations (Deut. 7:9). The Scripture which gave our hymn its title is Lamentations 3:22-23. It is because of the Lord's mercies that we are not consumed. It is because of our Lord's faithfulness that we are sustained.

The intensely personal expressions of faithfulness conclude the refrain. Over and over we are reminded that God is faithful unto me. The entire resources of the faithful God to the grandeur and majesty of His creation are expressed also to the least and the last of His creatures. It is good to know that the stability and regularity of God's guiding hand to the universe is of one and the same cloth that oversees the least of His children. The injunction of the gospel song, "Have Faith in God,"[9] is the underside of God's faithfulness to us. It is His faithfulness to us in the creation and the cross that invites and excites our having faith in God. He believed in us before we ever believed in Him. Creation, preservation, redemption, and eschatology are evidences of His faith in us. Our response of faith and our faithfulness to the commitments we make to Him are all His gifts. But these gifts unite and require our response and our participation. God is eternal. God is faithful.[10]

The eternal God who is faithful is also merciful. We do not often sing "There's a Wideness in God's Mercy. That is unfortunate, for the text and tune are among the loveliest in our hymnals.

There's a Wideness in God's Mercy

There's a wideness in God's mercy,
Like the wideness of the sea;
There's a kindness in his justice,
Which is more than liberty.

There is welcome for the sinner,
And more graces for the good;
There is mercy with the Savior;
There is healing in his blood.

But we make his love too narrow
By false limits of our own;
And we magnify his strictness
With a zeal he will not own.

For the love of God is broader
Than the measure of man's mind;
And the heart of the Eternal
Is most wonderfully kind.[11]

In the Old Testament, the Hebrew words for *mercy* are used more than the Hebrew words for *love.* It may well be said that the Old Testament idea of spiritual love is best expressed by the term *mercy.* Mercy is kindness. Mercy is looking with favor and delight on those from whom one has nothing to expect in return. It is said of the imprisoned Joseph that God "shewed him mercy, and gave him favour" (Gen. 39:21, KJV). And the results brought blessings unimagined. There is a word which has come recently into prominence in our speech. The term is *serendipity.* The idea of serendipity is of something unexpected and delightfully surprising. Mercy is God's serendipitous character. Numbers 14:18 ("The Lord is longsuffering, and of great mercy, forgiving iniquity and transgression," KJV) unites mercy with the forgiveness of sins.

Psalm 136 is a litany of mercy which reminds us with magnificent monotony, "His mercy endureth for ever" (KJV). Praise and thanksgiving are united in human response to the diverse manifestations of mercy. Mercy is not uninformed sentiment. Proverbs unites mercy and truth (Prov. 3:3; 14:22; 16:6). God's mercy is built on the actual and the factual. God is good and gracious to all. Especially is He merciful to those in need, who have no other source of comfort, acceptance, or help. Conditions in a country are desperate when "there is no truth, nor mercy, nor knowledge of God in the land" (Hos. 4:1, KJV).

The God who is merciful wants His people to be merciful. To be merciful is better than all ritual observances. God does not regard our religious rituals unless they are accompanied by gracious and merciful attitudes and actions towards others. God said to disobedient

Israel, and just as clearly to disobedient Christians, "For I desired mercy, and not sacrifice; and the knowledge of God more than burnt offerings" (Hos. 6:6, KJV). To Hosea's impassioned cry on behalf of God may be added Micah's simple statement, "He hath shewed thee, O man, what is good; and what doth the Lord require of thee, but to do justly, and to love mercy, and to walk humbly with thy God" (Mic. 6:8, KJV).

In the Old Testament mercy is intimately related to the covenant of God. It is God's mercy which has provided the covenant, and it is God's mercy that keeps the covenant (Deut. 7:9; 1 Kings 8:23; Neh. 1:5; 9:32). The psalmist recognized mercy as a central feature of God's character. One of the most beautiful descriptions about God in all biblical literature is Psalm 103. One of the central expressions of that hymn of praise says, "The Lord is merciful and gracious, slow to anger, and plenteous in mercy" (v. 8, KJV).

In the New Testament Luke, the hymnist, quoted the Old Testament in conjoining the mercy of the covenant God with the promise of the new covenant established in the person of God's Son (Luke 1:50, 54, 58, 72, 78). And Paul, the rabbinic scholar, remembered his instruction in Israel and found its completion in Christ. Paul saw God's mercy in Christ and prayed that the Gentiles might glorify God for His mercy (Rom. 15:9); he acknowledged that God's provision in Christ is given by "God, rich in mercy" (Eph. 2:4); and he predicated his apostolic greetings on the "Grace, mercy, and peace to you from God" (1 Tim. 1:2; 2 Tim. 1:2; Titus 1:4; See 1 Peter 1:3; 2 John 3; and Jude 2). Mercy is an essential characteristic of God according to Scripture.

Frederick Faber, in his lyrics quoted above, tapped into this biblical funding of God's mercy by a series of poetic images. God's mercy is wider than the sea, "more than liberty." God's mercy assures the sinner of a welcome and gives grace to the good. I enjoy especially the metaphor of extended space, the luxurious dimensions, and enlarging expressions of this hymn. Faber's comparisons are true. Our mercy and love are narrow, limited, and too strict. Our kindness has a zeal not promoted by love. I have often said, if God is not more forgiving and merciful than His church, we are all in trouble. The mysterious element is likewise expressed in Faber's words. It is a felicitous phrase which reminds us that "the love of God is broader/

Than the measure of man's mind." There are depths in God's mercy and there is an element of mystery we will discuss under the hymn, "Immortal, Invisible, God Only Wise." But first it is appropriate to hold together and relate God's mercy and His grace, for they are indeed siblings, if not identical twins.

Amazing Grace

Amazing grace! how sweet the sound,
That saved a wretch like me!
I once was lost, but now am found,
Was blind, but now I see.

'Twas grace that taught my heart to fear,
And grace my fears relieved;
How precious did that grace appear
The hour I first believed!

Thro' many dangers, toils, and snares,
I have already come;
'Tis grace that bro't me safe thus far,
And grace will lead me home.

The Lord has promised good to me,
His word my hope secures;
He will my shield and portion be
As long as life endures.

When we've been there ten thousand years,
Bright shining as the sun,
We've no less days to sing God's praise
Than when we first begun.[12]

What better hymnic expression of grace than this old gospel song which has even made the lists of popular musical selections in our secular society! Grace is one of those religious terms that we are better at using than we are at defining.[13]

If the Old Testament speaks less about grace and more about mercy, the New Testament reverses the situation. Yet both terms are essential to both Testaments. Grace is often defined as unmerited favor; but it is much more. Grace is the central disposition of God in relation to His world. To find grace in God's eyes is humanity's only hope of survival. Noah "found grace in the eyes of the Lord" (Gen. 6:8). Jacob prayed to find grace in God's sight (Gen. 33:10). Joseph found grace in Potiphar's sight because he had previously found grace in God's sight (Gen. 39:4). Moses found grace in God's sight

(Ex. 33:13-14), and as one graced of God, he prayed that all of God's people might find grace in God's sight (Ex. 33:16).

Moses' prayer was fully answered in the One upon whom the grace of God dwelt fully, Jesus Christ (Luke 2:40). Whereas the grace of the law was upon Moses, the full grace and truth of God dwelt among us in Jesus Christ (John 1:17). "Out of his full store we have all received grace upon grace" (John 1:16). The grace of "the Child" was extended to the children of the Father in numerous ways in the Book of Acts.[14]

Paul was the apostle *to* the Gentiles, but he was the apostle *of* God's grace. It requires almost one full column in a concordance to list Paul's use of the term grace. Grace was his greeting (Rom. 1:7, see also the salutations in all of his letters). It is the nature of God and the gift of God. Grace enables us to be (1 Cor. 15:10) and to be saved (Eph. 2:8-10). Grace enables our speech to be appropriate and our hearts to sing (Col. 4:6; 3:16).

Small wonder that John Newton's words have become a universal and ecumenical way of singing the gospel. Contemporary theologians have explored grace at great length.[15] The simple words of our hymn celebrate grace in a language all can appropriate. Grace is amazing, amazing because it is undeserved, unexpected, and essentially unexplainable. Grace teaches godly fear and relieves anxiety. Grace first leads us to God and leads us, at last, home with God. Grace promises that God "will my shield and portion be/As long as life endures." And then, in a higher key, grace reaches beyond earth to heaven where it becomes the key note in an eternal celebration.

Throughout church history Christians have argued much about the appropriation of God's grace. How do we receive grace? Some say especially through rituals of the church. Others say by a legal declaration and gift of God. Most would prefer to speak of grace as a relationship which God initiates and in which we cooperate. All of us would agree that grace is a gift of God. Our first grace from God is life. Our highest grace gift from God is eternal life through Jesus Christ, our Lord. Paul spoke of grace abounding (Rom. 5:20). John Bunyan celebrated the Pauline phrase and developed it into a basic book about God and the Christian life.[16]

Mercy and grace are twins. And they share an element of mystery. The mysterious nature of God's ways with His world is an essential element in our limited understanding of God. It is about that dimension of mystery we now must sing.

IMMORTAL, INVISIBLE, GOD ONLY WISE

Immortal, invisible, God only wise,
In light inaccessible hid from our eyes,
Most blessed, most glorious, the Ancient of Days,
Almighty, victorious, thy great name we praise.

Unresting, unhasting, and silent as light,
Nor wanting, nor wasting, thou rulest in might;
Thy justice like mountains high soaring above,
Thy clouds which are fountains of goodness and love.

To all, life thou givest, to both great and small;
In all life thou livest, the true life of all;
We blossom and flourish as leaves on the tree,
And wither and perish—but naught changeth thee.

Great Father of glory, pure Father of light,
Thine angels adore thee, all veiling their sight;
All praise we would render; O help us to see
'Tis only the splendor of light hideth thee![17]

At first glance we may suppose that mystery is not a biblical concept. There are twenty-seven references to the mystery(ies) of God in the New Testament. In these uses *mystery* refers to what is known only to the initiated. I would certainly want to affirm that those who know God in a vital relationship know more about God and understand the things of God better than others do. But this knowledge of the initiated is only one use of the term *mystery.* A more popular meaning of the term is something that we, or at least a clever detective, can resolve. That is not the meaning I want to convey. There is a category of the mysterious which will always remain unresolved, fascinating, and intriguing. There is something of this type of mystery in the nature of God. Two Old Testament passages celebrate this otherness of God which is always above and beyond the creature. "For my thoughts are not your thoughts,/and your ways are not my ways,/This is the very word of the Lord./For as the heavens are higher than the earth,/so are my ways higher than your ways/and my thoughts than your thoughts" (Isa. 55:8-9). "He hath made every thing beautiful in his time: also he hath set the world in their heart, so that no man can find out the work that God maketh from the beginning to the end" (Eccl. 3:11, KJV).

It is this "depth of unknowingness" and this height of God's ways that are celebrated in the hymn "Immortal, Invisible, God Only Wise." The title of the hymn is taken from 1 Timothy 1:17. Paul used the concept of immortality in 1 Corinthians 15:53, 54 and Romans 2:7. In these references the subject is humanity's immortality through Christ. In 2 Timothy 1:10 the reference is to Jesus Christ who brings us immortality. First Timothy 6:16 refers to immortality and light as expressions of God. This passage is indirectly referred to in the second and third line of the first stanza of our hymn. In Colossians 1:15 Christ is described as the image of the invisible God. And in 1 Timothy 1:17 the terms *immortal* and *invisible* are both ascribed to God. The author of Hebrews paid tribute to Moses who lived although he "saw the invisible God" (Heb. 11:27).

This small list exhausts the references to immortality and invisibility. But the insights to which these terms refer are many and significant. To begin, when we speak of God's immortality, we acknowledge God as the source of life, the giver of life, and energizing principle of all that is. It is therefore a linguistic and an actual absurdity to speak of the death of God in any way except metaphorically.[18] Immortal means not to be able to die. In that absolute sense God only is immortal. Through Jesus Christ God will call creation back into existence. But of ourselves, we are not immortal.[19]

Invisible means that God cannot be seen. It is a term that stresses God's otherness from the world. It is this otherness, this mystery, this beyondness that is suggested by these two terms. The element of mystery is necessary to preserve God's otherness. The fact of mystery is necessary to retain our interest in God. It is observable from childhood on, even to our second childhood, that we lose interest in those subjects, those people, and those things which we know all about, whom we have all figured out, and whom we can control.[20] God is not one of those. There is more to God than meets the eye. Years of too simple theology and too confident and supposedly exhaustive talk and preaching about God have made God banal and boring. J. B. Phillips's challenge to young people, who had lost interest in God because God had been presented in such a domesticated way, was *Your God Is Too Small.*[21]

It does us good to sing "Unresting, unhasting, and silent as light,/

Nor wanting, nor wasting, thou rulest in might." Faith and this kind of God go together. For "faith is the substance of things hoped for, the evidence of things not seen" (Heb. 11:1, KJV). Only when the term *God* is invested with absolutes and given embodiment in Christ do we have the God of Scripture—God, the Maker of heaven and earth; the God of Abraham, Isaac, and Jacob; and the God and Father of our Lord and Savior, Jesus Christ. A generation glutted on TV spectaculars needs a profound dose of the grandeur of God. There is that which cannot die because it is life. There is that which cannot be seen because it gives meaning to everything that can be seen. That "that" is God.

That God came to us in the person of One who was seen and who did die. But behind that mortal, visible face of God lies the other face of God—the fact of God who is other than we are, higher than we are, better than we are. We may serve that God all the days of our life, and then "ten thousand years," and then we may begin to understand and appreciate that His ways are not our ways and His thoughts are not our thoughts (Isa. 55:8). Robert Browning understood this otherness well when he said, "Ah, but a man's reach should exceed his grasp,/Or what's a heaven for?"[22] "Most blessed, most glorious, the Ancient of Days,/Almighty, victorious, thy great name we praise."[23]

The descriptive word about God which most closely parallels the terms *immortal* and *invisible* and stresses God's mystery and otherness is "holy."

HOLY, HOLY, HOLY

Holy, holy, holy! Lord God Almighty!
Early in the morning our song shall rise to thee;
Holy, holy, holy, merciful and mighty!
God in three Persons, blessed Trinity!

Holy, holy, holy! all the saints adore thee,
Casting down their golden crowns around the glassy sea;
Cherubim and seraphim falling down before thee,
Who wert, and art, and evermore shalt be.

Holy, holy, holy! tho the darkness hide thee,
Tho the eye of sinful man thy glory may not see;
Only thou art holy; there is none beside thee,
Perfect in pow'r, in love, and purity.

Holy, holy, holy! Lord God Almighty!
All thy works shall praise thy name, in earth, and sky, and sea;
Holy, holy, holy; merciful and mighty!
God in three Persons, blessed Trinity![24]

We use some words so often they become a part of us without our awareness of what they really mean. I believe *holy* is one of those words. Everything I said in the previous section about otherness, difference from creation, applies here as well. Holy is an elemental experience that involves awe, wonder, and fascination. Holiness is the exciting characteristic of God that should keep us on tenterhooks before God in expectancy. If we understand God's holiness, we know we can never put our full weight down in God's presence, for there is yet something more to be explored.

The word *holy* in the Old Testament means something that is cut off, separate, set apart from everything else. Holy is more than a call of seraphim in Isaiah's worship experience (Isa. 6:3). Holy is what God is and what God expects His people to be (Lev. 19:2). How is it possible for people to be holy? Only in a derivative way. God only is absolute holiness. God only is distinctive and set apart from all else. But because God is holy, in this sense, God holds forth fresh possibilities that things can be different for us and for God's world. Jerusalem is a holy city because it is set apart to a holy God. Christians are a "chosen generation, a royal priesthood, an holy nation, a peculiar people; that [they] should shew forth the praises of him who hath called you [them] out of darkness into his marvellous light" (1 Pet. 2:9, KJV).

As I suggested above, this means that saints are primarily people who are set apart to a holy God. God's holiness is a moral holiness, but God's holiness is primarily a way of being, a type of difference, a religious category.

Holiness, and those other terms for God which convey His otherness (glory, immortality, invisibility), needs to be reclaimed by many of our churches in their worship. Holiness does not require stiff formality, but it does appreciate a moment of silence. Holiness, the holiness of God, does not require intellectualism, but it needs moments for reflection. Holiness does not require a pipe organ, but it enjoys a singing heart that knows things can be different. Reginald Heber's text, "Holy, Holy, Holy" sung to John B. Dykes's tune

NICAEA is perhaps one of our most familiar hymns. Perhaps it is too familiar. Perhaps we have sung it so frequently that we do not believe "the darkness hide[s] thee," and that "the eye of sinful man thy glory may not see." We need to reflect very much on holiness, for it is the principal atmosphere of heaven. Holiness is what the angels sing, from the seraphim of Isaiah (6) to their counterparts who are still on this one song in Revelation (4:8).

Holiness speaks of God's transcendence. God is high and lifted up. God is also close and very present. The primary proof of God's presence is God's love.

O Love That Wilt Not Let Me Go

O Love that wilt not let me go,
I rest my weary soul in thee;
I give thee back the life I owe,
That in thine ocean depths its flow
May richer, fuller be

O Light that followest all my way,
I yield my flick'ring torch to thee;
My heart restores its borrowed ray,
That in thy sunshine's glow its day
May brighter, fairer be.

O Joy that seekest me through pain,
I cannot close my heart to thee;
I trace the rainbow thro' the rain,
And feel the promise is not vain
That morn shall tearless be.

O Cross that liftest up my head,
I dare not ask to hide from thee;
I lay in dust life's glory dead,
And from the ground there blossoms red
Life that shall endless be.[25]

George Matheson preserved something of the divine mystery in his text: "O Love That Wilt Not Let Me Go." There is an anonymous quatrain that also gives gratitude for God's love while confessing its mysterious quality.

That thou shouldst think so well of me
And be the God thou art
Is darkness to my intellect
But sunshine to my heart.

From a human point of view, and that is all we have without God's enlightenment, the love of God is unfathomable. God's kind of love does not make sense in our kind of world. But "this is [my] Father's world," and the love of God will redeem it despite our inability to understand such redemption.

The biblical vocabulary is full of expressions about love. The Old Testament stresses the intensity of God's love by the use of a word that means "to pant" or "eagerly desire." The love of the God of Israel is no cool, dispassionate attachment. God's love pursues. God's love grasps. God's love makes God jealous on behalf of the goodness of creation. God has a passionate attachment to judgment ("justice," Ps. 37:28), to righteousness (45:7). God is decidedly partisan on behalf of the good. And God expects His love to be returned. It is the primary command to love the Lord God with all the heart, mind, and soul (Deut. 6:5). God's love for Israel is reflected in Hosea's love for faithless Gomer. One finds a whole vocabulary of love in such terms as *pity, compassion,* and *lovingkindness.* The fervor and intensity of God's love for creation will not let it go. God purges the world with water (Gen. 6—8), consumes it with fire (Deut. 9:3), and pursues it with a Father's waiting love (Hos. 11:1-9).

These are strong words. God's love is a strong and constant pressure. This kind of love is related to zeal. It cannot be ignored. It shakes the foundations of the earth and pursues Elijah in a still small voice. Most of us would prefer something more romantic or controllable. But God's love is not at our convenience. It is at the center of His being and of ours. It "will not let us go." There is a claim on us to "give back the life we owe," "to trace the rainbow thro' the rain," to know "the promise is not vain"—all the promises of God.

In the New Testament there are a variety of words for love. The lowest level of love is lust, *epithumia;* it is akin to love only in its eager grasping. It is prevented from being love because what it desires so intensely it desires for selfish and destructive reasons. Lust has both God's intensity and demonic intentions. Lust is never used of God. It is the opposite of God's way of loving. Lust uses up. Love restores. Lust destroys. Love makes whole.

A second term for love in the New Testament era, *eros,* means to be attracted to something because of what it can do for one. *Eros* is discriminating. It asks: "What is in it for me?" *Eros* shops for bargains, gets its way, and looks out after number one. *Eros* does not appear in the New Testament, but it appears everywhere in the world. We may not recognize the Greek word, but we know much about the reality for which it stands. It is human love, our kind of love. And we are never totally without it. As I discussed above, we deceive ourselves when we suppose we are.

Phileo is the love of a friend. It is not to be despised. It is the high regard with which Jesus held Lazarus (John 11:3,36). And in John 5:20 it is used of God's love to Jesus. *Phileo* has the interest of the other in mind. You are fortunate if over the years you have had a few friends whom you can love and be loved by in this way.

The major New Testament term for God's love is *agape.* It was a colorless classical term into which the New Testament poured the great torrents of God's compassion and concern for creation. *Agape* flows outward regardless of the worth of the object. This is the mysterious unfathomable kind of love that just loves because its very nature is to love. When we understand this warm word of the New Testament, it, too, like the Old Testament expressions, will overwhelm us.[26] It defies our understanding as to why God keeps loving the loveless, keeps reaching out to the unresponsive, the uncaring. But that is precisely what God does. And because this is the case, God's love will not let "me," or any part of His creation, go.

Perhaps you are realizing that this type of love seems also to pose something of a threat. It does. The love of God keeps on pursuing. It is "the hound of heaven." To those who receive it and live out of it, this kind of love is nurture, the source of acceptance, the steady assurance of God's best will, and best intentions for all of His creation. To reject this love, to try to be neutral to it, to want to be involved with it in only convenient, superficial ways is to be "burned." Our God is a consuming fire (Deut. 4:24; Heb. 12:29). And the fire that warms can also burn. God's love is the other side of His wrath. Love and wrath are not consecutive. He does not first love you and then decide He will be angry with you. God's love and wrath are convertible. He pours out His intense holy love on all creation, and it will warm or burn depending on where one stands in relation to it.

God's love will redeem all creation. God's love gave people a choice. Love will save us. Love will condemn us. Wrath will save us.

Wrath will condemn us. If we accept His love and live from it, we are redeemed. If we spurn His love, we are miserable. If we are chastened by His wrath, we are also purified by it. If we resist His wrath, we meet the immovable force, God's holiness. In the holiness of God we are constituted by His all-encompassing love. In the holiness of God we are consumed by His settled opposition to sin, His wrath.

This is a paradox. We would rather have two clear and unambiguous ways of God with His world. It is easier to be in charge if we could barter, bribe, or be sure we have only God's love. Wrath, we suppose, is for the others. God is for us and against our enemies. God is God, and God's consistent holiness is expressed in both love and wrath. Romantic notions of God's love can always come to terms with God on our own conditions. Biblical realism knows that God is consistent, and we are not. Therefore, there is both a promise and threat in the hymn: "O Love That Wilt Not Let Me Go." "In the ocean depths," the flow of our lives "may richer, fuller be." If we are buoyed up by His swelling current, we will be carried into the fullness of His love. If we resist, we will understand the psalmist's words, "Out of the depths have I called unto thee, O Lord" (Ps. 130:1). In our life in history, we know both. If we are God's children, we are chastened. Those who refuse to be God's children are "drowned in a love" that is wrath. History is our time of decision. Eternity is God's time of the confirmation of our decisions.

I hope the depth of this discussion has not distressed you. I trust the intensity of the discussion has not frightened you. One thing we must do, if we are to understand God's love, is to know that it has everlasting consequences. We dare not domesticate God's love and compromise His holiness. "O Love That Wilt Not Let Me Go" is, in the last analysis, a world of comfort. It is one of the hymns I have requested for my funeral. It is not inappropriate to think about one's service of commemoration, if one knows, trusts, lives out of, and is chastened by the love of God.

A Mighty Fortress Is Our God

A mighty fortress is our God,
A bulwark never failing;
Our helper he, amid the flood

Of mortal ills prevailing:
For still our ancient foe
Doth seek to work us woe;
His craft and pow'r are great,
And, armed with cruel hate,
On earth is not his equal.

Did we in our own strength confide,
Our striving would be losing;
Were not the right Man on our side;
The Man of God's own choosing:
Dost ask who that may be?
Christ Jesus, it is he;
Lord Sabbaoth, his name,
From age to age the same,
And he must win the battle.

And tho this world, with devils filled,
Should threaten to undo us,
We will not fear, for God, hath willed
His truth to triumph thro us:
The Prince of Darkness grim,
We tremble not for him;
His rage we can endure,
For lo, his doom is sure,
One little word shall fell him.

That word above all earthly pow'rs,
No thanks to them, abideth;
The Spirit and the gifts are ours
Thro' him who with us sideth:
Let goods and kindred go,
This mortal life also;
The body they may kill:
God's truth abideth still,
His kingdom is forever.[27]

Martin Luther's famous Reformation hymn exudes confidence. In the midst of Luther's continuing crises, his confidence in God often seemed all he had left. Ordinarily, we think of being comforted by God's love and dismayed by His power. In biblical realism the power of God is our source of comfort, and that which should dismay us is how we are relating to His love. Both power and love are substantial; they, like glory, are heavy words and important aspects of who God is. There is a paradoxical element in all of God's ways with us. We who are God's children do not fear God's power. It is the primary source of strength for the universe and for ourselves. God's power is for us the ability whereby God can do what His love requires. Love without power is maudlin sentiment. Power without love is repressive force. God "has" no power without love. God "has" no love that is without power to accomplish His purpose. They go together: love and power.[28]

There are at least seven words used of God's power in the Old Testament. But an illustration is worth a thousand words. And the poetic notion of God's power as a rock is one of those illuminating illustrations. There are no more comforting words in Scripture than those which associate God, in a poetic way, with the strength of a rock. As usual, the Psalms (KJV) sum it up beautifully:

> The Lord is my rock, and my fortress, and my deliverer; my God, my strength, in whom I will trust; my buckler, and the horn of my salvation, and my high tower (18:2).
>
> For thou art my rock and my fortress; therefore for thy name's sake lead me, and guide me (31:3).
>
> He brought me up also out of an horrible pit, out of the miry clay, and set my feet upon a rock, and established my goings (40:2).
>
> I will say unto God my rock, Why hast thou forgotten me? why go I mourning because of the oppression of the enemy? (42:9).
>
> Be thou my strong habitation, whereunto I may continually resort: thou has given commandment to save me; for thou art my rock and my fortress (71:3).
>
> He brought streams also out of the rock, and caused waters to run down like rivers (78:16).

The strength of God, our rock, is extended in a messianic prophecy which tells what it is like when God, and His Messiah, are near. "A man shall be as an hiding place from the wind, and a covert from the tempest; as rivers of water in a dry place, as the shadow of a great rock in a weary land" (Isa. 32:2). Augustus Toplady's two-hundred-year-old hymn comes to mind. It is interesting to note that this, too, has been a great funeral hymn, perhaps one of those most frequently used to provide comfort in moments of bereavement.

ROCK OF AGES, CLEFT FOR ME

Rock of Ages, cleft for me,
Let me hide myself in thee;
Let the water and the blood,
From thy wounded side which flowed,

Be of sin the double cure,
Save from wrath and make me pure.

Not the labors of my hands
Can fulfill thy law's demands;
Could my zeal no respite know,
Could my tears forever flow,
All for sin could not atone;
Thou must save, and thou alone.

While I draw this fleeting breath,
When mine eyes shall close in death,
When I rise to worlds unknown,
And behold thee on thy throne,
Rock of Ages, cleft for me,
Let me hide myself in thee.[29]

It is important to know that the God who cares is the God who "can." "He is able to deliver thee." Daniel understood this (Dan. 3 and 6 have nine references to the delivering God). So should we. We especially should understand the power of God, we whose own natural powers have begun to fade. It is biblical realism to find comfort in the fact that the source of all power is kindly disposed to us and is graciously inclined especially to those who lack power.

In the New Testament there are three words for power. One (*kratos*) means force or power. *Dunameis* (we get our word *dynamite* from it) means an extraordinary kind of power. This term is usually translated "miracle." The third term is *exousia,* which means authority or rightful power. Suffice it to say, at this point, that God is able—able to do the strong (*kratos*), the spectacular (*dunameis*), and the steady, sustaining things that flow from His inner strength (*exousia*).

There are two special expressions of God's power that, for me, demonstrate the essence of strength. How strong is God? God is strong enough to exercise the incredible patience that will tolerate our mistakes and the mess we make of things personally, corporately, and cosmically. The patience of God may be for us a reassuring notion. The patience of God may be for us the major source of questions about the problem of evil. Sometimes it is both. It is comforting to know that in God's own way and in God's own time, God's own will will be done. It is frustrating, to the point of anger, to declare: If God can do something, why doesn't He?

How strong is God? God is strong enough to endure eternally a split in His creation. God is strong enough to permit us freedom enough to thwart His will for the sake of human will. That is what hell means. God does not will it. God has permitted it. God must endure it. It is God who suffers most because of hell. He has no delight in "the death of him that dieth" (Ezek. 18:32, KJV). He has no peace, in the sense of equanimity, because of what humans do to themselves, others, their environment, and God's world. He has no peace because of the lasting consequences of what humans do. He is strong enough to endure it. God is strong enough to accept the consequences of freedom. God is strong enough to create, strong enough to save, strong enough to permit the decisions of errant people. God is also strong enough to redeem.

Once to Every Man and Nation

Once to ev'ry man and nation
Comes the moment to decide,
In the strife of truth with falsehood,
For the good or evil side;
Some great cause, some great decision,
Off'ring each the bloom or blight,
And the choice goes by forever
'Twixt that darkness and that light.

Then to side with truth is noble,
When we share her wretched crust,
Ere her cause bring fame and profit,
And 'tis prosperous to be just;
Then it is the brave man chooses
While the coward stands aside,
Till the multitude make virture
Of the faith they had denied.

....

Tho the cause of evil prosper,
Yet the truth alone is strong;
Tho her portion be the scaffold,
And upon the throne be wrong:
Yet that scaffold sways the future,
And, behind the dim unknown,
Standeth God within the shadow,
Keeping watch above his own.[30]

There are not many great hymns about God's justice. The hymn I have chosen speaks more about our doing justice and walking humbly with our God (Mic. 6:8). James Russell Lowell puts the crisis of decision eloquently. We have many times to choose justice and to do mercy. But there are turns of "fate" which call for major decisions. As Shakespeare reminded us, "There is a tide in the affairs of men/ Which taken at the flood leads on to fortune/Omitted, all the voyage of their life/Is bound in shallows and in miseries./On such a full sea are we now afloat,/And we must take the current when it serves,/Or lose our ventures."[31] Once to every man and nation may not be enough. God's decision for justice is once and forever. God is just. Justice is not just something God loves or God dispenses. Like love and power, justice is something God is. Just as love without power is maudlin sentiment, so love without justice is romantic favoritism. And just as power without love is repressive force, so power without justice is despotism. They go together, love, power, and justice; for they are grounded in God. God is the Guarantor of justice and the Dispenser of judgment. Thank God! For only God is holy enough, able enough, and wise enough to be Judge. Justice is what a judge dispenses. Judgment is the decision and the confirmation of justice. It is supposed to be that way on earth. It is not always so. It is that way in heaven.

God is the standard of what is right. (The basic biblical words for right, righteous, righteousness, just, justice, and justification are essentially from the same stems.) Amos likened God to a plumbline beside which all else was crooked (Amos 7:7-9). Jesus declared God was right (John 17:25). Paul said it was God who justifies (Rom. 8:33). Monarchy is when one does what is right in the sight of the king. Anarchy is when one does what is right, each one, in one's own eyes. The final state is the kingdom of God. And the final state of the kingdom of God is justice.

It is all right to question what appears to be divine justice. So Abraham asked, "Shall not the judge of all the earth do what is just?" (Gen. 18:25). So did Eliphaz in Job, "Can mortal man be more just than God,/or the creature purer than his Maker?" (Job 4:17). But it is not all right to question the fact of justice, that it resides in God, that it should be practiced by God's friends, that it will at last be done in earth, as it is in heaven.

Because God is just we should find it noble "to side with truth," "Ere her cause bring fame and profit,/And 'tis prosperous to be just."

Because God is just we will not stand aside "Till the multitude make virtue/Of the faith they had denied." Because God is just, we must push upward still and onward, who would keep abreast of truth. God's justice guarantees the right. God's righteous Child, seemingly such a victim of injustice, will come to judge the world in righteousness. Therefore, we are justified by faith. Is this justice? Yes, it is God's justice, tempered with mercy and enforced by the power of holy love.

Classical theology talked in Latin terms about God's omnipresence, God's omnipotence, and God's omniscience. I have discussed the presence of God together with love. The section on God's power was "sung" with Luther's Reformation hymn and accompanied with all of the comfort an adequate understanding of God's power can bring. It is now time to turn attention to God's knowledge. We can approach it academically, or we can approach it devotionally. I would like to talk about God's knowledge devotionally in a way that will include the academic. There is a choice old hymn that does just that.

All Things Bright and Beautiful

All things bright and beautiful,
All creatures great and small,
All things wise and wonderful;
The Lord God made them all.

Each little flower that opens,
Each little bird that sings,
He made their glowing colors,
He made their tiny wings.

The purple-headed mountains,
The river running by,
The sunset, and the morning
That brightens up the sky,

The cold wind in the winter,
The pleasant summer sun,
The ripe fruits in the garden—
He made them every one.[32]

Cecil Alexander's text may seem a strange selection as an illustration for God's knowledge. In reality it is particularly appropriate. It carries the Old Testament implication that the maker of a thing has a kind of peculiar and intimate knowledge and awareness of a thing.

And it is this peculiar, intimate knowledge of the maker which predominates rather than the idea of knowing in an academic, intellectual sense. God made and therefore has a relational knowledge of all things. God made summer and winter (Ps. 74:17). God made leviathan to play with (Ps. 104:26; see Job 41). God made a covenant with Abraham (Gen. 12:1-7; 15; 17:2). The Lord made the Jordan River as a border between the Reubenites and the Gaddites (Josh. 22:25). God made Solomon king over Israel, according to the flattering words of Hiram of Tyre (2 Chron. 2:11). God chose Isaiah to remind Israel: "I am the Lord, your Holy One, your creator, Israel, and your King" (Isa. 43:15). The summary statement comes at the first of the Old Testament. "The Lord God made earth and heaven" (Gen. 2:5). All of the rest of the creation account and all of the rest of Scripture is commentary on the specifics.

God makes things, and God makes things happen. Therefore God knows. God knows the sorrows of the Israelites in Egypt (Ex. 3:7). God knows Moses, which means Moses found grace in God's sight (Ex. 33:12). God knows the way of the righteous (Ps. 1:6). God knows the birds of the mountains (Ps. 11:1). Jesus reminded His disciples that God knows the lilies of the field, the birds of the air, and the number of the hairs of one's head (Matt. 10:29-31). We need to know that the Father knows "what things" we have need of even before we ask (Matt. 6:8). God makes things. God knows things. "All things bright and beautiful,/All creatures great and small,/All things wise and wonderful,/The Lord God made [and knows] them all."

It is this kind of knowing that matters. If Jesus, God's Son at judgment does not "know" one, that one must depart from His presence and all possibility of fellowship. We never can depart from God's presence in actuality. Because it is the knowledge of God, no less than the presence and the power of God, which holds us in existence. God still "knows" what is going on in hell. God knows about humanity. But at Bethlehem, through Jesus Christ, God experienced humanity. Presence and knowing and power are as interrelated as love and power and justice.

We have great difficulty with God's knowledge because we assume two things that may not necessarily be so in the way we suppose them. First, we assume that God has to know like we have to know. If we would reflect on the matter carefully, we would know that is not necessarily correct. "For my thoughts are not your thoughts,/and your ways are not my ways./This is the very word of the Lord" (Isa. 55:8). Isaiah asked many perceptive questions. One of the most searching was "Who hath directed the spirit of the Lord? What counsellor stood at his side to instruct him?" (Isa. 40:13). Paul picked up on this mystery of the divine knowledge and repeated it in his benediction at the conclusion of Romans 9—11 (11:34). Our second mistake is assuming God's knowledge should be discussed in technical philosophical terms. Once we start asking how God knows and if God knows this first and that second, we have opened Pandora's box of Greek philosophical questions that make predestination a conundrum instead of a comfort. Moreover, when we stress God's knowledge as a formal/conceptual way of knowing rather than a biblical/relational way of knowing, we start arguments about intellect and leave aside the biblical insights about relationships. Discussions about how God conceptualizes and organizes His thoughts break up into sterile rationalism that can prove what it wants to about what God thinks while ignoring what God has done.

The important question for seniors is not, "What was God's first thought in eternity?" Much more significant is the question: "Does God know me?" And the all-inclusive answer is, "If a man love, he is acknowledged by God" (1 Cor. 8:3). "He has made everything [beautiful] to suit its time; moreover he has given men a sense of time past and futute, but no comprehension of God's work from beginning to end" (Eccl. 3:11).

These are the ways God acts and the words that express what God is. God is our help, from ages past. God is faithful. God is merciful. God is gracious and glorious. God is mysterious in His holiness and in His loving presence. God is present in wrath and love. God is powerful to accomplish what must be done and wise enough to know how to do it. These are ten words about God: (1) Eternal, (2) Faithful, (3) Merciful, (4) Gracious, (5) Mysterious, (6) Holy, (7) Loving, (8) Strong, (9) Just, and (10) Knowing. There are four ways of God with His world: (1) Creation, (2) Providence, (3) Election-Redemption, and (4) Eschatology.

If you still are singing—and why should we not be in the light of what these ten hymns have taught us about God?—there are songs you can sing of each of God's ways with us. For creation try: "This

Is My Father's World," "How Great Thou Art," "Praise to the Lord, the Almighty, the King of Creation!" "Morning Has Broken," "The Heavens Are Telling." For God's providential care enjoy "Children of the Heavenly Father," "He's Got the Whole World in His hand?" "Day by Day," "God Will Take Care of You," and especially "God Moves in a Mysterious Way His Wonders to Perform."

In gratitude for God's redemption hymn writers have penned: "Eternal Father, Strong to Save," "Praise Him! Praise Him!" "Praise the Lord! Ye Heavens, Adore Him," and "Ye Servants of God." God is the God of conclusions, too. We tend to associate eschatology, the last things primarily with Jesus. But God the Father is the Consummator as well. Few hymns celebrate "Gods part" in the last things. "Rejoice, the Lord Is King" and "The Lord Will Come" seem to refer both to the Father and the Son. Good Christian theology always refers to God, the Father;[33] God, the Son; and God, the Holy Spirit. And since I would like for this book to be a good Christian theology, there is yet another song to sing. That is a song about the threefoldness of God.

COME, THOU ALMIGHTY KING

Come, thou Almighty King,
Help us thy name to sing,
Help us to praise:
Father! all-glorious,
O'er all victorious,
Come, and reign over us,
Ancient of Days.

Come, thou Incarnate Word,
Gird on thy mighty sword,
Our prayer attend!
Come, and thy people bless,
And give thy word success:
Spirit of holiness,
On us descend.

Come, Holy Comforter,
Thy sacred witness bear
In this glad hour!
Thou, who almighty art,
Now rule in ev'ry heart,
And ne'er from us depart,
Spirit of pow'r.

To thee, great One in Three,
The highest praises be,
Hence evermore;
Thy sov'reighn majesty
May we in glory see,
And to eternity
Love and adore.[34]

God is threefold. It is easier to celebrate and sing about the threefoldness of God than it is to rationalize about it. The term most frequently used to describe the threefoldness of God is Trinity. Do not reach for the concordance. Trinity is not a biblical term. And trinity is not really about ice, water, and steam, or an egg (shell, white, yellow), or about equilateral triangles, or three-leaf clovers (visual signs often used to symbolize the Trinity). Trinity is about relationships, relationships among the "persons" of the Godhead and relationships between the threefold God and all of creation. The anonymous text writer put it well. There is a stanza to God, the Father (stanza 1), a stanza to God, the Son (stanza 2), and a stanza to God, the Spirit (stanza 3). The final stanza is a litany of praise to the "great One in Three." Well done, but hard to explain.

The major grace notes about God's threefoldness in the New Testament are benedictions. "The grace of the Lord Jesus Christ, and the love of God, and fellowship in the Holy Spirit, be with you all" (2 Cor. 13:14). "Now to him who is able to do immeasurably more than all we can ask or conceive, by the power which is at work among us [the Spirit], to him be glory in the church and in Christ Jesus from generation to generation evermore! Amen" (Eph. 3:20). Or the Trinitarian implications are given by way of introduction (Rom. 1:1-4; 1 Pet. 1:2). There is an implicit Trinitarian reference in 1 Timothy 3:16. The verse is primarily a hymn to Christ, but the work of the Spirit in vindication and the glorification by the Father in high heaven are needed to make the passage meaningful.[35]

The Trinity is about relationships and about figuring out the ways God has revealed Himself to us so that it fits—fits our experience, our common sense, and the things about God which need to be held together.[36]

God made the world. God became present to the world in a variety of ways.[37] God promised a fuller expression of Himself.[38] Jesus was born, and when He became a man He declared there was a special relationship between God and Himself. Jesus promised a fuller revelation of Himself. After Jesus' death and resurrection, the Holy Spirit empowered the early church at Pentecost. After Pentecost some arose in the early church (the New Testament writers) who declared in the power of the Spirit several important things: (1) That the Holy Spirit was the fuller revealer of Jesus. (2) That Jesus was the fuller revealer of God. (3) That Jesus was the Son of God in a distinct sense. (4) That the Spirit of God whom Jesus sent was both the Spirit of God and the Spirit of Christ. "They" are related. Two doctrines require some reflection about the threefoldness of God: (1) the distinctiveness of Jesus and His oneness with God; (2) the continuing presence and witness of the Spirit of God among the people of God bearing witness to Jesus as the Son of God.

From these basic affirmations Christians worked backwards and forwards. It was always this way. "In the beginning was the Word" (John 1:1). It will always be this way. Jesus offered Himself to God in the power of "eternal Spirit" (Heb. 9:14). What God wants for His creation is redemption. Only God can accomplish what must be done to redeem the world. And whom God chose from the beginning was the fullness of Himself in Jesus Christ, in whom we belong to God (Eph. 1:1-14). And we belong to God because the Spirit of God enables us to cry "Abba" Father through the sacrificial love of the Son (Rom. 8:15). "They" are together in this that we might be together with Him who is Father, Son, Spirit.

It is not mathematical or mystical. It is relational. Those who have been led of the Spirit through the Son to the Father can pray and sing "To thee, great One in Three,/The highest praises be." And in heaven the "Spirits" before the altar (a reference to the Holy Spirit in apocalyptic terms) and the "Lamb" beside the throne and "the Ancient of Days" (Dan. 7:9), who sits upon the throne (Rev. 4—5) will receive the praise of the church on earth that has union with God, the Three in One. And those about the throne reply: "Thou art worthy, O Lord, to receive glory and honour and power: for thou hast created all things, and for thy pleasure they are and were created" (Rev. 4:11, KJV).

One can either join the singing or stop and argue. It is more fun singing.

Notes

1. On the nature of God language, see Langdon Gilkey, "Dissolution and Reconstruction in Theology," *Christian Century,* 82 (1965), 135-139; "Cosmology, Ontology, and the Travail of Biblical Language," *Journal of Religion,* 41 (1961) 194-205; "The Concept of Providence in Contemporary Theology," *Journal of Religion,* 43 (1963), 171-192; "Symbols, Meaning, and the Divine Presence," *Theological Studies* 35 (1974), 249-267; and "Mystery of Being and Nonbeing: An Experimental Project," *Journal of Religion,* 58 (1978), 1-12.

2. See for example, A. H. Strong, *Systematic Theology,* 3 vols. in 1 (Philadelphia: Judson Press, 1951).

3. See Geoffrey Wainwright, *Doxology: The Praise of God in Worship, Doctrine, and Life: A Systematic Theology* (London: Epworth Press, 1980).

4. Isaac Watts, "O God, Our Help in Ages Past," 1719; Tune, ST. ANNE, William Croft, 1708. Unless otherwise noted, the texts of all hymns cited in this chapter follow the *Baptist Hymnal* (Nashville: Convention Press, 1975). On writers and tunes from the *Baptist Hymnal* see William Reynolds, *Companion to Baptist Hymnal* (Nashville: Broadman Press, 1976); for a theological assessment of several classical hymns see S. Paul Schilling, *The Faith We Sing* (Philadelphia: Westminster Press, 1983).

5. John Calvin, *The Institutes of the Christian Religion,* ed. John T. McNeill, trans. by Ford Lewis Battles (London: SCM Press, 1960) Book 1, chapter 1 (Title), vol. 1, pp. 35-39.

6. Henry F. Lyte, "Abide with Me," stanza 2, 1847.

7.

8. See Karl Barth (*Church Dogmatics,* vol. 3, pt. 3, trans. G. W. Bromiley and T. F. Torrance [Edinburgh: T. & T. Clark, 1961], Ch. 11, § 49, "God the Father as Lord of His Creature," pp. 58-288) on the faithfulness of the Creator to the creature.

9. B. B. McKinney, "Have Faith in God" (Broadman Press, 1934).

10. For discussions on the nature of faith and faithfulness see R. Bultmann, *pisteuo,* in Gerhard Friedrich, ed., *Theological Dictionary of the New Testament,* trans. and ed. Geoffrey W. Bromiley (Grand Rapids: Eerdmans, 1968), Vol. VI, pp. 174-228.

11. Frederick W. Faber, "There's a Wideness in God's Mercy," 1862. Tune WELLESLEY, Lizzie S. Tourjee, 1878.

12. John Newton, "Amazing Grace! How Sweet the Sound," *Virginia Harmony,* 1831; arranged, Edwin O. Excell, 1900.

13. For the linguistic background and usages see W. Zimmerli and H. Conzelmann, *chairo, ktl,* in Gerhard Friedrich, ed., *Theological Dictionary of the New Testament,* ed. and trans. G. W. Bromiley (Grand Rapids: Eerdmans, 1974), vol. 9, pp. 359-415, especially pp. 372-402.

14. Trace the uses of grace in a standard concordance, and you will be delighted to see this broadening of grace from a few in the Old Testament, to the supreme expression of grace in Jesus Christ, and through Him to the church, and from the church's witness it is extended to all who receive the graciousness of God in Jesus Christ.

15. See especially Edward Schillebeeckx, *Christ, The Experience of Jesus as Lord,* trans. John Bowden (New York: Seabury Press, 1980), pp. 81-644, for an extended discussion of grace which relates this important biblical idea about God to both Testaments and which spells out the relations of God's grace to our response of faith in devotional, liturgical (worship), and social ways.

16. John Bunyan, *Grace Abounding to the Chief of Sinners* (Grand Rapids: Zondervan, 1948).

17. Walter Chalmers Smith, "Immortal, Invisible, God Only Wise," 1867. See 1 Tim. 1:17.

18. See Thomas J. J. Altizer and William Hamilton, *Radical Theology and the Death of God* (Indianapolis: Bobbs-Merrill, 1966) and related literature, for example, Charles Bent, *The Death-of-God Movement: A Study of Gabriel Vahanian, William Hamilton, Paul Van Buren, and Thomas J. J. Altizer* (Westminster, Md.: Paulist Press, 1967); C. W. Christian (comp.), *Radical Theology: Phase Two: Essays in a Continuing Discussion* (Philadelphia: Lippincott, 1967); John Cooper, *Radical Christianity and Its Sources* (Philadelphia: Westminster Press, 1968); Jackson Lee Ice (comp.), *The Death of God Debate* (Philadelphia: Westminster Press, 1967); Thomas W. Ogletree, *The Death of God Controversy* (Nashville: Abingdon Press, 1966); Gabriel Vahanian, *No Other God* (New York: G. Braziller, 1966); John B. Cobb, Jr. (ed.), *The Theology of Altizer: Critique and Response* (Philadelphia: Westminster Press, 1970); and most recently Mark C. Taylor, *Erring: A Postmodern A/Theology* (Chicago: University of Chicago Press, 1984).

19. See the discussion in chapter 1 and the reference to Oscar Cullmann's book, *Immortality of the Soul: Or, Resurrection of the Dead? The Witness of the New Testament* (New York: Macmillan, 1958), esp. pp. 15-27.

20. See Rudolph Otto, *The Idea of the Holy: An Inquiry into the Non-rational Factor in the Idea of the Divine and Its Relation to the Rational,* trans. John W. Harvey, rev. ed. (New York: Oxford University Press, 1925) for a good discussion of the insights in this section and the next.

21. John Bertram Phillips, *Your God Is Too Small* (New York: Macmillan, 1952).

22. Robert Browning, "Andrea del Sarto," 1:51, in *The Oxford Dictionary of Quotations,* 3rd ed. (New York: Oxford University Press, 1979), p. 98.

23. Walter Chalmers Smith, "Immortal, Invisible, God Only Wise," (1867) stanza 1, lines 3-4; see 1 Tim. 1:17.

24. Reginald Heber, "Holy, Holy, Holy," 1826.

25. George Matheson, "O Love That Wilt Not Let Me Go," 1882.

26. For the word study materials on love and the other expressions about God used in this chapter, see Kittel's *Theological Dictionary of the New Testament,* 10 vols. Edited by Gerhard Kittel and Gerhard Friedrich, translated by Geoffrey W. Bromiley (Grand Rapids: Eerdmans, 1964-1976. *In loco.*

27. Martin Luther, "A Mighty Fortress Is Our God" [*"Ein' Feste Burg"*], 1529; trans. Federick H. Hedge, 1853; See Psalm 46.

28. See Paul Tillich's *Love, Power and Justice: Ontological Analyses and Ethical Applications* (New York: Oxford University Press, 1954).

29. Augustus M. Toplady, "Rock of Ages, Cleft for Me," 1775, 1776; see Ps. 94:22.

30. James Russell Lowell, "Once to Every Man and Nation," 1845, stanzas 1, 2, & 4 (text as modified in *Baptist Hymnal*), p. 385.

31. William Shakespeare, *Julius Caesar,* Act IV. Scene iii, 11.217-223, *The Oxford Dictionary of Quotations,* 3rd ed. (New York: Oxford University Press, 1979), p. 451.

32. Mrs. C. F. Alexander, *All Things Bright and Beautiful,* n.d., stanzas 1-4. Cited from *The Baptist Church Hymnal,* rev. ed. (London: Psalms and Hymns Trust, The Baptist Church House, 1933), pp. 678-679.

33. In using the term *Father,* we follow the biblical expression. Fatherhood of God does not refer to God's maleness. God is beyond sexuality. Fatherhood of God refers to the care, the compassion, and the concern of the Creator with the creation. Any idea of the "Fatherhood" of God which is read from human fatherhood is bound to contain all the weakness with which human fathers are afflicted. The dynamic and dependable

relationship of God and Jesus is the only adequate point from which to start any discussion of the Fatherhood of God. For objections to the use of the male term *father* and for examples of and suggestions about more inclusive language, see Vernard Eller, *The Language of Canaan and the Grammar of Feminism* (Grand Rapids: Eerdmans, 1982); Letty M. Russell (ed.), *Feminist Interpretation of the Bible* (Philadelphia: Westminster Press, 1985); Willem Adolph Visser't Hooft, *The Fatherhood of God in an Age of Emancipation* (Geneva: World Council of Churches, 1982); Johannes-Baptist Metz and Edward Schillebeeckx, *God as Father?* Marcus Lefebvre, English language editor (New York: Seabury Press, 1981); Casey Miller and Kate Swift, *Words and Women* (Garden City, N.Y.: Anchor Press, 1976); Denise Lardner Carmody, *Feminism and Christianity: A Two-Way Reflection* (Nashville: Abingdon, 1982); Elizabeth Schussler Fiorenza, *Bread Not Stone: The Challenge of Feminist Biblical Interpretation* (Boston: Beacon Press, 1985); and *An Inclusive Language Lectionary: Readings for Year A* and *Readings for Year B* (Atlanta: John Knox Press for the Cooperative Publication Association, 1983, 1984).

34. Anonymous, "Come, Thou Almighty King," 1757.

35. First John 5:7 does not appear in any of the ancient biblical manuscripts in Greek. Antitrinitarian groups will delight to point this out to you.

36. There are many ancient and modern books about the Trinity from the viewpoint of formal and philosophical thought. See Aurelius Augustine, *The Trinity,* trans. Stephen McKenna (Washington: Catholic University of America Press, 1963); Hilary, *The Trinity,* trans. Stephen McKenna (New York: Fathers of the Church, 1954); William G. Rusch (trans. and ed.), *The Trinitarian Controversy* (Philadelphia: Fortress Press, 1980); Jean Danielou, *God's Life in Us,* trans. Jeremy Leggat (Denville, N.J.: Dimension Books, 1969); Leonard Hodgson, *The Doctrine of the Trinity* (London: Nisbet & Co., 1943); Karl Barth, *Church Dogmatics,* vol. 1, pt. 1, trans. G. T. Thomson (Edinburgh: T. & T. Clark, 1936) chapter 2, part 1, "The Triune God," pp. 339-560; Robert W. Jenson, *The Triune Identity: God According to the Gospel* (Philadelphia: Fortress Press, 1982); Eberhard Jungel, *The Doctrine of the Trinity: God's Being Is in Becoming,* trans. Harton Harris (Grand Rapids: Eerdmans, 1976); James P. Mackey, *The Christian Experience of God as Trinity* (London: SCM Press, 1983) Bertrand de Margerie, *The Christian Trinity in History* (Still River, Mass.: St. Bede's Publications, 1981); Jurgen Moltmann, *The Trinity and the Kingdom: The Doctrine of God,* trans. Margaret Kohl (London: SCM Press, 1981); Karl Rahner, *The Trinity,* trans. Joseph Dunceel (New York: Herder and Herder, 1970); Cyril C. Richardson, *The Doctrine of the Trinity* (New York: Abingdon Press, 1958); Claude Welch, *In This Name: The Doctrine of the Trinity in Contemporary Theology* (New York: Scribner, 1952); Bernard Lonergan, *The Way to Nicaea: The Dialectical Development of Trinitarian Theology,* trans. Conn O'Donovan (London: Darton, Longman, & Todd, 1976); and Georges H. Tavard, *The Vision of the Trinity* (Lanham Md.: University Press of America, 1981).

37. See the concluding chapter for a discussion on revelation.

38. See the section on the long-awaited Child in chapter 7.

9

First Things Last

The reason children and old people survive is because they ask questions. Asking questions is not only the way to learn, it is also a way of surviving. My favorite theological question is, "Why?" When a student tells me he/she is full of the Spirit, I ask, "Why?" When someone tells me she/he does not believe the Bible or does believe the Bible in some unbelievable way, I ask, "Why?" This "why?" asking certainly leads to some interesting theological discussions.

But there are other questions which must be asked, questions that get at the roots of things, questions that reveal the basics, questions that are logically prior to all theological discussions. Four of those will be explored in this final chapter. Perhaps you are asking why this putting of first things last? Good question. Please read again the preface and the introduction to the first chapter. Let me remind you. This book has been a working through theology as life. We often learn, in the midst of living, and we need to learn, before we are through living, what the important questions are. In good theology the questions come out of experience. Formally speaking, that is called the inductive approach. The inductive approach means that you are in the midst of things, and you begin to discern and explain how they work. The inductive approach is in contrast to the deductive approach. The deductive approach is a way of sitting down and thinking through how things work before you start to do them. In life we need both approaches. In *A Theology for Children,* I used the deductive approach. It was all figured out for them in advance. This book uses the inductive approach because *A Theology of Aging* needs to be written from the midst of things and from a more modest position which knows that nobody but God has "it" all figured out in advance.

There are crucial questions; those will be explored first. Then we must ask, "Who said so?" That is the question of authority. "How does God speak?" is the question of revelation. And the final question is really the first question: "Where do you start?" That is the question of presuppositions. Seniors are good at asking questions. These are some questions worth asking.

Crucial Questions

There are four crucial questions to ask about anything and everything. What is? What is important? How do you know what is? How do you express what is, what is important, and what you know?

What is? Pardon the grammar, but two things "is": The Creator and the creation. This is the starting point of Scripture. This is the basic theological affirmation. God is. The world God made is. The Bible does not try to prove God. Proving first principles is *not* necessary. Demonstrating first principles *is* necessary. The Bible starts with the leap of faith that says, "In the beginning God." Biblical realism moves on quickly to the world and all that is therein. There are different kinds of reality and different kinds of created things. There are spiritual beings, angels.[1] Some people do not believe in angels because they have never "seen" one. The motto "seeing is believing" is bad news for faith. There are, according to Scripture (our primary source about angels) two kinds of angels. Those who apparently kept their first estate and "those who kept not their first estate (Jude 6, KJV)." That lofty language has usually been translated as the blessed angels and the fallen angels. This is not the place to argue their case. This is the place to list what is in the created order. There are three dimensions that created beings can have: physical, psychosocial, and spiritual. So far as we can discover from Scripture, angels have spiritual and psychosocial dimensions and may assume a physical dimension when serving as messengers in our world of time and space. Angels are one class of created things.

Humans are another. With that class we have all had some experience.[2] Humanity too is a creature of God. "It is he that hath made us, and not we ourselves" (Ps. 100:3, KJV) or, as the preferred Hebrew translation reads, "We are his." We are, as long as we are doing the defining, the most complete creation of God. We have a physical dimension, a psychosocial dimension, and a spiritual dimension. Next come the animals with physical and pyschosocial dimensions.

Finally, the plants and physical matter which have only, so far as we know, a physical dimension.[3]

The question about "what is" is the question of being. There is a technical term for everything. The technical term for being is *ontology* (from the Greek *ontos,* being). The question "What is?" is the ontological question. It is the simplest of the crucial questions. What is? God is. God's creation is. Within the spectrum of God's creation there are all kinds of things which exist in different ways. They make for a variety in life. Is cancer real? Are dreams real? Is imagination better than mere physical reflexes? Is worship the same kind of experience as work? I do not think so. If so, how can you say that humans worship and animals work? There are different kinds of experiences, and apparently different orders of creation undergo different kinds of experiences. Both humans and animals eat, but only humans, it seems, worry about how to pay for it. Ours is a complicated world with a variety of possibilities of experience. Even our experiences with God are radically different from those of others.[4] That is why, in the last analysis, experience can be a window through which to see reality, but cannot be our final authority.

There are those, to be sure, who deny one or the other of the two types of existence. There are those who deny the Creator. They are called atheists. There are those who deny the reality of existence. I call them impossible idealists. The question is: What is? The answer is: God is, and God's creation is.

What is important? The second crucial question is the question of value. What is important? We place higher value on diamonds than we do on glass. This is purely arbitrary and is based on the availability of the supply. We place higher value on humans than we do on animals, or we ought to. Values are very subjective things. An older woman was once showing us through her well-appointed home. She had some lovely antique china. We were impressed. Then she showed us a postcard from her granddaughter. She declared that the one small postcard meant much more to her than all of the china. She had a good sense of values.

Doubtless there are, in your home or room, some small mementos that have little monetary value or interest to others, but they are very important to you. A very threatening way to put the idea of value, as it pertains to possessions, is to ask the sensational question: "What one thing would you save if your house were burning?" I believe this question of values should be placed above the questions of "How do you know?" or "How do you express yourself?" Theories of value and their study are called *axiology*.

Many answers have been given to the axiological question. Some have said that *knowing* is most important. Obviously, one would expect a professor to list that first. Knowing is important. Knowing can help you, and what you do not know can hurt you (take for example an ignorance of hygiene and an unawareness of germs). Yet I do not place first priority on knowing in the academic, intellectual sense of that term. The business person's suggestion about what is important is *having*. Many people do place priority on what or how much a person, a corporation, a church, or a country has in terms of money, persons, or real estate. Our whole society tends to value bigness and wealth. And the rest of the world tends to value our wealth too. Bigness, strength, and prosperity are not wrong within themselves. Yet it is wrong, in my opinion, to grant having the highest priority to them.

Ours is an activist society. We prize *doing* as one of the highest priorities. A sports figure is valuable for and is paid on the basis of achievement. Churches are considered successful by how much they do, how many activities they promote. Programs, promotion, and performance seem to be the major criteria of success. Those who get worthy things done are certainly doing better than those who get no-things done. Yet activity can be mere busy work. The fact and act of doing does not necessarily mean that the busiest people are the happiest people. Both capitalism and communism prize production above all things. "Money is not important" says a certain brand of piety. My response is that money is not important if you have enough or if you are willing to starve. We cannot pretend that material does not matter. But we dare not suppose that material things matter most.

It seems to me that *relating* is the key word in value. Not just relating. But relating in such a way that the relationships of life are as they should be. The pattern for this idea of relating as a top priority is the biblical affirmation that we should love the Lord our God, with all our heart and mind and soul and our neighbor as ourselves (Deut. 6:4-5; Matt. 22:35-40). All of the answers we have explored to the axiological question have their merit. I am able to integrate the others best around the idea of adequate relationships. Knowing is important. But ignorance is not our primary problem; disobedience is. The knowledge of God in the sense of an obedient relationship is the beginning of knowledge and the highest good. To put this truth in an old cliché: it really is not what you know but whom you know. Having is essential to living. Having an adequate relationship with God is essential to abundant life, eternal life. Doing is the disposition that accomplishes things. Blessed are the makers and the shakers of life, for out of them come the accomplishments. Doing the will of God (Heb. 10:7-11) and doing the truth (1 John 1:6; 2:4; 3:18; in 1 John truth is something one *does*) are the highest values. So I would vote for *relating* as the most desirable category for integrating our values. It is relating what you know to God, others, and the self; relating what you have to God, others, and the self; relating what you do to God, others, and the self that is the highest good.

How do you know? Theology is primarily a word (*logos*) from God. Secondarily, theology is words (*rhemata*) about God. The person and the relationship precede the knowledge and the study. That is why I place how one knows as the third crucial question. How we know things must be asked. Whom we know (being) and why we know (value) need to be asked first.

There are four ways of knowing: by authority, by reflection, by experience, and by intuition. A great deal of what we know we have received by authority. We all say: "I read it in the paper." "I heard it on the news." "My parents taught me so." "Why, I learned that in the first grade!" This is received knowledge. It is secondary information. It is accepted by us because of confidence in our sources. Most of what we "know" we know by this received knowledge. If we had to figure out everything for ourselves or experiment with every technical device we use until we had a flash of insight about reality, most of us would not know much.

When we do put our minds to knowing, we use one and usually all of the three classical ways of knowing. Ways of knowing and theory of knowledge is called *epistemology*, so this is the epistemological question. Knowing by reflection is the most ancient of formal ways of knowing in Western thought. Formal logic was begun by Aristotle about 300 BC. Logic is a tool for thinking. Logic clarifies our thinking. Logic cannot guarantee the truth of our thinking. If your thoughts are correct, logic can help you put all knowledge into a coherent whole. Logic may also serve the purpose of propaganda and slanting things the way you want them. Aristotle's classic case helps us all. He said: All men are mortal. I am a man. Therefore I am mortal. That is good logic, and it is also a true conclusion. But take another instance: nobody likes a crying baby. All babies cry. Therefore nobody likes babies. The logic is technically correct, but the conclusion is not true. It is not true because the first sentence is wrong, "Nobody likes a crying baby." Where would we be if our mother had not liked a crying baby? Formal reflection, logic, is a helpful tool to aid us to put our thoughts together. But we need to be certain that the thoughts we are putting together are correct.

There is a second type of logic. It is not so formal, but it is even older. This is the logic of Socrates that asks probing questions, that tries to see both sides of a situation (it goes back and forth in its arguments so it is called *dialectic,* that which is read from the other view also). Back-and-forth thinking admits paradoxes (seeming logical contradictions). God can be both God and man. God can express both love and wrath. It is an incorrect choice to take one of these kinds of formal thinking to the exclusion of the other. Good thinkers use both. I must confess a preference for the back-and-forth kind of thinking, for I feel it is easier to express biblical insights with this tool for thinking. Both of these ways of reasoning are called deductive. If mathematics or philosophy are your gift, you will enjoy reasoning this way.

Another way of knowing things is by experiment or experience. This way of knowing is the most prevalent one for the last three centuries. This is the way products in laboratories are produced, social experiments are carried out, and the dynamics of the organization of groups are carried on. Most TV advertising appeals to this way of knowing. Experience can never be the final authority for Christian faith. There are many things in theology that we can never experience or experiment with. For example, the Trinity or what it is like to be a divine and human person. But on the other hand, one can never disallow one's own experience. However we may choose to describe our spiritual life-styles, I hope that each of us would want to trust our own experiences with God as confirmed by Scripture.

This book has been written primarily to Christians and has made a strong appeal to their experience. Experience is a valuable way of knowing, even if it is not our basic authority in the Christian faith.

Intuition is the fourth way of knowing, and it is the hardest way to describe. Older folks tend to trust their intuitions. We speak of "having a hunch." Intuition is what "one knows in one's bones." We often tend to dismiss this way of knowing as a valid or reliable one. And intuitions, like logic and experiments, can often be wrong. But a philosopher of science has said that most of the advances and discoveries in the realm of the physical sciences happened as a result of intuition.[5]

All complete and balanced forms of thought will use all four types of knowing. I have tried to use them. You use these four ways of thinking in the course of everyday living. The question of knowledge is important. How do you know? You receive many things on good authority. You reflect on things. You experiment with and experience things. Sometimes you just have a hunch. Good for you!

How do we express what is important and what we know? This is a question of methodology. You can value things. You can know things. But if you cannot express the things known and valued you are at a decided disadvantage. A philosopher of communications in the twentieth century, Marshall McLuhan, has said that the methodological question is the most important one.[6]

There are two primary methods by which we can express things. We can express things verbally and nonverbally. Authors have to express things to their readers in a verbal way. Words are carriers of meanings. It is important to ask what words are. They are symbols. Words point to or participate in reality and describe it. But they cannot exhaust or actually become the things they represent. There are three kinds of word symbols: (1) Words can be common symbols. *Water* is a common symbol word. It represents a liquid substance we cannot live without. But the word *water* is not the actual substance. It only represents it. (2) There are technical symbols. H_2O is a technical formula for water. Every first-year chemistry student recognizes this formula for water and realizes that this is a symbolic way of expressing water. (3) There are poetic symbols. Water of life is a poetic symbol. One kind of symbol is not better than another. They are different from one another.

All three kinds of symbols occur in the Bible. One of the primary problems in biblical interpretation is determining what kind of symbol the words of a passage are. If you understand that all words are symbols, it does not make much sense to ask whether one interprets the Bible literally or symbolically. All words are symbols. It would be better to ask, what kind of a symbol is this? Most of the Bible is written in common symbols. Common symbols usually mean just what they say. Some people would refer to this as "literal" interpretation. This verbal way of communication is a very powerful and a very effective method of communication.

Nonverbal communication is very powerful and effective too. Nonverbal communication is found in the arts, body language, logos, and signs. A picture is worth a thousand words. Well, some pictures are. But pictures can convey meaning. So does music. So do sculptures, films, mimes, photographs, and all other types of art. Body language tells you a great deal. Do you remember when your children were in the "adolescent slouch" period? They spoke volumes without speaking a word. Desmond Morris, a social anthropologist, has collected photos of body language from around the world.[7] You can communicate with sign language, if you have to.

I am writing this book as I am on sabbatic leave in Taiwan, a Chinese culture. I speak no Chinese. Recently I purchased some flea powder for a cat. I am too embarrassed to describe the contortions and sounds I went through to make a very amused Chinese merchant aware of my needs, but you can imagine. There are, of course, in every culture, thousands of speechless people whose communication is by signs. Every major business today has a logo. Many churches have them. Logos are initials, easily identified, and intended to be identified with a certain place or a certain product. The familiar three-circle sign of all wool is readily identified on the tag of a garment. So are the signs that tell you how to wash or iron them. There is a thick book of international signs that gives universally recognized signs. People can go around the world today and handle the necessities of life if they recognize these signs. Traffic signs, indicators, and signals have become universal. One does not have to know foreign words to locate a familiar and much-appreciated no smoking sign, the red *X* over a smoking cigarette. It may be that in the twenty-first century nonverbal language will become as important in international communication as verbal language. The churches can and should take more awareness of this method of communicating. And the church can profit from a dynamic and creative interchange with the arts.

These are the crucial questions: about being, about valuing, about knowing, about communicating. Now it is time for the big question: the question of authority.

Who Said So?

One of the first questions children learn to ask and one of the final, and most important questions the aging ask is, "Who said so?" That is the question of authority. Authority is necessary to the structure of existence, the well-being of life, an adequate sense of belongingness. How authority is used, what type of authority one has, and the source and power of authority are all very important to this discussion. Uninformed opinions about cancer can disturb us deeply. What we do not know or understand poses a great deal of threat to us. "Confidence in the doctor is half the cure." Second opinion is a recent term we have begun to use in medicine. In the "good old days," which really were not quite as good as nostalgia makes them, there were family doctors who had treated people for "forty years," and they referred to specialists as they were needed. Currently, there is the high mobility of the population and the knowledge explosion in medicine. These things have put the "country doctor" out of reach and incline many people toward a trust in new medical technology which must be supplied by a battery of experts, largely unknown to the patient. I want to use a medical analogy to explain some things about authority.

When a medical opinion is given in a situation of trust where patient and physician have known each other for some time and the physician has been kept current, as much as is possible in a busy schedule, that is a personal type of authority based on experience and good, objective medical research and practice. When a medical opinion is based only on a variety of diagnoses, lab tests, and a battery of experts, it is an impersonal authority while being objective, accurate, and expensive.

In our religious life we begin by receiving our opinions on the basis of authority. Those in Christian homes usually believe on and learn about God from parents, whom they trust. This process is continued by a church relationship where both parents and children are taught and nurtured by pastors and teachers whom they know personally and trust. They all use religious publications published by those they trust. Many of those pastors were taught in seminaries by specialists whom they know and trust. This process, like all good authority patterns, involves the objective (factual) and the subjective (experiential) approach. When this breaks down at any point, competing authorities, climates of distrust, and lack of a unified authority pertains. There are in the religious arena a wide variety of opinions, no less than in the medical arena. When a person or group of persons in a congregation begins to accept as their authority a famous television religious talk-show host or evangelist, they contrast and compare that to their pastor. It is often like comparing the "country doctor" to "general hospital." Allegiances shift to the stellar figures. Loyalties are divided. This pattern is true for religious sociology (group action) no less than for medical sociology. What is happening in such cases is a shift of authority.

We need to keep in mind the kind of authority, the way in which authority is expressed, and the source of authority. Religious authority is supposed to be dealing with matters of absolute and final truth, life and death, time and eternity. Religion is what is ultimately binding on a person or that which deals with ultimate concern. Please reread the last sentence. Do you prefer the term *ultimately binding* or the term *ultimate concern?* One is a stricter, more forceful expression: *ultimately binding.* One is a more personal, involved expression: *ultimate concern.* The phrase you chose is possibly a barometer to the type of authority you prefer. Religious authority is an authority that deals with very important matters. It has to be said that in our day and time there are many people who do not believe in a spiritual or religious dimension of life. Unless God changes them, or we are able to convince them, or some crisis in their lives occasions a shift of viewpoint, or all of these work together, they will not be convinced by any religious authority.

The way in which authority is expressed or applied makes a difference. People complain about or are drawn to a physician who is a no-nonsense, strict, will-have-no-arguments-out-of-you kind of authority. The same is true of preference in pastors, teachers, and writers. You might reflect on which kind of authority figures you like and why. Few persons would opt for the extremes. Few would choose the arrogant, powerful, ruthless figure, the Hitler. Few would choose the compliant, anything-goes, it-is-all-relative figure. I have discovered that those of one authority preference usually accuse those of the other camp of such extremes. There is a whole range of expressions of authority in between. Those who are in positions of authority need always to ask what is their way of using their authority.

The final question is the most important question. What is the source of authority? That is the bottom line. Who said so? The doctor said so! The pastor said so! My favorite TV religious program said so! The latest book I read said so! The teacher said so! All of these authority figures have only as much weight as we give them or as their source(s) allow. Where would a physician be without patients? Where would a pastor be without a congregation? Where would TV religious programming be without an audience? Where would an author be without readers? Where would a teacher be without students? The answer to all of those is easy: Without a job. But if all of these authority figures told people only what they wanted to hear, where would they be? Without authority.

I believe there is a fourfold source of authority for the Christian faith. The authority of the Christian community is: (1) the triune God as (2) revealed in Scripture, (3) conveyed in a heritage, and (4) made real in experience. All four parts of this authority statement are essential, but they are not equal. Experience is the fourth element. Things may be true whether we accept them or not.

It is not enough to say, "I believe." But it is true that unless *you* believe, the beliefs are not *your* authority. Some are always trying to flee their heritage (the course of events that shape us, parents, country, history, and so forth). Others are always trying to build a monument to it and to preserve it from all change. A healthier attitude than either of these is to live with our heritage, examine it critically, and submit it to a higher authority for comparison and evaluation. The higher authority than heritage or experience is the Bible. The Bible must inevitably be interpreted and applied by heritage and experience, but it should not be replaced or changed by them. We believe in the Bible as an inspired, historical, written norm for spiritual truth. Why do we believe in the Bible? Because it is the Word of God. It is God who is the final and ultimate authority of the Christian faith. Which God? The God who is above gods (idols of our own making). The God who made heaven and earth. The God of Abraham, Isaac, and Jacob. The God and Father of our Lord and Savior, Jesus Christ. The God who is Father, Son, and Spirit. That God!

Much mischief is done when we get the elements of this fourfold authority out of line. When we put the Bible in the place of God, there is trouble. When we put heritage above Scripture and/or God, there is double trouble. When we put our individual interpretation of the heritage and the Bible in the place of God, we have more trouble than one can imagine. There is a descending order of importance. God first, the Word of God under God. Our heritage (corporate experience) under these. Our individual experience of these under all of these.

There is a final point in our discussion of authority. Much is being made today about subjective versus objective authorities. Subjective is what is experienced and real to the subject, you or whoever else. Objective is what is out there, what is basic fact, what lies in the object. Attempts to separate these too widely fail to see that they must go together. To place the New Testament outside of all experience would be to place it outside of the experience of the people who receive it, and that would place it outside of our time, space, and awareness.[8]

Who said so? God said so. That should settle the issue, all issues. But it invites a further question. Children and the aging always go to the limit: children because they are finding out the limit and the aging because they are facing it. The next question is how does God speak? That question deserves a whole book. It is the question of revelation.

How Does God Speak?

We have all been subjected enough to supposedly funny entertainment about God speaking in grocery stores, in steam baths, from the clouds, and to misunderstanding people at the "burning bush." The question is too important to ignore. And it is too significant to answer in a cavalier fashion. We need to define carefully what we mean when we ask how does God speak? The theological name for the "speech of God" is revelation.

I want to share with you four important definitions.

1. *Revelation* is God revealing Himself and truths about God, which could not otherwise be known, for purposes of establishing a redemptive relationship with His creation.

2. *Manifestation* is God entering our time and space to give definitive acts, speech, and interpretation as to who God is and to what He wills to do.

3. *Inspiration* is God guiding certain persons rightly to receive, understand, interpret, record, and transmit the fact and meaning of His manifestations. The product of inspiration is the Bible.

4. *Illumination* is God enabling persons in postbiblical times to understand and receive the inspired manifestation (the Bible) in things sufficient to salvation.

Revelation is the whole process. Manifestation, inspiration, and illumination are parts of revelation.

Those are heavy and complicated definitions. They are technical terms. Let me explain them and their importance in everyday language. Those definitions, when adequately understood, answer the question: How does God speak? They answer the "how" in terms of why. They do not answer the "how" in terms of the way a thing works so that we could do it too, if we only knew the method.

There are at least three ways of asking questions: (1) The Greek way which requires verbal, formal, logical explanations. The Greek way felt it had exhausted a subject when it had adequately described it or gave a formal rational proof about it. (2) The Latin way which asked the technical how question of method so that it could reproduce or experiment with things. In the West, inventions and technology arose in Latin lands. (3) The Hebraic way. The Hebraic way of asking questions is concerned with what is the function and purpose of a thing. The Hebraic way of putting a question asks: "Does a thing accomplish what it is intended to do?" The Bible, both Old and New Testaments, is concerned more with the Hebraic way of asking questions than it is with the other two. Now that we are through the hard parts, let me talk about how God speaks.

Revelation. What is the "speech" of God like? The rabbis taught that God and the heavenly court spoke Hebrew. I have no doubt that God hears Hebrew. But we have "reason to believe" God speaks other languages too. Answering the question how God speaks by giving the answer "God speaks Hebrew" is a wrong way to go about answering the question. It is wrong because "speech" is more than words on paper or syllables that come out of a mouth. Speech is also act. "God spoke and it was done" (for example, Gen. 1:3). The highest words God spoke were what Jesus *did.* Speech is an event. Speech involves act, interaction, reception, interpretations. When you have had a quarrel with a loved one or a friend, silence is eloquent and very painful. The living Word of God is Jesus. The written Word of God is Scripture. The continuing implications of the Word of God are spelled out in and among the people of God. Paul said, "You are all the letter we need, a letter written on our heart; any man can see it for what it is and read it for himself. And as for you, it is plain that you are a letter that has come from Christ, given to us to deliver: a letter written not with ink but with the Spirit of the living God, written not on stone tablets but on the pages of the human heart" (2 Cor. 3:2-3).

God's speech involves God's acts and words. The diffuse speech of God is found in the grandeur of the world around us. Diffuse and unformed speech may be found in the good, the true, and the beautiful wherever these are found. But the focused speech of God is most clearly pronounced in Jesus, the *Logos* (meaningful statement about) of God. The redemptive speech of God is found in Scripture as inspired and as applied by God's Holy Spirit.

If we on our own could discover the final and definitive truth of God, we would call it discovery. We cannot. God has revealed it. Revelation comes from a term that means to draw back the curtain. The purpose of "drawing back the curtain" is to reveal who and what is behind it. Revelation deals with the truth of God which leads to salvation. Revelation is not intended to reveal truth as an abstraction. Nor is revelation designed to lead us to truths of a sort that humans can discover for themselves. The purpose of revelation is the redemption of the world. God who spoke the world into being has spoken to redeem the world through Jesus Christ.

Manifestation. The definitive manifestations (those which enable us to define God and describe God) come to us in history, our time and space. And before we can grasp these manifestations, they must be put in our language, human language whether Hebrew, Greek, Chinese, or English.

In coming into our time and space, God used all types of things. God used angels, men, bushes, stones, animals, dreams, words, acts, prophetic consciousness, and wisdom literature. God supremely and especially used the incarnation of Jesus Christ to speak to us. This speech of God is historical and redemptive. It unites our world and His purpose. The Bible is the story of *why* God speaks to His world rather than *how* God speaks to His world.

Inspiration. Inspiration means to breathe into. We use the terms *inspired, inspiring,* and *inspirational* in a very broad, loose sense today. We hear inspiring music. Artists speak of inspired painting. We have an "inspiration of the moment." I want to use the term *inspiration* in the specific way I defined it above.

God speaking to Moses (Ex. 3:4-10) is an example of manifestation. Moses receiving, understanding, interpreting, and transmitting what God wanted is inspiration. The product of inspiration is the Bible. The purpose of inspiration is the same as the purpose of revelation and manifestation; it is that God may redeem creation.

Moses was one of many primary receivers of God's manifestations. There were editors, compilers, commentators, and others who participated in the process of bringing the Bible together. The bringing of the biblical materials into written form was aided by the Holy Spirit. It is futile to ask the Latin question, "How did God do it?" The Bible itself presupposes its inspiration. In Scripture we find everywhere the implicit assumption that what is being recorded is from God. Such terms as "the word of the Lord came to me, saying," "God spoke," "And the Lord, God appeared in a vision to Abraham," etc., appear throughout the Old Testament. In the New Testament Jesus' claim is that He does and speaks the words, will, and way of the Father.

The English term *inspiration* occurs twice in the Authorized King James Version of the Bible:

"But there is a spirit in man: and the inspiration of the Almighty giveth them understanding" (Job 32:8, KJV).

"All scripture is given by inspiration of God, and is profitable for doctrine, for reproof, for correction, for instruction in righteousness" (2 Tim. 3:16, KJV).

Second Peter 1:19 is an important reference for inspiration and for how the New Testament writers saw the Old Testament. The

2 Timothy reference clearly relates the purpose and extent of inspiration to the redemptive purpose of God.

Christian history has given much attention to two questions about inspiration. How was the Bible inspired? And how can we "prove" the inspiration of Scripture? These are not biblical questions. And in my opinion, too much time has been spent propounding theories about these questions to the neglect of serious and applied study of the Bible.[9]

The faith statement that the Christian community makes about the inspiration of the Bible is indeed a faith statement. We start with a belief in the credibility and authority of the Bible. We "know" it is inspired, not because of a rational proof or because we demonstrate its superiority over other world religious literature on a literary basis. We speak of the inspiration of Scripture because it is a faith presupposition. Everybody lives out of faith presuppositions, even people who do not have faith. They have "faith" that their own intellect is the final and only word on every matter. That is often the epitome of "blind faith."[10]

There have been two ways to affirm the inspiration and authority of the Bible. One is the way I have just discussed. It is the way of affirming trust. This way begins with the authority of Scripture, lives out of it, and sees no reason why it should not. Inspiration in this way of thinking is proved by its content and its effectiveness rather than by its method or a logical theory of what Scripture has to be. (See Appendix B.)

The second way of proving inspiration is by devising a logical, foolproof method of what Scripture has to be in order to be inspired. This argument is applied only to the original manuscripts and is used as a safeguard against any criticism of Scripture. This way is the way of rational proof. I prefer the first way of affirming the inspiration of Scripture because I believe it is the way most people actually have and hold their confidence in biblical inspiration. The way of "affirming trust" is also closer to the way in which I perceive the "people of the Book" (both the Bible writers and the people who have lived out of the Book) have understood and worked with the authority of Scripture. There are two major dilemmas with the way of the logical proof method. That method seems to call into question the wisdom of God in not preserving the original manuscripts. And, logically, that method calls into question the absolute inspiration of Scripture in the Bibles we now have, since they are not the original autographs.

It is a loss of fruitful energy for Christians who believe in the inspiration of Scripture to argue over who believes the Bible more or who is absolutely right. If we read the Bible carefully, we would understand that God only is right. The inspiration of Scripture is tied to two other questions. How did we get the Scriptures? And how do we interpret the Scriptures?[11]

Occasionally, I ask my students where the Bible came from. They answer with one of two responses. They say either that it came from God, or that it came from the Baptist Book Store. The real question is: How did it get from God to the Baptist Book Store? That is the question of the canon. The study of the canon (rule or guide) is the determination of what books came to be in the Bible and what criteria were used in determining that process.[12] We need to know, since the Bible came in history, how it got put together in history. Notice that this process is a part of the above definition of inspiration. There were, as always, two levels of work going on. The Scriptures were brought together by persons in history who made decisions about which were and which were not "inspired writings." And, more importantly, there was the level of the working of the Holy Spirit who aided in the writing, editing, and compiling of Scripture and who also guided in the selection of what is Scripture. In the reception and writing of Scripture and in the collecting and reception of Scripture, there were the divine and the human dimensions. The analogy of the divine and human dimension combined in Christ is an appropriate analogy to be applied to the formation of the Scriptures.

Likewise urgent is the question of how to interpret Scripture. The science of interpretation is called hermeneutics. Even the devil can quote Scripture (Matt. 4:5-6; Luke 4:9-11). And even a good Christian can make a devilish use of Scripture by quoting it out of context. Most differences among Christians arise out of different interpretations of Scripture and not out of a lack of any basic belief and trust in the Bible.

There are many books of "rules" for interpreting Scripture. I would like to give the following suggestions: (1) The Bible usually uses common symbols; it means what it says. Take it at face value. (2) The

Bible does use technical religious terms. Try to translate these technical symbols into everyday terms nonreligious people can understand. (3) Recognize the poetic-symbol words of Scripture and enjoy their beauty. (4) Use a reliable translation or version of the Bible for serious Bible study. Do not use paraphrases to establish doctrine or to determine what the best ancient biblical manuscripts say. (5) Use Bible tools (concordances, dictionaries, commentaries, atlases, and notes) to help with the hard parts. Remember, all of these tools are from some recent hand. Do not let anyone's references or commentaries take on the authority of inspired Scripture for you. (6) Read enough of the passage to understand what the verse is saying. Do not use a verse out of context. (7) If you receive some personal benefit or application from reading a portion of the Bible, reflect on that impression and act on it. But do not insist that the impression you derived from your circumstances is the original meaning of Scripture or is valid for everyone else. (8) Find out all you can about the background of a passage of Scripture. (9) Read enough and often enough in the Bible that you can begin to see for yourself the interconnections of Scripture. The Bible is its own best commentary. (10) Do not begin teaching others primarily on the basis of what the Bible says to you. This is too subjective. Start your teaching on the basis of what the Bible actually says in its own setting and what it unambiguously means so that all can understand it.

The product of inspiration is Scripture. Scripture is more authoritative than tradition. What Scripture actually says is more authoritative than any individual's personal, private experience. There are many who are quick to say, "God told me!" If what "God" told them is incompatible with Scripture, they heard the wrong voice.

Illumination. To what extent does the Spirit of God, who inspired Scripture, assist people in understanding Scripture? I would say, "In matters sufficient to salvation." Anyone can understand God's redemptive purpose by reading the New Testament. No one individual or organization can understand all of the Bible completely all of the time and give an infallible interpretation for all time. No one has this kind of interpretation for the following reasons. (1) The Bible is not a book of doctrine. It is a book about God's dynamic purpose. God's purpose may be expressed in doctrines, but the expression of all formal doctrine is made by persons who are not inspired, at least not to the extent and in the fashion that Scripture is inspired. (2) The Bible may have differing applications for persons who come to it in differing circumstances. Your culture, your way of being, your own psychological makeup and that of other cultures and individuals asks different kinds of questions from Scripture and applies biblical answers to the readers' own situations. (3) To suppose that anyone understands all the Bible is to commit the sin of pride. That would be to assume that our minds are equal to that of God.

God will assist us in an illumined understanding of His Word. But God guarantees no one the last word, the only word, the complete "word" on His Word. There was a motto at the time of the Protestant Reformation which said, "God has yet more light to break (shine) forth from His Word." That is still true because truth is a living interacting thing rather than a frozen unchanging thing. Jesus had divine and human dimensions. So do manifestation, inspiration, and illumination. How does God speak? Very lovingly, very persistently, very comfortingly. And the purpose of God's speech is to bring the cosmos back to the Creator and back to His original assessment of it, that it was good. And we affirm, because of Scripture, that God's new world will be better.

In Christian history the question as to the place of illumination has been raised. Does illumination happen in the church as a corporate body? Does illumination happen via the reason of those who study Scripture? Does illumination come about through the intuition (feelings, emotions, hunches, experiences) of the people of God? Yes! All three. The fullness of the body of Christ utilizes all of the gifts of all of the people of God in determining what the Spirit says to the churches.

There is a final question. It is really the first question, so I have saved it for last. Where do you start?

Where Do You Start?

There is really only one answer to the question: "Where do you start?" At the beginning. Beginnings—real beginnings, the bases—are presuppositions. Presuppositions are basics with which you start. If you are baking a cake, you start with the ingredients. If you are building a bird house, have the tools and the lumber handy. If you are going to write a theology, know what your presuppositions are from the beginning. And although I have waited until the end to express them, there are six starting points I had worked out from the beginning. Without these six presuppositions, the Christian faith would not hang together. Let me share these presuppositions with you. See if you do not agree that they are basic assumptions to our faith. These are the six starting points of the Christian faith.

1. *God is.* "In the beginning God . . . " (KJV). There is an awesome absoluteness about that. "Prove it," say those who do not have eyes to see. What kind of proof do you require? Scientific experimental proof, mathematical logical proof, experiential pragmatic proof? That is not the way faith works. The Christian community does not ask one to accept an illogical nonmeaningful, cannot-be-demonstrated faith. But Christians do insist that God is there from the beginning, and unless one starts with this presupposition, there is no way of arriving at this conclusion. Those who do not intentionally and knowingly believe in God are called atheists. Those who do believe in God are called theists. Coercion does not help. Faith that has to *prove* its point by the sword, by reason only, or at the altar of scientific experiment has already surrendered her birthright.

2. *God speaks.* I like the title of one of Francis Schaeffer's books: *He Is There and He Is Not Silent.*[13] It is possible to be noncommittal about the possibility of God. That is an agnostic viewpoint. There are two crucial presuppositions of the Christian faith: God is there, and God speaks. It should have been evident from the first of the book that the author believed in God and that God spoke. It should have been apparent from the title of this book that this was the case. Why else would one write a theology, a meaningful statement about God?

3. *What God has spoken is adequately and fully represented in Scripture and the content of God's speech is redemptive in purpose.* From the first pages there was an appeal to Scripture. All the way through there have been biblical citations as though those established something. They do. They give us the Logos, the statement of God about God on our behalf. God tells us what we cannot discover for ourselves. God tells us what kind of God He is and what a redeeming, holy, loving God wants. What God wants God has supplied, namely the salvation of the world in Jesus Christ.

4. *Humans can understand and respond to God who speaks in Scripture for our redemption.* We are, in fact, response-able and responsible to God. The

God who made us does not leave us alone. God gives the possibility of faith. The threefold God in all His redemptive ways is the object of faith. What God requires, God provides. We may choose to cooperate with God, and in this choice we are opened to the fullness and meaning of life. All of these presuppositions are good news. They become personal news for us when we respond to God, who speaks for our redemption and who invites us to participate in it.

5. *We cannot know all about God, but what we do know of God, who speaks redemptively in Scripture and invites us to respond in faith, is true to who God really is.* If we could know all about God, "we would be as gods." And the flirting with that presupposition is the start of all our woes. There are no ultimate surprises about who God is. But there is mystery, and there is room to grow. There is always an otherness to God that makes God fascinating. There is in Jesus Christ, a hereness to God comforting. The Father who made the world, the Son who comes a second time to redeem it, and the Holy Spirit who will breathe upon creation to renew it is the God of whom Scripture speaks. God is truly like what the Bible says God is like. God is more; but God is not less.

6. *As God's world is now it is not what is was originally intended to be, and it is not what it is ultimately going to be.* Ours is a fallen world. If it were not, we would need no restoration. If we and our world needed no restoration, the entire content of Scripture would be meaningless. If this is the best of all possible worlds, we are in real trouble. But if this world is not, in some sense, the same as God's good world which He created, there is no basis for renewal.

We and our world are on the way. We are between innocence and perfection. We are not yet perfect. But we are on the way. And the way grows better, but not necessarily easier. But the way goes home, and that should encourage us to keep going.

Notes

1. See above in chapter 5, pp. 195-198 and Mortimer Adler's book, *The Angels and Us* (New York: Macmillan, 1982) for a "reasonable" defense of angels from one who is not formally in any religious group.

2. For an interesting tour de force, see the book by Fredrich Nietzsche *Human All-Too-Human* (excerpts translated by Walter Kaufmann, *Basic Writings of Nietzsche* [New York: The Modern Library, 1968], pp. 145-178; and *The Portable Nietzsche* [New York:

Viking Press, 1954], pp. 51-64) in which Nietzsche wants to humanize the spiritual and spiritualize the human. In order to accomplish that one would have to "kill God" and elevate man. That is a step Nietzsche also took, but it was not particularly effective as evidenced by the clever bumper sticker slogan: " 'God is dead' Nietzsche. 'Nietzsche is dead' God."

3. See the above discussion in chapter 3. I am repeating the essence of it here in order to assist the reader in remembering so as to have a complete discussion about the question of being.

4. See William James' classic, *The Varieties of Religious Experience: A Study in Human Nature* (New York: Longmans, Green, & Co., 1902) for an inductive account of these experiences.

5. Thomas S. Kuhn, *The Structure of Scientific Revolutions*, 2nd ed. (Chicago: University of Chicago Press, 1970).

6. See, Marshall McLuhan, *The Medium is the Massage* (New York: Bantam Books, 1967). He deliberately mispelled the title trying to make his point. Everyone knew he felt the medium was the message, and they would expect that (message, not massage) as the title of his book. He made his point when people usually correct the spelling to what they think he meant.

7. Desmond Morris, *ManWatching: A Field Guide to Human Behavior* (New York: Harry N. Abrams, Inc., 1977).

8. See the discussion of E. Schillebeeckx, "Do we begin with the New Testament or with present-day experience? A false alternative," in *Christ: The Experience of Jesus as Lord*, translated by John Bowden (New York: Seabury Press, 1980), pp. 71-81.

9. For a variety of views of theories of inspiration and the process of studying, defending, and arguing about inspiration, see Dewey M. Beegle, *The Inspiration of Scripture* (Philadelphia: Westminster Press, 1963); Carl F. H. Henry, *God, Revelation and Authority*, 6 vols, (Waco, Tex.: Word Books, 1976-1983), especially vol. 3, chapter 27, "The Bible as Propositional Revelation," pp. 455-481; Harold Lindsell, *The Battle for the Bible* (Grand Rapids: Zondervan, 1976), and *The Bible in the Balance* (Grand Rapids: Zondervan, 1979); Jack Rogers & Donald McKim, *The Authority and Interpretation of the Bible: An Historical Approach* (San Francisco: Harper & Row, 1979); and Benjamin Breckinridge Warfield, *Revelation and Inspiration* (New York: Oxford University Press, 1927).

10. C. S. Lewis directed many of his apologetic works and also his more effective literary and symbolic works against such people. One biography calls him *C. S. Lewis: The Apostle to the Skeptics* (Chad Walsh [New York: Macmillan Co., 1949]).

11. On the question of how we got the Scriptures, see Ira M. Price, *The Ancestry of Our English Bible: An Account of Manuscripts, Texts, and Versions of the Bible,* third rev. ed. by William A. Irwin & Allen P. Wikgren (New York: Harper & Brothers, 1956), note especially bibliography on pp. 331-334; James McKee Adams, *Biblical Backgrounds*, rev. Joseph Callaway (Nashville: Broadman Press, 1965); Ernest C. Colwell, *The Study of the Bible* (Chicago: University of Chicago Press, 1937); Walter A. Copinger, *The Bible and Its Transmission* (London: H. Southeran & Co., 1897); G. Adolf Deissmann, *Light From the Ancient East: The New Testament Illustrated by Recently Discovered Texts of the Greco-Roman World*, trans. Lionel R. M. Strachan (New York: Harper & Brothers, 1927); Helmut Koester, *Introduction to the New Testament*, 2 vols. (Philadelphia: Fortress Press, 1982); Ernst Sellin and Georg Fohrer, *Introduction to the Old Testament*, trans. David F. Green (Nashville: Abingdon Press, 1968); Brevard S. Childs, *Introduction to the Old Testament as Scripture* (Philadelphia: Fortress Press, 1979) and *The New Testament as Canon: An Introduction* (Philadelphia: Fortress Press, 1985); R. H. Charles, *The Apocrypha and Pseudepigrapha of the Old Testament in English* (Oxford: Clarendon Press, 1913); E. J. Goodspeed, *Modern Apocrypha*

(Boston: Beacon Press, 1956); Geddes MacGregor, *A Literary History of the Bible: From the Middle Ages to the Present Day* (Nashville: Abingdon Press, 1968); and Herbert G. May, *Our English Bible in the Making: The Word of Life in Living Language,* rev. ed. (Philadelphia: Westminster Press for the Cooperative Publication Association, 1965).

For an introduction to biblical hermeneutics, see Robert M. Grant and David Tracy, *A Short History of the Interpretation of the Bible,* 2nd ed. (Philadelphia: Fortress Press, 1984); Carl E. Braaten, *History and Hermeneutics* (Philadelphia: Westminster Press, 1966); René Marlé), *Introduction to Hermeneutics,* trans. E. Froment & R. Albrecht (New York: Herder & Herder, 1967); A. Berkeley Mickelsen, *Interpreting the Bible* (Grand Rapids: Eerdmans, 1963); E. A. Nida, *Bible Translating: An Analysis of Principles and Procedures* (New York: American Bible Society, 1947); Clark H. Pinnock, *The Scripture Principle* (San Francisco: Harper & Row, 1984); Bernard Ramm, *Protestant Biblical Interpretation: A Textbook of Hermeneutics for Conservative Prostestants,* 3rd rev. ed., (Grand Rapids: Baker Book House, 1970); James D. Smart, *The Strange Silence of the Bible in the Church: A Study in Hermeneutics* (Philadelphia: Westminster Press, 1970); Henry A. Virkler, *Hermeneutics: Principles and Processes of Biblical Interpretation* (Grand Rapids: Baker Book House, 1981).

For further study in historical and philosophical hermeneutics see Aurelius Augustine, *On Christian Doctrine,* trans. D. W. Robertson, Jr. (New York: Liberal Arts Press, 1958); Josef Bleicher, *Contemporary Hermeneutics: Hermeneutics as Method, Philosophy, and Critique* (Boston: Routledge & Kegan Paul, 1980); Jean Daniélou, *From Shadows to Reality: Studies in the Biblical Typology of the Fathers,* trans. Wulstand Hibberd (London: Burns & Oates, 1960); Hans-Georg Gadamer, *Essays in Philosophical Hermeneutics* (Berkeley, Calif.: University of California Press, 1977) and *Truth and Method,* trans. Garrett Barden and John Cumming (New York: Continuum, 1975); R. P. C. Hanson, *Allegory and Event: A Study of the Sources and Significance of Origen's Interpretation of Scripture* (Richmond: John Knox Press, 1959); Eric Donald Hirsch, Jr., *The Aims of Interpretation* (Chicago: University of Chicago Press, 1976); Edgar V. McKnight, *Meaning in Texts: The Historical Shaping of a Narrative Hermeneutics* (Philadelphia: Fortress Press, 1978); Richard E. Palmer, *Hermeneutics: Interpretation Theory in Schleiermacher, Dilthey, Heidegger, and Gadamer* (Evanston, Ill.: Northwestern University Press, 1969); Paul Ricoeur, *The Conflict of Interpretation: Essays in Hermeneutics,* ed. Don Ihde (Evanston, Ill.: Northwestern University Press, 1974) and *Essays on Biblical Interpretation,* ed. Lewis S. Mudge (Philadelphia: Fortress Press, 1980); James M. Robinson & John B. Cobb, Jr. (eds.), *The New Hermeneutic* (New York: Harper & Row, 1964); Robert B. Robinson, *Roman Catholic Exegesis Since Divino Afflante Spiritu: Hermeneutical Implications* (Ph.D. thesis, Yale University, 1982); Ann Arbor, Mich.: University Microfilms International); and Edward Schillebeeckx, *The Understanding of Faith: Interpretation and Criticism,* trans. N. D. Smith (London: Sheed & Ward, 1974); Robert L. Cate, *How to Interpret the Bible* (Nashville: Broadman Press, 1983); and James M. Efird, *How to Interpret the Bible* (Atlanta: John Knox Press, 1984).

12. See Floyd V. Filson, *Which Books Belong in the Bible? A Study of the Canon* (Philadelphia: Westmingter Press, 1957) and Hans von Campenhausen, *The Formation of the Christian Bible,* translated by J.A. Baker (Philadelphia: Fortress Press, 1972).

13. Francis Schaeffer, *He Is There And He Is Not Silent* (Wheaton, Ill.: Tyndale House, 1972). The title is, in my opinion, better than the method of approach Schaeffer uses in the book. See my review in *Southwestern Journal of Theology,* 15 (1972), p. 139.

Appendix A
Suicide

A Sermon Preached at the Immanuel Baptist Church, Wichita Kansas

SCRIPTURE: Judges 16:21-31

I want to say a few brief words about suicide and related ideas because I am firmly convinced that the church has got to start speaking to reality.

Suicide is serious business today—whether you accept the poem of Dorothy Parker, written in humorous vein,

Razors pain you,
Rivers are demp,
Acids stain you,
Drugs give you the cramps,
Guns are illegal,
Nooses give,
Gas smells awful,
You might as well live!"

or whether you take it as serious business and recognize that suicide is the tenth largest killer in the United States, there are many factors that enter in. Suicide in cities is more prevalent than it is in the country. It's more prevalent in certain parts of our country than it is in other parts. It is definitely more prevalent in the spring than it is in the winter. You may be safe through December. It's the safest month. April through June are the hazardous months. If you try before thirty-five, the chances are you won't make it. If you try after fifty, you will. And on and on the account goes. What is alarming among other things is to know that among college-age young people, suicide is the third largest killer after accidents and cancer.

Suicide has been around a long time. It refers to taking one's life. In the middle ages the body of one who committed suicide was taken and dragged through the town and buried in the crossroads with a stake in its heart so it wouldn't rise to disturb other people.

In the Roman communion, one who takes his own life is not permitted to be buried in holy ground because he has not lived to ask forgiveness through the church. It was in this very church—not this building, but this congregation—in the years of my youth that I was taught—and I really don't remember by whom, so you all are safe—that suicide was the unpardonable sin. I am glad to tell you this is incorrect. This has no basis in fact, and no basis in biblical teaching. Unpardonable sin refers to something else, and I don't have time for a sermon on that. But I assure you suicide is not the unpardonable sin. This used to be thought by our elders who didn't realize they got it from the Roman communion. And the reason it was considered sin among them was because they could not ask forgiveness through the church after they had committed it.

Now to those people who are members of the free church, and such we are, it is important that you would know that this sin is a sin—it is serious, it is against the law of God, for a reason that we shall assert; but it is not unforgivable. I do not know what would lead you to suppose that we who claim that we stand in the presence of Almighty God in the world to come would not be able to ask Him to forgive, through Christ, anything which we have done including that problem and that dilemma.

Now all of you may be wondering, but why should the church speak about this? It's such an unpleasant topic. We need to speak because it's such a real topic in our society. I think it is time the church is done with talking about irrelevant things that have no place in the lives of people. So far as I know there have not been recent suicides in this congregation, and now is the time to talk about what the church thinks and what the Bible says about suicide.

First of all, I want you to know that the basic term itself means to take one's own life. You should pause and reflect for a little while as to what that means. The little poem I quoted at the beginning of the sermon gave a variety of ways in which it could be done. However, I want to suggest that suicide is also more than a momentary thing. Have you ever heard someone say, "My job is killing me"? They probably are right. It is a form of suicide to be tied to a vocation and job which you thoroughly hate and which takes all of the joy out of living. Have you thought about that? Life is too short not to enjoy what you do.

Years ago I went to an allergist. He told me I was allergic to ragweed and careless weed. He then told me the story of a Methodist minister's wife who was allergic to her husband. It's possible, ladies. It's possible. Quite often, we have a way of shortening our own lives by doing things that are less than best. There are people who say, "Don't you know it's a sin to smoke; it will give you lung cancer." It is possible, and that may be true. It is also a sin to overeat. Gluttony is my vice, so I won't tarry long on that one. I want you to understand that suicide is more than one instantaneous act. It is a process that begins with birth, which some of us hasten unduly. I remember someone said one time within my hearing, and I will not express it further, "I will never forgive somebody." Something fine within that person died. To the extent that you harbor hatred, and guilt, and frustration, and lack of forgiveness, you are committing a type of suicide. You see, our categories have been so black and so white, we have assumed that the suicide is only the one who plunges the knife or shoots the gun. It is not true. There is a sense in which all of us are involved with the stewardship of living, and we are entering in this day and time of modern technology some new and interesting gray areas. I think it is time for the church to sit down to define them.

First of all, why is suicide wrong? Not only because of the command, "Thou shalt not kill," for behind this command lies the creation command, that life as God gave it is His gift, and it is good. It is for this reason that suicide is wrong because it denies the Creator's right and denies the affirmation which is first in all the Scripture, "God saw that it was good."

I recognize that sometimes the circumstance of life is not good, but life itself and the fact that we can live and do live is good. And we should reverence it as such. We should live it as fully as we can in the days which God has given us to live. One thing about us Baptists (and I am glad we are emerging from it; I hope we are) is that we have trained our young people very well in one area, that is, we know what we don't do. That's very bad. I think it is time that we are emerging into a new day with Baptist young people when we teach them what they may do to make life enjoyable and full and rich and pleasurable. It is what I call affirming creation. Therefore, live, love, live long fruitfully and well in the things you do which God has given you. Today is your only day of opportunity. For this reason, know that it is wrong to shorten life by greed and hatred, by intemperate living; it is wrong to commit suicide gradually or suddenly. But know likewise it is no unpardonable sin. It is no sin which God will not forgive. The Scripture says nothing of this in anyplace.

Then, I want to ask you a question: What is life? You say well—and I'm familiar with that teenage blurb from some years back—"That tough. What's tough? Life's tough! What's life? Life's a magazine! Where do you get it? At the drugstore—cost's 35¢. I've only got a quarter. That's tough! What's tough? Life's tough!" And it kept on going for hours on end literally. And that's the way some life is. It is time for the people of God to start making a difference between living and existing. In the Fort Worth zoo there is a squirrel, poor little fellow. He's on a treadmill; and he gets on that thing and runs like crazy, just around and around and around; and if I could speak his language I don't know if I would tell him that he's not really going anyplace. But I do speak your language; and I want to tell your heart and mine—because we need to know—quite often what we are doing is not living, it's just existing. Existing so we can have food so we can get strength to work so we can have food so we can get strength to work—it's just a treadmill, and that's not life as God intended it to be.

I think sometimes we are too busy. I have a host of students who are, and I have been so guilty myself, busy about the things of God to such an extent that they can't appreciate the passing scene and take time to enjoy life. There is something wrong, even in the service of God, when one does not enjoy the life that's one's to live. Now, I believe that life, human life, is the ability to respond to God. That's what makes us different. There is a time at our birth and until we are mature enough when it may be said that a child, though breathing, is not fully alive in the sense in which I am talking about life. The sense in which the biblical materials speak about life is more than breath. Obviously, these children must go on breathing or they'll never learn to live. They must go on taking food or they'll never learn to savor what is good. But there is a time at the beginning of life—I think you understand what I'm saying—where people just have to exist. As a little girl said about her baby brother, "He's not good for much. He has no hair, no teeth, can't talk, or run and play. But we will keep him." We know what their potential is. We are aware of the joys which are theirs and the opportunities and the dilemmas. So I suggest to you we had better keep our babies.

Yet there is another problem. It's a problem that many of you have not thought about yet; some of you perhaps will begin to think about it. That is the fact that we had better start building the kind of lives while we are active that can go on, so far as possible, as long as we are living. I'm talking about the other end of life. What should be, and sometimes are called, the golden years have turned out to be hellish years for many people because they did not prepare to live well and to enjoy life while it was here. This is true, also, because of a great many other tragic things that I am going to speak of in just a moment.

There is a new problem that's rising among us. What about those who are half alive? I cannot decide for anyone else, but I have already decided and expressed to my family for myself something along the following lines. You see, the church is not speaking to the medical profession, and the medical profession would love for it to speak. We are not speaking words that are helpful and instructive. While I was in Chicago on a study leave, a doctor turned to me and said, "I had a decision to make last week. What should I have done?" He told me what he did. He didn't ask me before. I'm glad that he didn't, coward that I am. But it's this kind of decision the church ought to be helping to make. He said, "I had two patients, one of them was a living vegetable. I kept that patient alive by a breathing machine—never conscious, never any medical possibility aside from divine intervention of regaining consciousness. He was costing his family a fortune. He had a lot of young children, and they needed the money. He was going to die soon. Across the hall there was another man who had a full life ahead of him and a large family which needed him. He had a defective kidney and was dying of uremic poisoning, but he could have been cured and helped if he had had the kidney from the man who was doomed to die. What should I do? Should I pull the plug?" Now, that's the question to which the church ought to be speaking.

I want to tell you what I think. I think each person must make this kind of decision for himself, register it with his family and official persons before that decision has to be made. It is not fair that a physician should have to make it. It is not fair that a family that is mourning and loving people should have to make it. As for me and my house, when one lapses into a coma from which there are no medical possibilities of survival, it's the same as being a vegetable, and I have left instructions for the plug to be pulled. Now, this is talking where people live. It is not life to us at the other end where we are not able to respond to God. Better to go into His presence and be with Him than to exist in mere vegetable state and be a liability to those whom we love and enjoy most.

Baptist people have said that January is will-making month. That's correct. I would suggest that things like this be incorporated in Baptist wills as well as other things. You say, "But, preacher, this is such an awful thing." I understand, but it's as real as life, and it's as real as death.

Now, two other ingredients, and I'll try to say something nice before we close. I want to suggest that the world in which we live, of which you and I are a part, is engaged in a demonic conspiracy today to rob others of the joy of living. You say, "Not me, preacher, I'm not doing anything. I'm hoeing my own row." No, I suggest that all of us are responsible of a demonic conspiracy that's robbing a large part of our people of the joy of living. It is twofold: we are pushing the pressures of society down on our children in a stage and at a time when they are least able to bear them; and we are cutting off people from their maturing years. We give them no sense that they are needed or wanted or should be considered. I mean this most seriously, and I want to illustrate what I mean.

The medical profession is calling to our attention that never before have there been as many babies, infants, and preschool children with ulcers. Are you aware of the fact that we are teaching calculus in the second grade now? Well, almost. You ought to try this modern math sometime. It is most interesting. I am not objecting to that. I think all of these technological advances are necessary. But I think we are robbing our children of their childhood, and it's a sin before Almighty God.

We are robbing our children of their childhood! We recently sat down in our home and understood what our little boy was saying. He finally got through to us. "Daddy, all I want to do is play." Now, that doesn't mean that's all he wants to do, though he acts like it sometimes. It does mean that in his schedule there wasn't any place for being a child. There's a creek behind our house which the city, prosaically enough, is cementing up; and he never had the value of enjoying the creek, of looking at the leaves, of finding fossils, of doing things that children just sort of like to do. You see, there are piano lessons, speech lessons, this lesson, that lesson, and all of the lessons, and church eight nights a week. Yes, yes, and he hasn't had time to be a child. I suggest that's demonic. That is demonic!

Do you know that there are now thirteen million people over seventy in the United States, and before the end of this century, there will be twenty million people? Do you know the group that is most out of employment? It is not the high school dropouts, though they are pretty bad off. It is the man who has been professionally and well trained who has reached the age of fifty. How about that? He suddenly is severed from employment and cannot find work, or he is put out to pasture, as it were, at the age of fifty-five. I am quite interested to note that in the last fifteen years the only person that any of our churches have wanted is a man who is under thirty and has a doctor's degree. That's most interesting. Most interesting!

My Christian friends, we are part of a conspiracy that is ruining life at both ends. And I suggest we quit it. We should quit it by making those people who have come into what should be as King Lear said, "the time of honor and of joy," to have a little honor and a little joy and a little understanding and a little comfort. They must not be shoved off some place and be made to feel as though, even though they do not express it, they are no longer wanted or needed. It is time for us to begin to capture some of the imaginativeness of childhood. One of the deepest problems of my theological students is not that they can't read. That's one of their problems, but that's not their worst problem. The worst problem is they lack that one essential quality that is necessary to understand the Bible, and that is imaginativeness. That's one reason we don't understand our Bible any better.

The Bible is a Book that was born and came out of the oriental setting in which it was given substance; and it requires imaginativeness to understand it. I remember the student who came storming into class and knew all about the Book of Revelation. Beware, anybody who knows all about the Book of Revelation! He knew all about the Book of Revelation, and he said, "I have just discovered how many people are going to get to heaven." He took the angels' measuring rods—they are in there if you want to figure it up—then he took the square feet of the city foursquare, tall as it is broad, and so forth, and he got the cubed square feet of it. Then he took the square inches in a given soul and figured out how many souls could get in the heavenly city. Now, there wasn't anything wrong with his math, but his theology was atrocious. Just atrocious! You don't figure heaven on a slide rule. It's time we gave up trying. You cannot put the methods of a technological society into your spiritual experience and expect to come out with anything but chaos.

Now, I've meddled, twiddled, and chased rabbits. What about our text? Have you ever thought of Samson as a suicide? There are seven mentioned in the Bible, and this is the first one. From Samson to Judas, and to our text there should be appended a New Testament expression, "Judas went and hanged himself."

I would suggest that suicide is wrong because it robs us of your possession which God has given to you, namely, life. I would also suggest that the way in which many of us live—without purpose, without joy, without help, without encouragement—is terribly, tragically, wrong before Almighty God.

I would suggest that the things we do to our children, and the things we are doing to our aged, are terribly, tragically wrong, and it is time for the church of the living God to stand to say that there should be dignity in death and joy in life. These are both important. It is not just whether one takes the knife but whether one controls a knifelike tongue all through life that matters too. It is not just whether one should die a lingering, purposeless death, but whether you should not do something about living a joyous, vital, and energizing life. Basically, the choice of death is not ours unless we choose to take it and to distort what God has given. Basically, our choice is life—what we ought to do. This is the day which the Lord hath made. Let us rejoice and be glad therein. Restore unto me, said the psalmist, the joy of my salvation.

"Oh, God our help in ages past,/Our hope for years to come,/Our shelter from the stormy blast/And our eternal home," grant to us this joy. Help us, our Father, not so much to complain as to live. Help us, our Father, not so much to worry about dying as to be sure that we are good stewards of life. Help us, our Father, to know that it is wrong to do anything that terminates the breath you've given to us so that we may respond to thee. And help us, O God, also to know that it's wrong to take the breath You've given to us and waste it in a hundred different foolish ways.

Give us strength and guidance and help us as a church and as Thy children, Lord, to renew our vows and recreate within us, O God, a clean heart and to renew a right spirit within us.

We pray in Jesus' name. Amen.

Appendix B

Two Models of Biblical Authority

Grace and peace from our Lord Jesus Christ. It is important to have an adequate view of the authority of the Christian faith. The authority of the Christian faith is the triune God as revealed in Scripture, as conveyed in a heritage, and as made real in experience, corporate experience and personal experience.

It is also important to understand how we know things. There are four ways of knowing. The first of them is knowing by *authority.* Most of us know most of what we know on this basis. That is, we believe our teachers, our pastors, those people who have studied and/or are expert in the various skills they bring to us. When the lights do not come on, most of us depend upon the authority and the skills of the persons at the electric company to know what to do and how to do it. Most of us also receive our first impressions and our concepts of Scripture from those we love and those we trust. We began with the Bible as a matter of authority, the authority of those who loved the Bible and loved us, and have passed their love for the Bible on to us. Most of us believe in Scripture on the basis of this authority and learn our first attitudes toward Scripture from those we trust.

A second way of knowing is by *intuition.* The way of intuition says there are some inherent or particular moments of insight that come to us and we have, as a result of them, certain kinds of feelings and certain kinds of confidence. Our grandfathers used to say, "I feel it in my bones." That saying indicates there is a kind of intuitive awareness about people and things that matter to us. The intuitive type of knowledge is very important in marital relationships, in all interpersonal relationships, and in the awareness of what is most important in life. Thomas Kuhn's book *Structures of Scientific Revolutions* demonstrates that every major scientific advance was made on the basis of some intuition.

A third way of knowing is by *deduction.* The deductive way of knowing requires conscious reflecting and thinking about a problem and putting it together by formal logic.

The fourth way of knowing is the *inductive* method. This method supposes that we are in the midst of a circumstance and begin to experiment and reflect upon it in such fashion that we are able to make sense of it. These four ways of knowing are very important for our two models of biblical authority.

Model A: 1 + 1 = 2

I call the first model of biblical authority the 1 + 1 = 2 model. It has the following characteristics. It is basically a *mathematical* model. This model requires that the matter of biblical authority can be positively demonstrated in a logical way. Numbers and figures are not things; they are logical constructs, but they do add up to precise, demonstrable, and accurate ways which can be checked by mathematical methods. When one looks at the Bible this way, it gives the same kind of logical certainty that mathematical equations and calculations give.

Model A is *logical* in the formal sense of Aristotle's straight-line thinking. Logic is related to mathematics in that it is a precise science and provides tools for reflective thought. Model A (1 + 1 = 2) is based on Aristotle's straight-line thinking in such a way that this view of Scripture can be demonstrated by all persons who hold to this way as a primary means of thinking.

The third characteristic of Model A is that it is *deductive.* It sits down in advance and thinks as to how it can protect and preserve the integrity of biblical authority. This is an *a priori* method.

The fourth characteristic of this model of biblical authority is that is is *purely propositional.* This means that this model conceives of revelation as a series of propositions which form a coherent whole and which can be logically expressed and explained in a completely rational system. Carl F. H. Henry once told me that he felt that Aristotelian logic was the one divinely prepared vehicle for the understanding of the gospel in every age.

The fifth characteristic of Model A is the assumption that the *Bible contains a complete, rational, and logically demonstrable systematic theology.* This means that one would be able to find the answers to all doctrinal questions in such a fashion as to leave no loose ends in a complete, unified body of propositions that teach us everything about God, our world, and anything that might be included in a traditional systematic theology.

This model has several distinct advantages. It *gives certainty* to its followers. It gives certainty in the same way that mathematics gives when one adds up a column of figures. Whichever way one goes, top or bottom, the sums are correct; and that is the only answer which can be given.

The second advantage (and these advantages are from the viewpoint of the adherents of Model A) is that it *stresses the cognitive side of God's revelation.* There is definitely an intellectual and rational priority in this model. It wants to have a system which is complete and coherent in every detail.

The third advantage of this model is that it is *objective* in the prescientific sense of Kantian philosophy. It lays claim to being outside of the individual consciousness, and its affirmations concern the object itself, namely Scripture.

The fourth advantage of this model is that it is *rationally consistent.* It proves its propositions in a straightforward, syllogistic way. Formal reasoning is the major and exclusive tool of Model A as it pertains to biblical authority.

There are, however, several disadvantages to this model. The first one is that it may be *questioned as to its source.* The source of this model lies in Greek philosophy and Protestant scholastic rationalism. It does not lie within the biblical framework of thought itself.

The second objection or disadvantage to this model is that it does not have a formal place for personal interaction and relationship. This does not mean that those who hold the model do not have a vital relationship with God. But it does mean that their relationship with God may have little to do with their formal theory of biblical inspiration.

The third objection to the $1 + 1 = 2$ model is that to be logically consistent this model requires a divinely inspired hermeneutic to regulate and interpret the *one* systematic theology found in Scripture. This is necessary in order to ensure the mathematical and rational completion of this model of biblical inspiration. In other words, it will not do, if there is *one* systematic theology within the Scriptures, for various interpretations of that theology to be proposed since such proposals would represent a failure to define the one message found in biblical inspiration. To be logically complete, unified message requires a unified interpretation. There are those who have claimed that their hermeneutic, their method of biblical interpretation, was, indeed, the divinely inspired one, or at least was the only rational, coherent one. By and large, however, most people who hold to the $1 + 1 = 2$ model do not want to make this claim for themselves even though the logic of their position requires it.

A fourth objection to this model is that it is very difficult in the missionary task to assume that Greek, rational, philosophical theology is appropriate and understandable by all cultures and languages. For example, when I was teaching at our seminary in Taiwan, I presented these models and all of the precise words that had been used in history concerning biblical inspiration. When I had finished, my translator said that it was a very difficult day. I asked why. She replied, "Because there is a word in Chinese for inspiration, but there are no words that give precise meanings to terms such as inerrancy, infallibility, plenary, intuitive, and other such words." The question then becomes, must we teach Asian persons, one fifth of the world who use the Chinese language, to think in terms of Greek philosophical insights before we can assure their biblical orthodoxy or permit them to have an adequate understanding of the biblical materials?

The fifth disadvantage of this model is, in my opinion, the major and conclusive disadvantage. The $1 + 1 = 2$ model is not based on the Bible we have. Only the original autographs are assumed to be inerrant and infallible, and that, of course, is all that anyone with an awareness of biblical languages would propose. Yet we do not have the original autographs. According to this model, this means that what we have is less than inerrant and infallible. And I do not feel that we can speak that way. I think that it is at this point that the model breaks down. It does no good to say that, given the variations in the manuscripts and the small amount of substantial difference that these make on doctrine, we have a reasonably inerrant Scripture. In the mathematical and rational model, if there is one exception or if the theory breaks down at any point, the entire game is lost. When you are adding up the column of figures, and it is supposed to be 100, it has to be 100. Ninety-nine percent will not do.

Model B: I Love You

The second model, Model B, I call the "I Love You" model. Basically, its characteristics are as follows. It gives attention primarily to relational categories, that is, how the divine and His creation interact.

The second characteristic is that it uses a variety of ways of knowing. It does not eschew formal, philosophical thinking, but it is aware that there are other types of logic and thinking that are appropriate in the biblical materials and in life itself. To quote Pascal, the French philosopher, "The heart has reasons that reason knows not of." This second model uses modern, phenomenological patterns and procedures in understanding human consciousness. There is the recognition today that the idea of the subjective/objective dichotomy in the Kantian sense is no longer a viable category for modern thinking.

The third characteristic of this model is that it is *inductive.* This model starts where we are and with the Bible which we actually have. It reflects on the circumstances in which we find ourselves and the kind of Scripture, the actual Bible, which God in His providence has seen fit to give us.

This means, in the fourth place, that this is an *a posteriori* model. It reflects upon the circumstances after they have arisen. After all, there are no formal theories of biblical inspiration in Scripture itself. Scripture is the Word of God because it is God's Word and because it has come in His interaction and interrelationship with His creation. And it is left for us to figure this out later. In Model B it is not necessary, as it is in Model A, to have an *a priori* system of biblical authority worked out before one can come to Scripture.

The fifth characteristic of this model is that it is both relational and propositional. There is no predisposition of this model to want to say that revelation is not propositional. That is self-defeating. If revelation could not be expressed in propositions, it could not be passed on from one human generation to another. Nevertheless, the impetus behind revelation and the reality of grasping revelation is found in the relational aspect of the confrontation of God and His creation, of the interaction we have with Him through Scripture and in our own experience.

Sixth, the Bible contains the narrative of God's redemptive purpose. This is what the Bible itself says it is for. Second Timothy 3:16

informs us why Scripture is inspired, and it has to do with redemptive relationships and ethical activity. The Bible makes no claim for itself that it is a fountain of scientific wisdom or of any other type of wisdom except the knowledge that leads to God.

The first disadvantage of this model, and it is from the viewpoint of the adherents of Model A, is that this model gives assurance rather than certainty. Assurance is a basic kind of equanimity that comes from confidence, but it is not the kind of certainty that comes from adding up figures in a mathematical column. I can understand why those who are seeking objectivity in Model A would feel that this mere assurance of Model B is a disadvantage. Obviously, I do not agree with them.

The second disadvantage of Model B, from the viewpoint of Model A, is that this model stresses the affective elements of human life. That is, it does not deal primarily with the cognitive and the intellectual. Model A people find Model B people too much lacking in formal logic and in demonstrable logical proofs. I would indicate that I understand this; but it seems to me that the majority of people to whom we witness and whom we win to Christ are won on the basis of an authoritative Bible through whom God speaks and acts in their very lives. Their relationship with God does not wait upon a prescribed, formal theory of biblical authority.

The third disadvantage, from the viewpoint of Model A, is that Model B (the "I Love You" model) stresses the interactive, confrontational aspects of revelation. It does not put priority upon logical consistency and rational proofs. Model B talks about why God came into His creation and into the arena of time and space. The reason for His revelation is that He might redeem us. All of those things which humanity can discover by mathematics, by logic, by experimentation are well and good. But the one thing that is required from an adequate view of inspiration is what is found in the Scriptures themselves, namely that God confronts us with His revelation in Jesus Christ and convicts us on the basis of that revelation by His Holy Spirit.

The fourth disadvantage of the "I Love You" model from the viewpoint of the $1 + 1 = 2$ model is that it does not have one exclusive philosophical, logical system as a basis for its thought. I would simply have to confess that that this is correct. It uses many logical, philosophical systems as the basis for its thought. And often it is aware that the revelation of God can be presented, defended, and lived without any formal philosophical definitions and defenses.

The advantage of Model B, in my opinion, are:

1. That it is true to the biblical experience. It is biblically based. It is expressed in biblical categories and is on target in its insistence that the purpose of God in entering our arena is not to guarantee us infallibility but to grant us salvation.

2. The second advantage of this viewpoint is that it maintains this relational aspect of biblical revelation, which it has received on authority and has expressed through the working out of life in the light of God's Word.

3. The third advantage of this viewpoint is that it can and does tolerate diversity in the biblical materials and in the interpretation of them. This model recognizes different ways of understanding and different ways of communicating. It does not feel there are contradictions in Scripture. It is a contradiction of definitions to say that an authority is mistaken in matters in which it is an authority. And if we come to the Bible as an ultimate authority in matters in which it does not claim to be an authority, we are misusing it. Model B is aware that God is God and that, since His Word is given to us for redemption, everyone may find in Scripture an understanding of things sufficient to salvation. But the assumption of this model is that no one has an infallible and inerrant interpretation of all of Scripture. The reason for this is the fragmentation of sin in the human life and because the finite is not fully capable of grasping the infinite mind. If we knew what God knows in the way in which He knows it and knew all of it, we would be as God. That we can know in this way is not an assumption that I feel the Bible warrants.

4. The fourth and final advantage of Model B is simply that it deals with the Bible which we have. This view holds that inspiration also involves the process of bringing the canon together. This "I Love You" model confesses that what God has given to us is adequate for our salvation. It says that the Scriptures which we have must be translated, that the manuscripts behind them may be reevaluated, and that God by the continuing guidance of His Spirit is authentically in this process. God does not permit us to nail down either His Word or our interpretation of it in such fashion that there are no loose ends,

no mystery. God ceases to be God when we can, by our minds, grasp and exhaust Him.

It is my firm feeling that persons in both Models A and B have a serious and dedicated desire to serve God and to learn from His Word, Holy Scripture. My prayer is that the God of Scripture may enlighten and enlarge all of us as, in love, we speak the truth as we see it one to another.

Selected Bibliography

Books

Argyle, Michael. *Religious Behavior.* London: Routledge & Kegan Paul, 1958.

Bradburn, Norman M. and Caplovitz, David. *Reports on Happiness: A Pilot Study of Behavior Related to Mental Health.* Chicago: Aldine Publishing Co., 1965.

Buhler, Charlotte. *Psychology for Contemporary Living.* Translated by Hella Freud Bernays. New York: Hawthorn Books, Inc., 1968.

Butler, Robert N. "The Life Review: An Interpretation of Reminiscence in the Aged." In *Middle Age and Aging,* pp. 486-496. Edited by Bernice L. Neugarten. Chicago: The University Press, 1968.

Cavan, R. S.; Burgess, E. W.; Havighurst, R. J.; and Goldhamer, H. *Personal Adjustment in Old Age.* Chicago: Science Research Associates, 1949.

Chiriboga, David. "Perception of Well-Being." In *Four Stages of Life,* pp. 84-98. Edited by Marjorie Fiske Lownthal, Majda Thurnher, David Chiriboga, and Associates. San Francisco: Jossey-Bass Publishers, 1975.

Chown, Sheila M. "Morale, Careers and Personal Potentials." In *Handbook of the Psychology of Aging,* pp. 672-691. Edited by James E. Birren and K. Warner Schaie. New York: Van Nostrand Reinhold Co., 1977.

Culver, Elsie Thomas. *New Church Programs with the Aging.* New York: Association Press, 1961.

Cumming, Elaine. "Further Thoughts on the Theory of Disengagement." In *Aging in America,* pp. 19-41. Edited by Cary S. Kart and Barbara B. Manard. N.p.: Alfred Publishing Co., Inc., 1976.

Cumming, Elaine and Henry, William E. *Growing Old.* New York: Basic Books, Inc., 1961.

Geist, Harold. *The Psychological Aspects of the Aging Process.* St. Louis: Warren H. Green, Inc., 1968.

Gray, Robert M. and Moberg, David O. *The Church and the Older Person.* Grand Rapids: William B. Eerdmans Publishing Co., 1977.

Havighurst, Robert J. "Personal and Social Adjustment in Old Age." In *The New Frontiers of Aging,* pp. 172-179. Edited by Wilma Donahue and Clark Tibbitts. Ann Arbor: The University of Michigan Press, 1957.

———. "Successful Aging." In *Process of Aging,* pp. 299-320. Edited by R. H. Williams, C. Tibbitts, and W. Donahue. New York: Atherton Press, 1963.

Havighurst, R. J., and Albrecht, Ruth. *Older People.* New York: Longmans, Green, 1953.

Havighurst, Robert J.; Neugarten, Bernice L.; and Tobin, Sheldon S. "Disengagement and Patterns of Aging." In *Middle Age and Aging,* pp. 161-172. Edited by Bernice L. Neugarten. Chicago: The University Press, 1968.

Hays, William L. *Statistics for Psychologists.* New York: Holt, Rhinehart, and Winston, 1963.

Hendricks, Jon, and Hendricks, C. Davis. *Aging in Mass Society.* Cambridge: Winthrop Publishers, Inc., 1977.

Kutner, B.; Fanshel, D.; Togo, A. M.; and Langer, T. S. *Five Hundred Over Sixty.* New York: Russell Sage Foundation, 1956.

Lawton, M. Powell. "The Dimensions of Morale." In *Research Planning and Action for the Elderly: The Power and Potential of Social Science,* pp. 144-165. Edited by Donald P. Kent, Robert Kastenbaum, and Sylvia Sherwood. New York: Behavioral Publications, Inc., 1972.

Lidz, Theodore. *The Person: His Development Throughout the Life Cycle.* New York: Basic Books, Inc., 1976.

Moberg, David O. *The Church as a Social Institution.* Englewood Cliffs: Prentice-Hall, Inc., 1962.

Neugarten, Bernice L. "Personality and Aging." In *Handbook of the Psychology of Aging,* pp. 626-649. Edited by James E. Birren and K. Warner Schaie. New York: Van Nostrand Reinhold Co., 1977.

______. "Personality and Patterns of Aging." In *Middle Age and Aging,* pp. 173-177. Edited by Bernice L. Neugarten. Chicago: The University Press, 1968.

Neugarten, Bernice L.; Havighurst, Robert J.; and Tobin, Sheldon S. "The Measurement of Life Satisfaction." In *Aging in America,* pp. 123-147. Edited by Cary S. Kart and Barbara B. Manard. N.p.: Alfred Publishing Co., Inc., 1976.

Newman, Barbara M., and Newman, Phillip R. *Development Through Life: A Psychosocial Approach.* 3rd ed. Homewood, Ill.: The Dorsey Press, 1984.

Pfeiffer, Eric. "Psychopathology and Social Pathology." In *Handbook of the Psychology of Aging,* pp. 650-671. Edited by James E. Birren and K. Warner Schaie. New York: Van Nostrand Reinhold Co., 1977.

Reichard, Suzanne; Livson, Florine; and Peterson, Paul G. *Aging and Personality.* New York: John Wiley & Sons, Inc., 1962.

Roscoe, John T. *Fundamental Research Statistics for the Behavioral Sciences.* 2nd ed. New York: Holt, Rinehart, and Winston, Inc., 1975.

Sheldon, Henry D., and Tibbitts, Clark. *The Older Population of the United States.* New York: John Wiley & Sons, Inc., 1958.

Southern Baptist Convention. *The 1979 Annual of the Southern Baptist Convention.* Houston, Tex.: n.p., 1979.

Williams, Richard H., and Loeb, Martin B. "The Adult's Social Life Space and Successful Aging: Some Suggestions for a Conceptual Framework." In *Middle Age and Aging,* pp. 379-381. Edited by Bernice L. Neugarten. Chicago: The University of Chicago Press, 1968.

Journals

Adams, David L. "Analysis of a Life Satisfaction Index." *Journal of Gerontology* 24 (October 1969): 470-474.

______. "Correlates of Satisfaction Among the Elderly." *The Gerontologist* 11 (Winter 1971, part 2): 64-68.

Alston, J. P., and Dudley, C. J. "Age, Occupation and Life Satisfaction," *The Gerontologist* 13 (Spring 1973): 58-61.

Barfield, Richard E., and Morgan, James N. "Trends in Satisfaction with Retirement." *The Gerontologist* 18 (February 1978): 14-23.

Blazer, Dan, and Palmore, Erdman. "Religion and Aging in a Longitudinal Panel." *The Gerontologist* 16 (February 1976): 82-85.

Bortner, Rayman, and Hultsch, David F. "A Multivariate Analysis of Correlates of Life Satisfaction in Adulthood." *Journal of Gerontology* 25 (January 1970): 41-47.

Bull, C. Neil, and Aucoin, Jackie B. "Voluntary Association Participation and Life Satisfaction: A Replication Note." *Journal of Gerontology* 30 (January 1975): 73-76.

Carp, Frances M. "Impact of Improved Housing on Morale and Life Satisfaction." *The Gerontologist* 15 (December 1975): 511-515.

Cohn, Richard M. "Age and the Satisfaction from Work." *Journal of Gerontology* 34 (March 1979): 264-272.

Conner, Karen A.; Powers, Edward A.; and Bultena, Gordon L. "Social Interaction and Life Satisfaction: An Empirical Assessment of Late-Life Patterns." *Journal of Gerontology* 34 (January 1979): 116-121.

Cumming, Elaine; Dean, L.; and Newell, D. S. "What is Morale? A Case History of a Validity Problem." *Human Organization* 17 (Summer (1958): 3-8.

Cutler, Neal A. "Age Variations in the Dimensionality of Life Satisfaction." *Journal of Gerontology* 34 (July 1979): 573-578.

Cutler, Stephen J. "Membership in Different Types of Voluntary Associations and Psychological Well-Being." *The Gerontologist* 16 (August 1976): 335-339.

______. "Transportation and Changes in Life Satisfaction." *The Gerontologist* 15 (April 1975): 155-159.

Dobson, Cynthia; Powers, Edward A.; Kuth, Patricia; and Goudy, Willis J. "Anomia, Self-esteem, and Life Satisfaction: Interrelationships Among Three Scales of Well-Being." *Journal of Gerontology* 34 (July 1979): 569-572.

Edwards, J. N., and Klemmach, D. L. "Correlates of Life Satisfaction: A Re-examination." *Journal of Gerontology* 28 (October 1973): 497-502.

Gould, Roger L. "The Phases of Adult Life: A Study in Developmental Psychology." *American Journal of Psychiatry* 129 (November (1972): 521-531.

Graney, Marshall J. "Happiness and Social Participation in Aging." *Journal of Gerontology* 30 (November 1975): 701-706.

Gubrium, Taber F. "Environmental Effects on Morale in Old Age and the

Resources of Health and Solvency." *The Gerontologist* 10 (Winter (1970): 294-297.

Guinan, Sister St. Michael. "Aging and Religious Life." *The Gerontologist* 12 (Spring 1972): 21.

Havighurst, Robert J. "The Social Competency of Middle-Aged People." *Genetic Psychology Monographs* 56 (November 1957): 297-375.

______. "Successful Aging." *The Gerontologist* 1 (March 1961): 8-13.

Kline, Chrysee. "The Socialization Process of Women: Implications for a Theory of Successful Aging." *The Gerontologist* 15 (December 1975): 486-492.

Knapp, Martin R. J. "Predicting the Dimension of Life Satisfaction." *Journal of Gerontology* 31 (September 1976): 595-604.

Kuhlen, R. G. "Age Trends in Adjustment During the Adult Years as Reflected in Happiness Ratings." *American Psychologist* 3 (July 1948): 307.

Kurtz, John J., and Wolk, Stephen. "Continued Growth and Life Satisfaction." *The Gerontologist* 15 (April 1975): 129-131.

Larson, Reed. "Thirty Years of Research on the Subjective Well-Being of Older Americans." *Journal of Gerontology* 33 (January 1978): 109-125.

Lawton, M. Powell. "The Philadelphia Geriatic Center Morale Scale: A Revision." *Journal of Gerontology* 30 (Jaauary 1975): 85-89.

Lemon, Bruce W.; Bengtson, Vern L.; and Peterson, James A. "An Exploration of the Activity Theory of Aging: Activity Types and Life Satisfaction Among In-Movers to a Retirement Community." *Journal of Gerontology* 27 (October 1972): 511-523.

Lohmann, Nancy. "Correlation of Life Satisfaction, Morale and Adjustment Measures." *Journal of Gerontology* 32 (January 1977): 73-75.

Markides, Kyriakos, and Martin, Harry W. "A Causal Model of Life Satisfaction Among the Elderly." *Journal of Gerontology* 34 (January 1979): 86-93.

Medley, Morris L. "Satisfaction with Life among Persons Sixty-five Years and Older: A Causal Model." *Journal of Gerontology* 31 (July 1976): 448-455.

Mindel, Charles H., and Vaughan, C. Edwin. "A Multidimensional Approach to Religiosity and Disengagement." *Journal of Gerontolgoy* 33 (January 1978): 103-108.

Moberg, David O. "Church Membership and Personal Adjustment in Old Age." *Journal of Gerontology* 8 (April 1953): 207-211.

______. "Needs Felt by the Clergy for Ministries to the Aging." *The Gerontologist* 15 (April 1975): 170-175.

______. "Religiosity in Old Age." *The Gerontologist* 5 (June (1965): 78-87.

Morris, John N., and Sherwood, Sylvia. "A Retesting and Modification of the Philadelphia Geriatric Center Morale Scale." *Journal of Gerontology* 30 (January 1975): 77-84.

Neugarten, Bernice L.; Havighurst, Robert J.; and Tobin, Sheldon S. "The Measurement of Life Satisfaction." *Journal of Gerontology* 16 (April 1961): 134-143.

Orbach, Harold L. "Aging and Religion." *Geriatrics* 16 (October (1961): 530-540.

Palmore, Erdman, and Kivett, Vira. "Change in Life Satisfaction: A Longitudinal Study of Persons Aged 46-70." *Journal of Gerontology* 32 (May 1977): 311-316.

Peters, R. George. "Self-Conception of the Aged, Age Identification and Aging." *The Gerontologist* 11 (Winter 1971): 69-73.

Pierce, Robert C., and Chiriboga, David A. "Dimensions of Adult Self-concept." *Journal of Gerontology* 34 (January 1979): 80-85.

Pollman, A. William. "Early Retirement: Relationship of Variation in Life Satisfaction." *The Gerontologist* 11 (Spring 1971): 43-47.

Schonfield, David. "Future Commitments and Successful Aging: I. The Random Sample." *Journal of Gerontology* 28 (April 1973): 189-196.

______. "Geronting: Reflections on Successful Aging." *The Gerontologist* 7 (December 1967): 270-273.

Schonfield, David, and Hooper, Allen. "Future Committments and Successful Aging: II. Special Groups." *Journal of Gerontology* 28 (1973): 197-201.

Smith, K. J., and Lipman, A. "Constraint and Life Satisfaction." *Journal of Gerontology* 27 (January 1972): 77-82.

Spakes, Patricia R. "Family, Friendship, and Community Interaction as Related to Life Satisfaction of the Elderly." *Journal of Gerontological Social Work* 1 (Summer 1979): 279-293.

Spreitzer, E., and Snyder, E. "Correlates of Life Satisfaction Among the Aged." *Journal of Gerontology* 29 (July 1974): 454-458.

Storandt, Martha; Wittels, Ilene; and Botwinick, Jack. "Predictors of a Dimension of Well-Being in the Relocated Healthy Aged." *Journal of Gerontology* 30 (Jaauary 1975): 97-102.

Tallmer, Margot, and Kutner, Bernard. "Disengagement and Morale." *The Gerontologist* 10 (Winter 1970): 317-320.

Teaff, Joseph D.; Lawton, M. Powell; Nahemow, Lucille; and Carlson, Diane. "Impact of Age Integration on the Well-Being of Elderly Tenants in Public Housing." *Journal of Gerontology* 33 (January 1978): 126-133.

Toseland, Ron, and Sykes, James. "Senior Citizen Center Participation and Other Correlates of Life Satisfaction." *The Gerontologist* 17 (June 1977): 235-241.

Wingrove, C. Ray, and Alston, Jon P. "Age, Aging, and Church Attendance." *The Gerontologist* 11 (Winter 1971): 356-358.

Wolk, Stephen, and Telleen, Sharon. "Psychological and Social Correlates of Life Satisfaction as a Function of Residential Constraint." *Journal of Gerontology* 31 (January 1976): 89-98.

Wood, Vivian; Wylie, Mary L.; and Sheafor, Bradford. "An Analysis of a Short Self-Report Measure of Life Satisfaction: Correlation with Later Judgments." *Journal of Gerontology* 24 (October 1969): 465-469.

Wylie, Mary. "Life Satisfaction as a Program Impact Criterion." *Journal of Gerontology* 25 (January 1970): 36-40.

Youmans, E. Grant. "Age Stratification and Value Orientations." *International Journal of Aging and Human Development* 4 (Winter 1973): 53-65.

Unpublished Material

Ferguson, Larry Neil. "Life-Satisfaction among the Elderly as a Function of Participation in Organized Religious Activities." Ph.D. dissertation, Fuller Theological Seminary, 1975.